Ezekiel, Daniel, and the Minor Prophets Volume 26

EXPOSITIONS OF HOLY SCRIPTURE

EXPOSITIONS OF HOLY SCRIPTURE

ALEXANDER MACLAREN, D. D., Litt. D.

EZEKIEL, DANIEL, AND THE MINOR PROPHETS

A. Maclaren

HODDER & STOUGHTON
NEW YORK
GEORGE H. DORAN COMPANY

CONTENTS

THE BOOK OF EZEKIEL

THE BOOK OF DANIEL

HOSEA

AMOS

JONAH

CONTENTS

MICAH

HABAKKUK

ZEPHANIAH

HAGGAI

ZECHARIAH

CONTENTS

THE BOOK OF EZEKIEL

CHAMBERS OF IMAGERY

'Then said He unto me, Son of man, hast thou seen what the ancients of the house of Israel do in the dark, every man in the chambers of his imagery?'— EZEKIEL viii. 12.

THIS is part of a vision which came to the prophet in his captivity. He is carried away in imagination from his home amongst the exiles in the East to the Temple of Jerusalem. There he sees in one dreadful series representations of all the forms of idolatry to which the handful that were left in the land were cleaving. There meets him on the threshold of the court 'the image of jealousy,' the generalised expression for the aggregate of idolatries which had stirred the anger of the divine husband of the nation. Then he sees within the Temple three groups representing the idolatries of three different lands. First, those with whom my text is concerned, who, in some underground room, vaulted and windowless, were bowing down before painted animal forms upon the walls. Probably they were the representatives of Egyptian worship, for the description of their temple might have been taken out of any book of travels in Egypt in the present day. It is only an ideal picture that is represented to Ezekiel, and not a real fact. It is not at all probable that all these various forms of idolatry were found at any time within the Temple itself. And the whole cast of the vision suggests that it is an ideal picture, and not reality, with which we have to do. Hence the number of these idolaters

A

was seventy—the successors of the seventy whom
Moses led up to Sinai to see the God of Israel! And
now here they are grovelling before brute forms painted
on the walls in a hole in the dark. Their leader bears
a name which might have startled them in their apos-
tasy, and choked their prayers in their throats, for
Jaazan-iah means 'the Lord hears.' Each man has a
censer in his hand — self-consecrated priests of self-
chosen deities. Shrouded in obscurity, they pleased
themselves with the ancient lie, 'The Lord sees not;
He hath forsaken the earth.' And then, into that San-
hedrim of apostates there comes, all unknown to them,
the light of God's presence; and the eye of the prophet
marks their evil.

I have nothing to do here with the other groups which
Ezekiel saw in his vision. The next set were the representatives of the women of Israel, who, false at once to
their womanhood and to their God, were taking part in
the nameless obscenities and abominations of the worship of the Syrian Adonis. And the next, who from
their numbers seem to be intended to stand for the
representatives of the priesthood, as the former were
of the whole people, represent the worshippers who had
fallen under the fascinations of a widespread Eastern
idolatry, and with their backs to the house of the Lord
were bowing before the rising sun.

All these false faiths got on very well together. Their
worshippers had no quarrel with each other. Poly-
theism, by its very nature and the necessity of its
being, is tolerant. All its rabble of gods have a mutual
understanding, and are banded together against the
only One that says, 'Thou shalt have none other gods
beside Me.'

But now, I take this vision in a meaning which the

prophet had no intention to put on it. I do not often do that with my texts, and when I do I like to confess frankly that I am doing it. So I take the words now as a kind of symbol which may help to put into a picturesque and more striking form some very familiar and homely truths. Look at that dark-painted chamber that we have all of us got in our hearts; at the idolatries that go on there, and at the flashing of the sudden light of God who marks, into the midst of the idolatry. 'Hast thou seen what the ancients of the children of Israel do in the dark, each man in the chambers of his imagery?'

I. Think of the dark and painted chamber which we all of us carry in our hearts.

Every man is a mystery to himself as to his fellows. With reverence, we may say of each other as we say of God—'Clouds and darkness are round about Him.' After all the manifestations of a life, we remain enigmas to one another and mysteries to ourselves. For every man is no fixed somewhat, but a growing personality, with dormant possibilities of good and evil lying in him, which up to the very last moment of his life may flame up into altogether unexpected and astonishing developments. Therefore we have all to feel that after all self-examination there lie awful depths within us which we have not fathomed; and after all our knowledge of one another we yet do see but the surface, and each soul dwells alone.

There is in every heart a dark chamber. Oh, brethren! there are very, very few of us that dare tell all our thoughts and show our inmost selves to our dearest ones. The most silvery lake that lies sleeping amidst beauty, itself the very fairest spot of all, when drained off shows ugly ooze and filthy mud, and all manner of creeping abominations in the slime. I wonder what we should see if our hearts were, so to speak, drained off, and the very bottom layer of every thing brought into the light. Do you think you could stand it? Well, then, go to God and ask Him to keep you from unconscious sins. Go to Him and ask Him to root out of you the mischiefs that you do not know are there, and live humbly and self-distrustfully, and feel that your only strength is: 'Hold Thou me up, and I shall be saved.' 'Hast thou seen what they do in the *dark*?'

Still further, we may take another part of this description with possibly permissible violence as a symbol of another characteristic of our inward nature. The walls of that chamber were all painted with animal forms, to which these men were bowing down. By our memory, and by that marvellous faculty that people call the imagination, and by our desires, we are for ever painting the walls of the inmost chambers of our hearts with such pictures. That is an awful power which we possess, and, alas! too often use for foul idolatries.

I do not dwell upon that, but I wish to drop one very earnest caution and beseeching entreaty, especially to the younger members of my congregation now. You, young men and women, especially you young men, mind what you paint upon those mystic walls! Foul things, as my text says, 'creeping things and abominable beasts,' only too many of you are tracing there. Take care, for these figures are ineffaceable. No repentance will obliterate them. I do not know whether even Heaven can blot them out. What you love, what you desire, what you think about, you are photographing on the walls of your immortal soul. And just as to-day, thousands of years after the artists have been gathered to the dust, we may go into Egyptian temples

and see the figures on their walls, in all the freshness
of their first colouring, as if the painter had but laid
down his pencil a moment ago; so, on your hearts,
youthful evils, the sins of your boyhood, the pruriences
of your earliest days, may live in ugly shapes, that no
tears and no repentance will ever wipe out. Nothing
can do away with 'the marks of that which once hath
been.' What are you painting on the chambers of
imagery in your hearts? Obscenity, foul things, mean
things, low things? Is that mystic shrine within you
painted with such figures as were laid bare in some
chambers in Pompeii, where the excavators had to
cover up the pictures because they were so foul? Or,
is it like the cells in the convent of San Marco at Flor-
ence, where Fra Angelico's holy and sweet genius has
left on the bare walls, to be looked at, as he fancied,
only by one devout brother in each cell, angel imagin-
ings, and noble, pure celestial faces that calm and
hallow those who gaze upon them? What are you
doing, my brother, in the dark, in your chambers of
imagery?

II. Now look with me briefly at the second thought
that I draw from this symbol,—the idolatries of the
dark chamber.

All these seventy grey-bearded elders that were bowing there before the bestial gods which they had portrayed, had, no doubt, often stood in the courts of the
Temple and there made prayers to the God of Israel,
with broad phylacteries, to be seen of men. Their true
worship was their worship in the dark. The other was
conscious or unconscious hypocrisy. And the very
chamber in which they were gathered, according to the
ideal representation of our text, was a chamber in, and
therefore partaking of the consecration of, the Temple,

So their worship was doubly criminal, in that it was
sacrilege as well as idolatry.   Both things are true
about us.

A man's true worship is not the worship which he
performs in the public temple, but that which he offers
down in that little private chapel, where nobody goes
but himself.   Worship is the attribution of supreme
excellence to, and the entire dependence of the heart
upon, a certain person.   And the people or the things
to which a man attributes the highest excellence, and
on which he hangs his happiness and well-being, these
be his gods, no matter what his outward profession is.
You can find out what these are for you, if you will ask
yourself, and honestly answer, one or two questions.
What is that I want most?   What is it which makes
my ideal of happiness?   What is that which I feel that
I should be desperate without?   What do I think about
most naturally and spontaneously, when the spring is
taken off, and my thoughts are allowed to go as they
will?   And if the answer to none of these questions is
'God!' then I do not know why you should call yourself a worshipper of God.   It is of no avail that we
pray in the temple, if we have a dark underground
shrine where our true adoration is rendered.

Oh, dear brethren! I am afraid there are a great many
of us nominal Christians, connected with Christian
Churches, posing before men as orthodox religionists,
who keep this private chapel where we do our devotion
to an idol and not to God.   If our real gods could be
made visible, what a pantheon they would make!   All
the foul forms painted on that cell of this vision would
be paralleled in the creeping things, which crawl along
the low earth and never soar nor even stand erect, and
in the vile, bestial forms of passion to which some of

us really bow down. Honour, wealth, literary or other
distinction, the sweet sanctities of human love dis-
honoured and profaned by being exalted to the place
which divine love should hold, ease, family, animal
appetites, lust, drink—these are the gods of some of us.
Bear with my poor words and ask yourselves, not whom
do you worship before the eye of men, but who is the
God to whom in your inmost heart you bow down?
What do you do in the dark? That is the question.
Whom do you worship there? Your other worship is
not worship at all.

Do not forget that all such diversion of supreme love
and dependence from God alone is like the sin of these
men in our text, in that it is sacrilege. They had taken
a chamber in the very Temple, and turned it into a
temple of the false gods. Whom is your heart made to
enshrine? Why! every stone, if I may so say, of the
fabric of our being bears marked upon it that it was laid
in order to make a dwelling-place for God. Whom are
you meant to worship, by the witness of the very constitution of your nature and make of your spirits? Is
there anybody but One who is worthy to receive the
priceless gift of human love absolute and entire? Is
there any but One to whom it is aught but degradation
and blasphemy for a man to bow down? Is there any
being but One that can still the tumult of my spirit,
and satisfy the immortal yearnings of my soul? We
were made for God, and whensoever we turn the hopes,
the desires, the affections, the obedience, and that
which is the root of them all, the confidence that ought
to fix and fasten upon Him, to other creatures, we
are guilty not only of idolatry but of sacrilege. We
commit the sin of which that wild reveller in Babylon
was guilty, when, at his great feast, in the very mad-

ness of his presumption he bade them bring forth the sacred vessels from the Temple at Jerusalem; 'and the king and his princes and his concubines drank in them and praised the gods.' So we take the sacred chalice of the human heart, on which there is marked the sign manual of Heaven, claiming it for God's, and fill it with the spiced and drugged draught of our own sensualities and evils, and pour out libations to vain and false gods. Brethren! Render unto Him that which is His; and see even upon the walls scrabbled all over with the deformities that we have painted there, lingering traces, like those of some dropping fresco in a roofless Italian church, which suggest the serene and perfect beauty of the image of the One whose likeness was originally traced there, and for whose worship it was all built.

III. And now, lastly, look at the sudden crashing in upon the cowering worshippers of the revealing light.

Apparently the picture of my text suggests that these elders knew not the eyes that were looking upon them. They were hugging themselves in the conceit, 'the Lord seeth not; the Lord hath forsaken the earth.' And all the while, all unknown, God and His prophet stand in the doorway and see it all. Not a finger is lifted, not a sign to the foolish worshippers of His presence and inspection, but in stern silence He records and remembers.

And does that need much bending to make it an impressive form of putting a solemn truth? There are plenty of us—alas! alas! that it should be so—to whom it is the least welcome of all thoughts that there in the doorway stand God and His Word. Why should it be, my brother, that the properly blessed thought of a divine eye resting upon you should be to you like the thought of a policeman's bull's-eye to a thief? Why should it not be rather the sweetest and the most calming and strength-giving of all convictions —'Thou God seest me'? The little child runs about the lawn perfectly happy as long as she knows that her mother is watching her from the window. And it ought to be sweet and blessed to each of us to know that there is no darkness where a Father's eye comes not. But oh! to the men that stand before bestial idols and have turned their backs on the beauty of the one true God, the only possibility of composure is that they shall hug themselves in the vain delusion :—'The Lord seeth not.'

I beseech you, dear friends, do not think of His eye as the prisoner in a cell thinks of the pin-hole somewhere in the wall, through which a jailer's jealous inspection may at any moment be glaring in upon him, but think of Him your Brother, who 'knew what was in man,' and who knows each man, and see in Christ the all-knowing Godhood that loves yet better than it knows, and beholds the hidden evils of men's hearts, in order that it may cleanse and forgive all which it beholds.

One day a light will flash in upon all the dark cells. We must all be manifest before the judgment-seat of Christ. Do you like that thought? Can you stand it? Are you ready for it? My friend! let Jesus Christ come to you with His light. Let Him come into the dark corners of your hearts. Cast all your sinfulness, known and unknown, upon Him that died on the Cross for every soul of man, and He will come; and His light, streaming into your hearts, like the sunbeam upon foul garments, will cleanse and bleach them white by its shining upon them. Let Him come into

your hearts by your lowly penitence, by your humble
faith, and all these vile shapes that you have painted
on its walls will, like phosphorescent pictures in the
daytime, pale and disappear when the 'Sun of Righteousness, with healing in His beams, floods your soul,
leaving no part dark, and turning all into a temple
of the living God.'

A COMMON MISTAKE AND LAME EXCUSE

'. . . He prophesieth of the times that are far off.'—EZEKIEL xii. 27.

HUMAN nature was very much the same in the exiles
that listened to Ezekiel on the banks of the Chebar
and in Manchester to-day. The same neglect of God's
message was grounded then on the same misappre-
hension of its bearings which profoundly operates in
the case of many people now. Ezekiel had been proclaiming the fall of Jerusalem to the exiles whose
captivity preceded it by a few years; and he was con-
fronted by the incredulity which fancied that it had a
great many facts to support it, and so it generalised
God's long-suffering delay in sending the threatened
punishment into a scoffing proverb which said, 'The
days are prolonged, and every vision faileth.' To
translate it into plain English, the prophets had cried
'Wolf! wolf!' so long that their alarms were dis-
believed altogether.

Even the people that did not go the length of utter
unbelief in the prophetic threatening took the com-
fortable conclusion that these threatenings had reference to a future date, and they need not trouble
themselves about them. And so they said, according
to my text, 'They of the house of Israel say, The

vision that he sees is for many days to come, and he prophesieth of the times that are far off.' 'It may be all quite true, but it lies away in the distant future there; and things will last our time, so we do not need to bother ourselves about what he says.'

So the imagined distance of fulfilment turned the edge of the plainest denunciations, and was like wool stuffed in the people's ears to deaden the reverberations of the thunder.

I wonder if there is anybody here now whom that fits, who meets the preaching of the gospel with a shrug, and with this saying, 'He prophesies of the times that are far off.' I fancy that there are a few; and I wish to say a word or two about this ground on which the widespread disregard of the divine message is based.

I. First, then, notice that the saying of my text— in the application which I now seek to make of it—is a truth, but it is only half a truth.

Of course, Ezekiel was speaking simply about the destruction of Jerusalem. If it had been true, as his hearers assumed, that that was not going to happen for a good many years yet, the chances were that it had no bearing upon them, and they were right enough in neglecting the teaching. And, of course, when I apply such a word as this in the direction in which I wish to do now, we do bring in a different set of thoughts; but the main idea remains the same. The neglect of God's solemn message by a great many people is based, more or less consciously, upon the notion that the message of Christianity—or, if you like to call it so, of the gospel; or, if you like to call it more vaguely, religion—has to do mainly with blessings and woes beyond the grave, and that there is plenty of time to attend to it when we get nearer the end.

Now is it true that 'he prophesies of times that are far off'? Yes! and No! Yes! it is true, and it is the great glory of Christianity that it shifts the centre of gravity, so to speak, from this poor, transient, contemptible present, and sets it away out yonder in an august and infinite future. It brings to us not only knowledge of the future, but certitude, and takes the conception of another life out of the region of perhapses, possibilities, dreads, or hopes, as the case may be, and sets it in the sunlight of certainty. There is no more mist. Other faiths, even when they have risen to the height of some contemplation of a future, have always seen it wrapped in nebulous clouds of possibilities, but Christianity sets it clear, definite, solid, as certain as yesterday, as certain as to-day.

It not only gives us the knowledge and the certitude of the times that are afar off, and that are not times but eternities, but it gives us, as the all-important element in that future, that its ruling characteristic is retribution. It 'brings life and immortality to light,' and just because it does, it brings the dark orb which, like some of the double stars in the heavens, is knit to the radiant sphere by a necessary band. It brings to light, with life and immortality, death and woe. It is true—'he prophesies of times that are far off,' and it is the glory of the gospel of Christ's revelation, and of the religion that is based thereon, that its centre is beyond the grave, and that its eye is so often turned to the clearly discerned facts that lie there.

But is that all that we have to say about Christianity? Many representations of it, I am free to confess, from pulpits and books and elsewhere, do talk as if that *was*

all, as if it was a magnificent thing to have when you
came to die. As the play has it, 'I said to him that I
hoped there was no need that he should think about
God yet,' because he was not going to die. But I urge
you to remember, dear brethren, that all that prophesying of times that are far off has the closest bearing
upon this transient, throbbing moment, because, for one
thing, one solemn part of the Christian revelation about
the future is that Time is the parent of Eternity, and
that, in like manner as in our earthly course 'the child
is father of the man,' so the man as he has made himself is the author of himself as he will be through the
infinite spaces that lie beyond the grave. Therefore,
when a Christian preacher prophesies of times that are
afar off, he is prophesying of present time, between
which and the most distant eternity there is an iron
nexus—a band which cannot be broken.

Nor is that all. Not only is the truth in my text but
a half truth, if it is supposed that the main business of
the gospel is to talk to us about heaven and hell, and
not about the earth on which we secure and procure
the one or the other; but also it is a half truth because,
large and transcendent, eternal in their duration, and
blessed beyond all thought in their sweetness as are
the possibilities, the certainties that are opened by the
risen and ascended Christ, and tremendous beyond all
words that men can speak as are the alternative possibilities, yet these are not all the contents of the gospel
message; but those blessings and penalties, joys and
miseries, exaltations and degradations, which attend
upon righteousness and sin, godliness and irreligion
to-day are a large part of its theme and of its effects.
Therefore, whilst on the one hand it is true, blessed be
Christ's name! that 'he prophesies of times that are

far off'; on the other hand it is an altogether inadequate description of the gospel message and of the
Christian body of truth to say that the future is its
realm, and not the present.

II. So, then, in the second place, my text gives a very
good reason for prizing and attending to the prophecy.

If it is true that God, speaking through the facts of
Christ's death and Resurrection and Ascension, has
given to us the sure and certain hope of immortality,
and has declared to us plainly the conditions upon
which that immortality may be ours, and the woful
loss and eclipse into the shadow of which we shall
stumble darkling if it is not ours, then surely that is
a reason for prizing and laying to heart, and living
by the revelation so mercifully made. People do not
usually kick over their telescopes, and neglect to look
through them, because they are so powerful that they
show them the craters in the moon and turn faint
specks into blazing suns. People do not usually neglect
a word of warning or guidance in reference to the
ordering of their earthly lives because it is so comprehensive, and covers so large a ground, and is so certain
and absolutely true. Surely there can be no greater
sign of divine loving-kindness, of a Saviour's tenderness and care for us, than that He should come to each
of us, as He does come, and say to each of us, 'Thou
art to live for ever; and if thou wilt take Me for thy
Life, thou shalt live for ever, blessed, calm, and pure.'
And we listen, and say, 'He prophesies of times that
are far off!' Oh! is that not rather a reason for coming
very close to, and for grappling to our hearts and
living always by the power of, that great revelation?
Surely to announce the consequences of evil, and to
announce them so long beforehand that there is plenty

of time to avoid them and to falsify the prediction, is the token of love.

Now I wish to lay it on the hearts of you people who call yourselves Christians, and who are so in some imperfect degree, whether we do at all adequately regard, remember, and live by this great mercy of God, that He *should* have prophesied to us ' of the times that are far off.' Perhaps I am wrong, but I cannot help feeling that, for this generation, the glories of the future rest with God have been somewhat paled, and the terrors of the future unrest away from God have been somewhat lightened. I hope I am wrong, but I do not think that the modern average Christian thinks as much about heaven as his father did. And I believe that his religion has lost something of its buoyancy, of its power, of its restraining and stimulating energy, because, from a variety of reasons, the bias of this generation is rather to dwell upon, and to realise, the present social blessings of Christianity than to project itself into that august future. The reaction may be good. I have no doubt it was needed, but I think it has gone rather too far, and I would beseech Christian men and women to try and deserve more the sarcasm that is flung at us that we live for another world. Would God it were true—truer than it is! We should see better work done in this world if it were. So I say, that ' he prophesieth of times that are far off' is a good reason for prizing and obeying the prophet.

III. Lastly, this is a very common and a very bad reason for neglecting the prophecy.

It does operate as a reason for giving little heed to the prophet, as I have been saying. In the old men-of-war, when an engagement was impending, they used to bring up the hammocks from the bunks and pile them into the nettings at the side of the ship, to defend it from boarders and bullets. And then, after these had served their purpose of repelling, they were taken down again and the crew went to sleep upon them. That is exactly what some of my friends do with that misconception of the genius of Christianity which supposes that it is concerned mainly with another world. They put it up as a screen between them and God, between them and what they know to be their duty—viz., the acceptance of Christ as their Saviour. It is their hammock that they put between the bullets and themselves; and many a good sleep they get upon it!

Now, that strange capacity that men have of ignoring a certain future is seen at work all round about us in every region of life. I wonder how many young men there are in Manchester to-day that have begun to put their foot upon the wrong road, and who know just as well as I do that the end of it is disease, blasted reputation, ruined prospects, perhaps an early death. Why! there is not a drunkard in the city that does not know that. Every man that takes opium knows it. Every unclean, unchaste liver knows it; and yet he can hide the thought from himself, and go straight on as if there was nothing at all of the sort within the horizon of possibility. It is one of the most marvellous things that men have that power; only beaten by the marvel that, having it, they should be such fools as to choose to exercise it. The peasants on the slopes of Vesuvius live very careless lives, and they have their little vineyards and their olives. Yes, and every morning when they come out, they can look up and see the thin wreath of smoke going up in the dazzling blue,

and they know that some time or other there will be a
roar and a rush, and down will come the lava. But 'a
short life and a merry one' is the creed of a good many
of us, though we do not like to confess it. Some of
you will remember the strange way in which ordinary
habits survived in prisons in the dreadful times of the
French Revolution, and how ladies and gentlemen,
who were going to have their heads chopped off next
morning, danced and flirted, and sat at entertainments,
just as if there was no such thing in the world as the
public prosecutor and the tumbril, and the gaoler going
about with a bit of chalk to mark each door where were
the condemned for next day.

That same strange power of ignoring a known future,
which works so widely and so disastrously round about
us, is especially manifested in regard to religion. The
great bulk of English men and women who are not
Christians, and the little sample of such that I have
in my audience now, as a rule believe as fully as
we do the truths which they agree to neglect. Let me
speak to them individually. You believe that death
will introduce you into a world of two halves—that if
you have been a good, religious man, you will dwell
in blessedness; that if you have not, you will not—
yet you never did a single thing, nor refrained from a
single thing, because of that belief. And when I, and
men of my profession, come and plead with you and
try to get through that strange web of insensibility
that you have spun round you, you listen, and then
you say, with a shrug, 'He prophesies of things that
are far off,' and you turn with relief to the trivialities
of the day. Need I ask you whether that is a wise
thing or not?

Surely it is not wise for a man to ignore a future

B

that is certain simply because it is distant. So long as it is certain, what in the name of common-sense has the time when it begins to be a present to do with our wisdom in regard to it? It is the uncertainty in future anticipations which makes it unwise to regulate life largely by them, and if you can eliminate that element of uncertainty — which you can do if you believe in Jesus Christ—then the question is not when is the prophecy going to be fulfilled, but is it true and trustworthy? The man is a fool who, because it is far off, thinks he can neglect it.

Surely it is not wise to ignore a future which is so incomparably greater than this present, and which also is so connected with this present as that life here is only intelligible as the vestibule and preparation for that great world beyond.

Surely it is not wise to ignore a future because you fancy it is far away, when it may burst upon you at any time. These exiles to whom Ezekiel spoke hugged themselves in the idea that his words were not to be fulfilled for many days to come; but they were mistaken, and the crash of the fall of Jerusalem stunned them before many months had passed by. We have to look forward to a future which must be very near to some of us, which may be nearer to others than they think, which at the remotest is but a little way from us, and which must come to us all. Oh, dear friends, surely it is not wise to ignore as far off that which for some of us may be here before this day closes, which will probably be ours in some cases before the fresh young leaves now upon the trees have dropped yellow in the autumn frosts, which at the most distant must be very near us, and which waits for us all.

What would you think of the crew and passengers of some ship lying in harbour, waiting for its sailing orders, who had got leave on shore, and did not know but that at any moment the blue-peter might be flying at the fore — the signal to weigh anchor — if they behaved themselves in the port as if they were never going to embark, and made no preparations for the voyage? Let me beseech you to rid yourselves of that most unreasonable of all reasons for neglecting the gospel, that its most solemn revelations refer to the eternity beyond the grave.

There are many proofs that man on the whole is a very foolish creature, but there is not one more tragical than the fact that believing, as many of you do, that 'the wages of sin is death, and the gift of God is eternal life through Jesus Christ,' you stand aloof from accepting the gift, and risk the death.

The 'times far off' have long since come near enough to those scoffers. The most distant future will be present to you before you are ready for it, unless you accept Jesus Christ as your All, for time and for eternity. If you do, the time that is near will be pure and calm, and the times that are far off will be radiant with unfading bliss.

THE HOLY NATION

'Then will I sprinkle clean water upon you, and ye shall be clean: from all your filthiness, and from all your idols, will I cleanse you. 26. A new heart also will I give you, and a new spirit will I put within you: and I will take away the stony heart out of your flesh, and I will give you an heart of flesh. 27. And I will put My Spirit within you, and cause you to walk in My statutes, and ye shall keep My judgments, and do them. 28. And ye shall dwell in the land that I gave to your fathers; and ye shall be My people, and I will be your God. 29. I will also save you from all your uncleannesses: and I will call for the corn, and will increase it, and lay no famine upon you. 30. And I will multiply the fruit of the tree, and the increase of the field, that ye shall receive no more reproach of famine among the heathen. 31. Then shall ye remember your own evil ways, and your doings that

were not good, and shall loathe yourselves in your own sight for your iniquities
and for your abominations. 32. Not for your sakes do I this, saith the Lord God,
be it known unto you: be ashamed and confounded for your own ways, O house
of Israel. 33. Thus saith the Lord God; In the day that I shall have cleansed you
from all your iniquities I will also cause you to dwell in the cities, and the wastes
shall be builded. 34. And the desolate land shall be tilled, whereas it lay desolate
in the sight of all that passed by. 35. And they shall say, This land that was
desolate is become like the garden of Eden; and the waste and desolate and
ruined cities are become fenced, and are inhabited. 36. Then the heathen that
are left round about you shall know that I the Lord build the ruined places, and
plant that that was desolate: I the Lord have spoken it, and I will do it. 37. Thus
saith the Lord God; I will yet for this be enquired of by the house of Israel, to do
it for them; I will increase them with men like a flock. 38. As the holy flock, as
the flock of Jerusalem in her solemn feasts; so shall the waste cities be filled with
flocks of men: and they shall know that I am the Lord.'—EZEKIEL xxxvi. 25-38.

THIS great prophecy had but a partial fulfilment,
though a real one, in the restored Israel. The land
was given back, the nation *was* multiplied, fertility
again blessed the smiling fields and vineyards, and,
best of all, the people *were* cleansed 'from all their
idols' by the furnace of affliction. Nothing is more
remarkable than the transformation effected by the
captivity, in regard to the idolatrous propensities of
the people. Whereas before it they were always
hankering after the gods of the nations, they came
back from Babylon the resolute champions of monotheism, and never thereafter showed the smallest
inclination for what had before been so irresistible.

But the fulness of Ezekiel's prophecy is not realised
until Jeremiah's prophecy of the new covenant is
brought to pass. Nor does the state of the militant
church on earth exhaust it. Future glories gleam
through the words. They have a 'springing accomplishment' in the Israel of the restoration, a fuller in
the New Testament church, and their ultimate realisation in the New Jerusalem, which shall yet descend to
be the bride, the Lamb's wife. The principles involved
in the prophecy belong to the region of purely spiritual
religion, and are worth pondering, apart from any
question of the place and manner of fulfilment.

First comes the great truth that the foundation, so far as concerns the history of a soul or of a community, of all other good is divine forgiveness (v. 25). Ezekiel, the priest, casts the promise into ceremonial form, and points to the sprinklings of the polluted under the law, or to the ritual of consecration to the priesthood. That cleansing is the removal of already contracted defilement, especially of the guilt of idolatry. It is clearly distinguished from the operation on the inward nature which follows; that is to say, it is the promise of forgiveness, or of justification, not of sanctification.

From what deep fountains in the divine nature that ' clean water' was to flow, Ezekiel does not know; but we have learned that a more precious fluid than water is needed, and have to think of Him ' who came not by water only, but by water and blood,' in whom we have redemption through His blood, even the forgiveness of our sins. But the central idea of this first promise is that it must be God's hand which sprinkles from an evil conscience. Forgiveness is a divine prerogative. He only can, and He will, cleanse from all filthiness. His pardon is universal. The most ingrained sins cannot be too black to melt away from the soul. The dye-stuffs of sin are very strong, but there is one solvent which they cannot resist. There are no ' fast colours' which God's ' clean water' cannot move. This cleansing of pardon underlies all the rest of the blessings. It is ever the first thing needful when a soul returns to God.

Then follows an equally exclusively divine act, the impartation of a new nature, which shall secure future obedience (vs. 26, 27). Who can thrust his hand into the depths of man's being, and withdraw one life-principle and enshrine another, while yet the individu-

ality of the man remains untouched? God only. How
profound the consciousness of universal obstinacy and
insensibility which regards human nature, apart from
such renewal, as possessing but a 'heart of stone'!
There are no sentimental illusions about the grim facts
of humanity here. Superficial views of sin and rose-
tinted fancies about human nature will not admit the
truth of the Scripture doctrine of sinfulness, alienation
from God. They diagnose the disease superficially, and
therefore do not know how to cure it. The Bible can
venture to give full weight to the gravity of the sickness, because it knows the remedy. No surgery but
God's can perform that operation of extracting the
stony heart and inserting a heart of flesh. No system
which cannot do that can do what men want. The
gospel alone deals thoroughly with man's ills.

And how does it effect that great miracle? 'I will
put My Spirit within you.' The new life-principle is
the effluence of the Spirit of God. The promise does
not merely offer the influence of a divine spirit, working
on men as from without, or coming down upon them as
an afflatus, but the actual planting of God's Spirit in
the deep places of theirs. We fail to apprehend the
most characteristic blessing of the gospel if we do not
give full prominence to that great gift of an indwelling
Spirit, the life of our lives. Cleansing is much, but is
incomplete without a new life-principle which shall
keep us clean; and that can only be God's Spirit, enshrined and operative within us; for only thus shall
we 'walk in His statutes, and keep His judgments.'
When the Lawgiver dwells in our hearts, the law will
be our delight; and keeping it will be the natural outcome and expression of our life, which is His life.

Then follows the picture of the blessed effects of

obedience (vs. 28-30). These are cast into the form
appropriate to the immediate purpose of the prophecy,
and received fulfilment in the actual restoration to the
land, which fulfilment, however, was imperfect, inasmuch as the obedience and renewal of the people's
hearts were incomplete. These can only be complete
under the gospel, and, in the fullest sense, only in
another order than the present. When men fully keep
God's judgments, they shall dwell permanently in a
good land. Israel's hold on its country was its obedience, not its prowess. Our real hold on even earthly
good is the choosing of God for our supreme good.
In the measure in which we can say ' Thy law is within
my heart,' all things are ours; and we may possess all
things while having nothing in the vulgar world's sense
of having. Similarly that obedience, which is the fruit
of the new life of God's Spirit in our spirits, is the condition of close mutual possession in the blessed recipro-
city of trust and faithfulness, love bestowing and love
receiving, by which the quiet heart knows that God is
its, and it is God's. If stains and interruptions still
sometimes break the perfectness of obedience and continuity of reciprocal ownership, there will be a further
cleansing for such sins. ' If we walk in the light, the
blood of Jesus Christ His Son cleanseth us from all sin '
(v. 29).

The lovely picture of the blessed dwellers in their
good land is closed by the promise of abundant harvests
from corn and fruit-tree ; that is, all that nourishes or
delights. The deepest truth taught thereby is that he
who lives in God has no unsatisfied desires, but finds in
Him all that can sustain, strengthen, and minister to
growth, and all that can give gladness and delight. If
we make God our heritage, we dwell secure in a good

land; and 'the dust of that land is gold,' and its harvests ever plenteous.

Very profoundly and beautifully does Ezekiel put as the last trait in his picture, and as the upshot of all this cornucopia of blessings, the penitent remembrance of past evils. Undeserved mercies steal into the heart like the breath of the south wind, and melt the ice. The more we advance in holiness and consequent blessed communion with God, the more clearly shall we see the evil of our past. Forgiven sin looks far blacker because it is forgiven. When we are not afraid of sin's consequences, we see more plainly its sinfulness. When we have tasted God's sweetness, we think with more shame of our ingratitude and folly. If God forgets, the more reason for us to remember our transgressions. The man who 'has forgotten that he was purged from his old sins' is in danger of finding out that he is not purged from them. There is no gnawing of conscience, nor any fearful looking for of judgment in such remembrance, but a wholesome humility passing into thankful wonder that such sin is pardoned, and such a sinner made God's friend.

The deep foundation of all the blessedness is finally laid bare (v. 32) as being God's undeserved mercy. 'For Mine holy name' (v. 22) is God's reason. He is His own motive, and He wills that the world should know His name,—that is, His manifested character,—and understand how loving and long-suffering He is. So He wills, not because such knowledge adds to His glory, but because it satisfies His love, since it will make the men who know His name blessed. The truth that God's motive is His own name's sake may be so put as to be hideous and repellent; but it really proclaims that He is love, and that His motive is His poor creatures' blessing.

To this great outline of the blessings of the restored nations are appended two subsidiary prophecies, marked by the recurring 'Thus saith the Lord.' The former of these (vs. 33-36) deals principally with the new beauty that was to clothe the land. The day in which the inhabitants were cleansed from their sins was to be the day in which the land was to be raised from its ruin. Cities are to be rebuilt, the ground that had lain fallow and tangled with briers and thorns is to be tilled, and to bloom like Eden, a restored paradise. How far the fulfilment has halted behind the promise, the melancholy condition of Palestine to-day may remind us. Whether the literal fulfilment is to be anticipated or no seems less important than to note that the experience of forgiveness (and of the consequent blessings described above) is the precursor of this fair picture. Therefore, the Church's condition of growth and prosperity is its realisation in the persons of its individual members, of pardon, the renewal of the inner man by the indwelling Spirit, faithful obedience, communion with God, and lowly remembrance of past sins. Where churches are marked by such characteristics, they will grow. If they are not, all their 'evangelistic efforts' will be as sounding brass and a tinkling cymbal.

The second appended prophecy (vs. 37, 38) is that of increase of population. The picture of the flocks of sheep for sacrifice, which thronged Jerusalem at the feasts, is given as a likeness of the swarms of inhabitants in the 'waste cities.' The point of comparison is chiefly the number. One knows how closely a flock huddles and seems to fill the road in endless procession. But the destination as well as the number comes into view. All these patient creatures, crowding the ways, are meant for sacrifices. So the inhabitants of the land then shall all yield themselves to God, living sacrifices. The first words of our text point to the priesthood of all believers; the last words point to the sacrifice of themselves which they have to offer.

'For this moreover will I be inquired of by the house of Israel.' The blessings promised do not depend on our merits, as we have heard, but yet they will not be given without our co-operation in prayer. God promises, and that promise is not a reason for our not asking the gifts from Him, but for our asking. Faith keeps within the lines of God's promise, and prayers which do not foot themselves on a promise are the off-spring of presumption, not of faith. God 'lets Himself be inquired of' for that which is in accordance with His will; and, accordant with His will though it be, He will not 'do it for them,' unless His flock ask of Him the accomplishment of His own word.

THE DRY BONES AND THE SPIRIT OF LIFE

'The hand of the Lord was upon me, and carried me out in the spirit of the Lord, and set me down in the midst of the valley which was full of bones, 2. And caused me to pass by them round about: and, behold, there were very many in the open valley; and, lo, they were very dry. 3. And He said unto me, Son of man, can these bones live? And I answered, O Lord God, Thou knowest. 4. Again He said unto me, Prophesy upon these bones, and say unto them, O ye dry bones, hear the word of the Lord. 5. Thus saith the Lord God unto these bones; Behold, I will cause breath to enter into you, and ye shall live: 6. And I will lay sinews upon you, and will bring up flesh upon you, and cover you with skin, and put breath in you, and ye shall live; and ye shall know that I am the Lord. 7. So I prophesied as I was commanded: and as I prophesied, there was a noise, and behold a shaking, and the bones came together, bone to his bone. 8. And when I beheld, lo, the sinews and the flesh came up upon them, and the skin covered them above: but there was no breath in them. 9. Then said He unto me, Prophesy unto the wind, prophesy, son of man, and say to the wind, Thus saith the Lord God; Come from the four winds, O breath, and breathe upon these slain, that they may live. 10. So I prophesied as He commanded me, and the breath came into them, and they lived, and stood up upon their feet, an ex-ceeding great army. 11. Then He said unto me, Son of man, these bones are the whole house of Israel: behold, they say, Our bones are dried, and our hope is lost: we are cut off for our parts. 12. Therefore prophesy and say unto them, Thus saith the Lord God; Behold, O My people, I will open your graves, and cause you to come up out of your graves, and bring you into the land of Israel. 13. And ye shall know that I am the Lord, when I have opened your graves, O My people, and brought you up out of your graves, 14. And shall put My spirit in you, and ye shall live, and I shall place you in your own land: then shall ye know that I the Lord have spoken it, and performed it, saith the Lord.'— EZEKIEL xxxvii. 1-14.

THIS great vision apparently took its form from a despairing saying, which had become a proverb among the exiles, 'Our bones are dried up, and our hope is lost: we are clean cut off' (v. 11). Ezekiel lays hold of the metaphor, which had been taken to express the hopeless destruction of Israel's national existence, and even from it wrings a message of hope. Faith has the prerogative of seeing possibilities of life in what looks to sense hopeless death. We may look at the vision from three points of view, considering its bearing on Israel, on the world, and on the resurrection of the body.

I. The saying, already referred to, puts the hopelessness of the mass of the exiles in a forcible fashion. The only sense in which living men could say that their bones were dried up, and they cut off, is a figurative one, and obviously it is the national existence which they regarded as irretrievably ended. The saying gives us a glimpse into the despair which had settled down on the exiles, and against which Ezekiel had to contend, as he had also to contend against its apparently opposite and yet kindred feeling of presumptuous, misplaced hope. We observe that he begins by accepting fully the facts which bred despair, and even accentuating them. The true prophet never makes light of the miseries of which he knows the cure, and does not try to comfort by minimising the gravity of the evil. The bones *are* very many, and they *are* very dry. As far as outward resources are

concerned, despair was rational, and hope as absurd as
it would have been to expect that men, dead so long
that their bones had been bleached by years of ex-
posure to the weather, should live again.

But while Ezekiel saw the facts of Israel's powerless-
ness as plainly as the most despondent, he did not
therefore despair.   The question which rose in his
mind was God's question, and the very raising it
let a gleam of hope in.   So he answered with that
noble utterance of faith and submission, 'O Lord
God, Thou knowest.'   'With God all things are
possible.'   Presumption would have said 'Yes';
Unbelief would have said 'No'; Faith says, 'Thou
knowest.'

The grand description of the process of resurrection
follows the analogy of the order in the creation of
man, giving, first, the shaping of the body, and afterwards the breathing into it of the breath which is life.
Both stages are wholly God's work.   The prophet's
part was to prophesy to the bones first; and his word,
in a sense, brought about the effect which it foretold,
since his ministry was the most potent means of re-
kindling dying hopes, and bringing the *disjecta membra*
of the nation together again.   The vivid and gigantic
imagination of the prophet gives a picture of the
rushing together of the bones, which has no superior
in any literature.   He hears a noise, and sees a
'shaking' (by which is meant the motion of the bones
to each other, rather than an 'earthquake,' as the
Revised Version has it, which inserts a quite irrelevant
detail), and the result of all is that the skeletons are
complete.   Then follows the gradual clothing with
flesh.   There they lie, a host of corpses.

The second stage is the quickening of these bodies

with life, and here again Ezekiel, as God's messenger, has power to bring about what he announces; for, at his command, the breath, or wind, or spirit, comes, and the stiff corpses spring to their feet, a mighty army. The explanation in the last verses of the text somewhat departs from the tenor of the vision by speaking of Israel as buried, but keeps to its substance, and point the despairing exiles to God as the source of national resurrection. But we must not force deeper meaning on Ezekiel's words than they properly bear. The spirit promised in them is simply the source of life,—literally, of physical life; metaphorically, of national life. However that national restoration was connected with holiness, that does not enter into the prophet's vision. Israel's restoration to its land is all that Ezekiel meant by it. True, that restoration was to lead to clearer recognition by Israel of the name of Jehovah, and of all that it implied in him and demanded from them. But the proper scope of the vision is to assure despairing Israelites that God would quicken the apparently slain national life, and replace them in the land.

II. We may extend the application of the vision to the condition of humanity and the divine intervention which communicates life to a dead world, but must remember that no such meaning was in Ezekiel's thoughts. The valley full of dry bones is but too correct a description of the aspect which a world 'dead in trespasses and sins' bears, when seen from the mountain-top by pure and heavenly eyes. The activities of godless lives mask the real spiritual death, which is the condition of every soul that is separate from God. Galvanised corpses may have muscular movements, but they are dead, notwith-

standing their twitching. They that live without God
are dead while they live.

Again, we may learn from the vision the preparation
needful for the prophet, who is to be the instrument
of imparting divine life to a dead world. The sorrow-
ful sense of the widespread deadness must enter into
a man's spirit, and be ever present to him, in order
to fit him for his work. A dead world is not to be
quickened on easy terms. We must see mankind in
some measure as God sees them if we are to do God's
work among them. So-called Christian teachers, who
do not believe that the race is dead in sin, or who,
believing it, do not feel the tragedy of the fact, and
the power lodged in their hands to bring the true life,
may prophesy to the dry bones for ever, and there will
be no shaking among them.

The great work of the gospel is to communicate
divine life. The details of the process in the vision
are not applicable in this respect. As we have pointed
out, they are shaped after the pattern of the creation
of Adam, but the essential point is that what the world
needs is the impartation from God of His Spirit. We
know more than Ezekiel did as to the way by which
that Spirit is given to men, and as to the kind of life
which it imparts, and as to the connection between
that life and holiness. It is a diviner voice than
Ezekiel's which speaks to us in the name of God, and
says to us with deeper meaning than the prophet of
the Exile dreamed of, 'I will put my Spirit in you, and
ye shall live.'

But we may note that it is possible to have the
outward form of a living body, and yet to have no life.
Churches and individuals may be perfectly organised
and perfectly dead. Creeds may be articulated most

correctly, every bone in its place, and yet have no vitality in them. Forms of worship may be punctiliously proper, and have no breath of life in them. Religion must have a body, but often the body is not so much the organ as the sepulchre of the spirit. We have to take heed that the externals do not kill the inward life.

Again, we note that this great act of life-giving is God's revelation of His name,—that is, of His character so far as men can know it. 'Ye shall know that I am the Lord' (vs. 13, 14). God makes Himself known in His divinest glory when He quickens dead souls. The world may learn what He is therefrom, but they who have experienced the change, and have, as it were, been raised from the grave to new life, have personal experience of His power and faithfulness so sure and sweet that henceforward they cannot doubt Him nor forget His grace.

III. As to the bearing of the vision on the doctrine of the resurrection little need be said. It does not necessarily presuppose the people's acquaintance with that doctrine, for it would be quite conceivable that the vision had revealed to the prophet the thought of a resurrection, which had not been in his beliefs before. The vision is so entirely figurative, that it cannot be employed as evidence that the idea of the resurrection of the dead was part of the Jewish beliefs at this date. It does, however, seem most natural to suppose that the exiles were familiar with the idea, though the vision cannot be taken as a revelation of a literal resurrection of dead men. For clear expectations of such a resurrection we must turn to such scriptures as Daniel xii. 2, 13.

THE RIVER OF LIFE

'Waters issued out from under the threshold of the house . . .

EZEKIEL xlvii. 1.

UNLIKE most great cities, Jerusalem was not situated
on a great river. True, the inconsiderable waters of
Siloam — 'which flow softly' because they were so
inconsiderable—rose from a crevice in the Temple rock,
and beneath that rock stretched the valley of the
Kedron, dry and bleached in the summer, and a rainy
torrent during the rainy seasons; but that was all.
So, many of the prophets, who looked forward to the
better times to come, laid their finger upon that one
defect, and prophesied that it should be cured. Thus
we read in a psalm: 'There is a river, the divisions
whereof make glad the City of our God.' Faith saw
what sense saw not. Again, Isaiah says: 'There'
—that is to say, in the new Jerusalem—'the glorious
Lord shall be unto us a place of broad rivers and
streams.' And so, this prophet casts his anticipations
of the abundant outpouring of blessing that shall come
when God in very deed dwells among men, into this
figure of a river pouring out from beneath the Temple-
door, and spreading life and fertility wherever its waters
come. I need not remind you how our Lord Himself
uses the same figure, and modifies it, by saying that whosoever believeth on Him, 'out of him shall flow rivers of
living waters'; or how, in the very last words of the
Apocalyptic seer, we hear again the music of the ripples
of the great stream, 'the river of the water of life
proceeding out of the Throne of God and of the Lamb.'
So then, all through Scripture, we may say that we
hear the murmur of the stream, and can catch the line

of verdure upon its banks. My object now is not only
to deal with the words that I have read as a starting-
point, but rather to seek to draw out the wonderful
significance of this great prophetic parable.

I. I notice, first, the source from which the river
comes.

I have already anticipated that in pointing out that
it flows from the very Temple itself. The Prophet sees
it coming out of the house—that is to say, the Sanctuary.
It flows across the outer court of the house, passes the
altar, comes out under the threshold, and then pours
itself down on to the plain beneath. This is the symbolical dress of the thought that all spiritual blessings,
and every conceivable form of human good, take their
rise in the fact of God's dwelling with men. From
beneath the Temple threshold comes the water of life ;
and wherever it is true that in any heart—or in any
community—God dwells, there will be heard the tinkling of its ripples, and freshness and fertility will come
from the stream. The dwelling of God with a man,
like the dwelling of God in humanity in the Incarnation of His own dear Son, is, as it were, the opening of
the fountain that it may pour out into the world. So,
if we desire to have the blessings that are possible for
us, we must comply with the conditions, and let God
dwell in our hearts, and make them His temples; and
then from beneath the threshold of that temple, too,
will pour out, according to Christ's own promise, rivers
of living water which will be first for ourselves to
drink of and be blessed by, and then will refresh and
gladden others.

Another thought connected with this source of the
river of life is that all the blessings which, massed
together, are included in that one word 'salvation'—

which is a kind of nebula made up of many unresolved
stars—take their rise from nothing else than the deep
heart of God Himself. This river rose in the House of
the Lord, and amidst the mysteries of the Divine
Presence; it took its rise, one might say, from beneath
the Mercy-seat where the brooding Cherubim sat in
silence and poured itself into a world that had not
asked for it, that did not expect it, that in many of its
members did not desire it and would not have it. The
river that rose in the secret place of God symbolises
for us the great thought which is put into plainer
words by the last of the apostles when he says, 'We
love Him because He first loved us.' All the blessings
of salvation rise from the unmotived, self-impelled,
self-fed divine love and purpose. Nothing moves Him
to communicate Himself but His own delight in giving
Himself to His poor creatures; and it is all of grace
that it might be all through faith.

Still further, another thought that may be suggested
in connection with the source of this river is, that that
which is to bless the world must necessarily take its
rise above the world. Ezekiel has sketched, in the last
portion of his prophecy, an entirely ideal topography
of the Holy Land. He has swept away mountains and
valleys, and levelled all out into a great plain, in the
midst of which rises the mountain of the Lord's House,
far higher than the Temple hill. In reality, opposite it
rose the Mount of Olives, and between the two there
was the deep gorge of the Valley of the Kedron. The
Prophet smooths it all out into one great plain, and
high above all towers the Temple-mount, and from it
there rushes down on to the low levels the fertilising,
life-giving flood.

That imaginary geography tells us this, that what is

to bless the world must come from above the world. There needs a waterfall to generate electricity; the power which is to come into humanity and deal with its miseries must have its source high above the objects of its energy and its compassion, and in proportion to the height from which it falls will be the force of its impact and its power to generate the quickening impulse. All merely human efforts at social reform, rivers that do not rise in the Temple, are like the rivers in Mongolia, that run for a few miles and then get sucked up by the hot sands and are lost and nobody sees them any more. Only the perennial stream, that comes out from beneath the Temple threshold, can sustain itself in the desert, to say nothing of transforming the desert into a Garden of Eden. So moral and social and intellectual and political reformers may well go to Ezekiel, and learn that the 'river of the water of life,' which is to heal the barren and refresh the thirsty land, must come from below the Temple threshold.

II. Note the rapid increase of the stream.

The Prophet describes how his companion, the interpreter, measured down the stream a thousand cubits—about a quarter of a mile—and the waters were ankle-deep another thousand, making half a mile from the start, and the water was knee-deep. Another thousand —or three-quarters of a mile—and the water was waist-deep; another thousand—about a mile in all—and the water was unfordable, 'waters to swim in, a river that could not be passed over.' Where did the increase come from? There were no tributaries. We do not hear of any side-stream flowing into the main body. Where did the increase come from? It came from the abundant welling-up in the sanctuary. The fountain was the mother of the river—that is to say, God's ideal for the world, for the Church, for the individual Christian, is rapid increase in their experience of the depth and the force of the stream of blessings which together make up salvation. So we come to a very sharp testing question. Will anybody tell me that the rate at which Christianity has grown for these nineteen centuries corresponds with Ezekiel's. vision—which is God's ideal? Will any Christian man say, 'My own growth in grace, and increase in the depth and fulness of the flow of the river through my spirit and my life correspond to that ideal'? A mile from the source the river is unfordable. How many miles from the source of *our* first experience do we stand? How many of us, instead of having 'a river that could not be passed over, waters to swim in,' have but a poor and all but stagnant feeble trickle, as shallow as or shallower than it was at first?

I was speaking a minute ago about Mongolian rivers. Australian rivers are more like some men's lives. A chain of ponds in the dry season—nay! not even a chain, but a series, with no connecting channel of water between them. That is like a great many Christian people; they have isolated times when they feel the voice of Christ's love, and yield themselves to the powers of the world to come, and then there are long intervals, when they feel neither the one nor the other. But the picture that ought to be realised by each of us is God's ideal, which there is power in the gospel to make real in the case of every one of us, the rapid and continuous increase in the depth and in the scour of 'the river of the water of life,' that flows through our lives. Luther used to say, 'If you want to clean out a dunghill, turn the Elbe into it.' If you desire to have your hearts cleansed

of all their foulness, turn the river into it. But it needs
to be a progressively deepening river, or there will be
no scour in the feeble trickle, and we shall not be a bit
the holier or the purer for our potential and imperfect
Christianity.

III. Lastly, note the effects of the stream.

These are threefold: fertility, healing, life. Fertility.
In the East one condition of fertility is water. Irrigate
the desert, and you make it a garden. Break down
the aqueduct, and you make the granary of the world
into a waste. The traveller as he goes along can
tell where there is a stream of water, by the verdure
along its banks. You travel along a plateau, and it is
all baked and barren. You plunge into a wâdy, and
immediately the ground is clothed with under-growth
and shrubs, and the birds of the air sing among the
branches. And so, says Ezekiel, wherever the river
comes there springs up, as if by magic, fair trees 'on
the banks thereof, whose leaf shall not fade, neither
shall the fruit thereof be consumed.'

Fertility comes second, the reception of the fertilising
agent comes first. It is wasted time to tinker at our
characters unless we have begun with getting into our
hearts the grace of God, and the new spirit that will
be wrought out by diligent effort into all beauty of life
and character. Ezekiel seems to be copying the first
psalm, or *vice versa*, the Psalmist is copying Ezekiel.
At any rate, there is a verbal similarity between them,
in that both dwell upon the unfading leaf of the tree
that grows planted by rivers of water. And our text
goes further, and speaks about perennial fruitfulness
month by month, all the year round. In some tropical
countries you will find blossoms, buds in their earliest
stage, and ripened fruit all hanging upon one laden

branch. Such ought to be the Christian life—continuously fruitful because dependent upon continual drawing into itself, by means of its roots and suckers, of the water of life by which we are fructified.

There is yet another effect of the waters—healing. As we said, Ezekiel takes great liberties with the geography of the Holy Land, levelling it all, so his stream makes nothing of the Mount of Olives, but flows due east until it comes to the smitten gorge of the Jordan, and then turns south, down into the dull, leaden waters of the Dead Sea, which it heals. We all know how these are charged with poison. Dip up a glassful anywhere, and you find it full of deleterious matter. They are the symbol of humanity, with the sin that is in solution all through it. No chemist can eliminate it, but there is One who can. 'He hath made Him to be sin for us, who knew no sin, that we might be made the righteousness of God in Him.' The pure river of the water of life will cast out from humanity the malignant components that are there, and will sweeten it all. Ay, all, and yet not all, for very solemnly the Prophet's optimism pauses, and he says that the salt marshes by the side of the sea are not healed. They are by the side of it. The healing is perfectly available for them, but they are not healed. It is possible for men to reject the influences that make for the destruction of sin and the establishment of righteousness. And although the waters are healed, there still remain the obstinate marshes with the white crystals efflorescing on their surface, and bringing salt and barrenness. You can put away the healing and remain tainted with the poison.

And then the last thought is the life-giving influence of the river. Everything lived whithersoever it went.

Contrast Christendom with heathendom. Admit all the hollowness and mere nominal Christianity of large tracts of life in so-called Christian countries, and yet why is it that on the one side you find stagnation and death, and on the other side mental and manifold activity and progressiveness? I believe that the difference between 'the people that *sit* in darkness' and 'he people that *walk* in the light is that one has the light and the other has not, and activity befits the light as torpor befits the darkness.

But there is a far deeper truth than that in the figure, a truth that I would fain lay upon the hearts of all my hearers, that unless we our own selves have this water of life which comes from the Sanctuary and is brought to us by Jesus Christ, 'we are dead in trespasses and sins.' The only true life is in Christ. 'If any man thirst, let him come unto Me, and drink. He that believeth on Me, as the Scripture hath said, out of his heart shall flow rivers of living water.'

THE BOOK OF DANIEL

YOUTHFUL CONFESSORS

'But Daniel purposed in his heart that he would not defile himself with the portion of the king's meat, nor with the wine which he drank: therefore he requested of the prince of the eunuchs that he might not defile himself. 9. Now God had brought Daniel into favour and tender love with the prince of the eunuchs. 10. And the prince of the eunuchs said unto Daniel, I fear my lord the king, who hath appointed your meat and your drink: for why should he see your faces worse liking than the children which are of your sort? then shall ye make me endanger my head to the king. 11. Then said Daniel to Melzar, whom the prince of the eunuchs had set over Daniel, Hananiah, Mishael, and Azariah, 12. Prove thy servants, I beseech thee, ten days; and let them give us pulse to eat, and water to drink. 13. Then let our countenances be looked upon before thee, and the countenance of the children that eat of the portion of the king's meat: and as thou seest, deal with thy servants. 14. So he consented to them in this matter, and proved them ten days. 15. And at the end of ten days their countenances appeared fairer and fatter in flesh than all the children which did eat the portion of the king's meat. 16. Thus Melzar took away the portion of their meat, and the wine that they should drink; and gave them pulse. 17. As for these four children, God gave them knowledge and skill in all learning and wisdom: and Daniel had understanding in all visions and dreams. 18. Now at the end of the days that the king had said he should bring them in, then the prince of the eunuchs brought them in before Nebuchadnezzar. 19. And the king communed with them: and among them all was found none like Daniel, Hananiah, Mishael, and Azariah: therefore stood they before the king. 20. And in all matters of wisdom and understanding, that the king enquired of them, he found them ten times better than all the magicians and astrologers that were in all his realm. 21. And Daniel continued even unto the first year of king Cyrus.'—DANIEL i. 8-21.

DANIEL was but a boy at the date of the Captivity, and little more at the time of the attempt to make a Chaldean of him. The last verse says that he 'continued even unto the first year of king Cyrus,' the date given elsewhere as the close of the Captivity (2 Chron. xxxvi. 22; Ezra i. 1; vi. 3). From Daniel x. 1 we learn that he lived on till Cyrus's third year, if not later; but the date in i. 21 is probably given in order to suggest that Daniel's career covered the whole

period of the Captivity, and burned like a star of hope
for the exiles. The incident in our passage is a noble
example of religious principle applied to small details
of daily life, and shows how God crowns such conscientious self-restraint with success. The lessons
which it contains are best gathered by following the
narrative.

I. The heroic determination of the boyish confessor
is first set forth. The plan of taking leading young
men from the newly captured nation and turning
them into Babylonians was a stroke of policy as heartless and high-handed as might be expected from a
great conqueror. In some measure, the same thing
has been done by all nations who have built up a
world-wide dominion. The new names given to the
youths, the attaching of them to the court, their
education in Babylonish fashion, all were meant for
the same purpose,—to denationalise them, and strip
them of their religion, and thus to make them tools for
more easily governing their countrymen.

Most men would yield to the influences, and be so
lapped in the comforts of their new position as to
become pliable as wax in the conqueror's hands; but
here and there he would come across a bit of stiffer
stuff, which would break rather than bend. Such an
obstinate piece of humanity was found in the Hebrew
youth, of some fifteen years, whose Hebrew name ('God
is my judge') expressed a truth that ruled him, when
the name was exchanged for one that invoked Bel.
It took some firmness for a captive lad, without friends
or influence, to take Daniel's stand; for the motive
of his desire to be excused from taking the fare
provided can only have been religious. He was
determined, in his brave young heart, not to 'defile'

himself with the king's meat. The phrase points to
the pollution incurred by eating things offered to idols,
and does not imply scrupulousness like that of Phari-
saic times, nor necessarily suggest a late date for the
book. Probably there had been some kind of religious
consecration of the food to Babylonian gods, and
Daniel, in his solitary faithfulness, was carrying out
the same principles which Paul afterwards laid down
for Corinthian Christians as to partaking of things
offered to idols. Similar difficulties are sure to
emerge in analogous cases, and do so, on many mission
fields.

The motive here, then, is distinctly religious. Common life was so woven in with idolatrous worship that
every meal was in some sense a sacrifice. Therefore
'Touch not, taste not, handle not,' was the inevitable
dictate for a devout heart. Daniel seems to have been
the moving spirit; but as is generally the case, he was
able to infuse his own strong convictions into his companions, and the four of them held together in their
protest. The great lesson from the incident is that
religion should regulate the smallest details of life,
and that it is not narrow over-scrupulousness, but
fidelity to the highest duty, when a man sets his foot
down about any small matter, and says, 'No, I dare
not do it, little as it is, and pleasant as it might be to
sense, because I should thereby be mixed up in a
practical denial of my God.' 'So did not I, because of
the fear of God' (Neh. v. 15), is a motto which will
require from many a young man abstinence from
many things which it would be much easier to
accept.

II. This young confessor was as prudent as he was
brave; and the story goes on to show how wisely he

played his part, and how willing he was to accept all
working compromises which might smooth his way.
He did not at all want to pose as a martyr, and had no
pleasure in making a noise. The favour which he had
won with the high officer who looked after the lads
before their formal examination (graduation we might
call it), is set down in the narrative to the divine favour;
but that favour worked by means, and no doubt the
lad had done his part to win the important good
opinion of his superior. The more firm is our determination to take no step beyond the line of duty, the
more conciliatory we should be. But many people
seem to think that heroism is shown by rudeness, and
that if we are afraid that we shall some time have to
say 'No' very emphatically, we should prepare for
it by a great many preliminary and unnecessary
negatives. The very stern need for parting company,
when conscience points one way and companions
another, is a reason for keeping cordially together
whenever we can.

'The prince of the eunuchs' made a very reasonable
objection. He had been appointed to see after the
health of the lads, and had ample means at his disposal; and if they lost their health in this chase after
what he could only think a superstitious fad, the
despot whom he served would think nothing of making him answer with his head. His fear gives a striking side-light as to the conditions of service in such a
court, where no man's head was firm between his
shoulders. Why should the prince of the eunuchs
have supposed that the diet asked for would not
nourish the lads? It was that of the bulk of men
everywhere, and he had only to go out into the streets
or the nearest barrack in Babylon to see what thews

and muscles could be nurtured on vegetable diet and water. But whatever the want of ground in his objection, it was enough that he made it. Note that he puts it entirely on possible harmful results to himself, and that silences Daniel, who had no right to ask another to run his head into the noose, into which he was ready to put his own, if necessary. Martyrs by proxy, who have such strong convictions that they think it somebody else's duty to run risk for them, are by no means unknown.

This boy was made of other metal. So, apparently, he gives up the prince of the eunuchs, and turns to another of the friends whom he had made in his short captivity—the person in whose more immediate charge he and his three friends were. He is named Melzar in the Authorised Version; but the Revised Version more accurately takes that to be a name of office, and translates it as 'steward.' He did the catering for them, and was sufficiently friendly to listen to Daniel's reasonable proposal to try the vegetable diet for 'ten days'—probably meaning an indefinite period, sufficiently long to test results, which a literal ten days would perhaps scarcely be. So the good-natured steward let the lads have their way, much wondering in his soul, no doubt, why they should take as much trouble to avoid good living as most youths would have taken to get it.

III. The success of the experiment comes next. We do not need to suppose a miracle as either wrought or suggested by the narrative. The issue might have taught the steward a wholesome lesson in dietetics, which he and a great many of us much need. 'A man's life consisteth not in the abundance of the things which he possesseth,' and his bodily life consisteth not in the abundance and variety of the things that he eateth. The teaching of this lesson is, not that vegetarianism or total abstinence is obligatory, for diet is here regarded only as part of idolatrous worship; but certainly a secondary conclusion, fairly drawn from the story, is that vigorous health is best kept up on very simple fare. Many dinner-tables, over which God's blessing is formally asked, are spread in such a fashion as it is hard to suppose deserves His blessing. The simpler the fare, the fewer the wants; the fewer the wants, the greater the riches; the freer the life, the more leisure for higher pursuits, and the more sound the bodily health.

But the rosy faces and vigorous health of Daniel and his friends may illustrate, by a picturesque example, a large truth—that God suffers no man to be a loser by faithfulness, and more than makes up all that is surrendered for His sake. The blessing of God on small means makes them fountains of truer joy than large ones unblessed. No man hath left anything for Christ's sake but he receives a hundredfold in this life, if not in the actual blessings surrendered, at all events in the peace and joy of heart of which they were supposed to be bearers. God fills places emptied by Himself, and those emptied by us for His sake.

IV. The conscientious abstinence of Daniel had limits. The learning of the 'Chaldeans' was largely ritualistic, and magic, incantations, divination, and mythology constituted a most important part of it. Did not the conscience, which could not swallow idolatrous food, resent being forced to assimilate idolatrous learning? No; for all that learning could be acquired by a faithful monotheist, and could be used against the system which gave it birth. Like

Moses, or like the young Pharisee Saul, these Jewish boys nurtured their faith by knowledge of their enemies' belief, and used their childhood's lessons as weapons in fighting for God's truth. It is not every man's duty to become familiar with error, or to master anti-Christian systems. But if it become ours, we are not to turn away from the task, nor to doubt that God will keep His own truth alight in our minds, if we realise the danger of the position, and seek to cling to Him.

V. So we have the last scene in the youths' appearance before Nebuchadnezzar. A three years' curriculum was considered necessary to turn a Jewish boy into a Chaldean expert, fit to be a traitor to his nation, an apostate from his God, and a tool of the tyrant. So far as knowledge of the priestly and astronomical science went, the four Hebrews came out at the top of the lists. The great king himself, with that personal interference in all departments which makes a despot's life so burdensome, put them through their paces, and was satisfied. His object had been to get instruments with which he could work on the Captivity, and, no doubt, also to secure servants who had no links with anybody in Babylon. Foreigners, 'kinless loons,' are favourites with despots, for plain reasons. But Nebuchadnezzar could not fathom the hearts of the lads. An incarnation of unbridled will would find it difficult to understand a life guided by conscience, and religious scruples would have sounded as an unknown tongue to him. But yet, as he and they stood face to face, who was stronger, the conqueror or the youths who feared God, and none besides? They were in their right place at the head of the examination lists. They had not said, 'We do not believe in all this rubbish, and we are not going to trouble ourselves to master it,' but they had set themselves determinedly to work, and been all the more persevering because of their objection to the diet. If a young man has to be singular by reason of his religion, let him be singularly diligent in his work, and seek to be first, not merely for his own glory, but for the sake of the religion which he professes.

'Plain living and high thinking' ought to go together. England and America have many names carved high on their annals, and written deep on their citizens' hearts, who have nourished a sublime, studious youth in poverty, 'cultivating literature on a little oatmeal,' and who all their lives have 'scorned delights and lived laborious days.' It is the temper which is most likely to succeed, but which, whether it succeeds or not, brings the best blessings to those who cultivate it. Such a youth will generally be followed by an honoured manhood like Daniel's, but will, at all events, be its own reward, and have God's blessing.

'Daniel continued unto the first year of king Cyrus.' These simple words contain volumes. During all the troubles of the nation, from the king's insanity, and the murders of his successors, amidst whirling intrigues, envies, plots, and persecutions, this one man stood firm, like a pillar amid blowing sands. So God keeps the steadfast soul which is fixed on Him; and while the world passeth away, and the fashion thereof, **he that doeth the will of God abideth for ever.**

THE IMAGE AND THE STONE

'This is the dream; and we will tell the interpretation thereof before the king.
37. Thou, O king, art a king of kings: for the God of heaven hath given thee a
kingdom, power, and strength, and glory. 38. And wheresoever the children of
men dwell, the beasts of the field and the fowls of the heaven hath He given into
thine hand, and hath made thee ruler over them all. Thou art this head of gold.
39. And after thee shall arise another kingdom inferior to thee, and another third
kingdom of brass, which shall bear rule over all the earth. 40. And the fourth
kingdom shall be strong as iron: forasmuch as iron breaketh in pieces and sub-
dueth all things: and as iron that breaketh all these, shall it break in pieces and
bruise. 41. And whereas thou sawest the feet and toes, part of potters' clay, and
part of iron, the kingdom shall be divided; but there shall be in it of the strength
of the iron, forasmuch as thou sawest the iron mixed with miry clay. 42. And as
the toes of the feet were part of iron, and part of clay, so the kingdom shall be
partly strong, and partly broken. 43. And whereas thou sawest iron mixed with
miry clay, they shall mingle themselves with the seed of men: but they shall not
cleave one to another, even as iron is not mixed with clay. 44. And in the days
of these kings shall the God of heaven set up a kingdom, which shall never be
destroyed: and the kingdom shall not be left to other people, but it shall break in
pieces and consume all these kingdoms, and it shall stand for ever. 45. Forasmuch
as thou sawest that the stone was cut out of the mountain without hands, and
that it brake in pieces the iron, the brass, the clay, the silver, and the gold; the
great God hath made known to the king what shall come to pass hereafter: and
the dream is certain, and the interpretation thereof sure. 46. Then the king
Nebuchadnezzar fell upon his face, and worshipped Daniel, and commanded that
they should offer an oblation and sweet odours unto him. 47. The king answered
unto Daniel, and said, Of a truth it is, that your God is a God of gods, and a Lord
of kings, and a revealer of secrets, seeing thou couldest reveal this secret. 48. Then
the king made Daniel a great man, and gave him many great gifts, and made him
ruler over the whole province of Babylon, and chief of the governors over all the
wise men of Babylon. 49. Then Daniel requested of the king, and he set Shadrach,
Meshach, and Abed-nego, over the affairs of the province of Babylon: but Daniel
sat in the gate of the king.'—DANIEL ii. 36-49.

THE colossal image, seen by Nebuchadnezzar in his
dream, was a reproduction of those which met his
waking eyes, and still remain for our wonder in our
museums. The mingled materials are paralleled in
ancient art. The substance of the dream is no less
natural than its form. The one is suggested by familiar
sights; the other, by pressing anxieties. What more
likely than that, 'in the second year of his reign' (v. 1),
waking thoughts of the future of his monarchy should
trouble the warrior-king, scarcely yet firm on his
throne, and should repeat themselves in nightly
visions? God spoke through the dream, and He is
not wont to answer questions before they are asked,

63

nor to give revelations to men on points which they have not sought to solve. We may be sure that Nebuchadnezzar's dream met his need.

The unreasonable demand that the 'Chaldeans' should show the dream as well as interpret it, fits the character of the king, as an imperious despot, intolerant of obstacles to his will, and holding human life very cheap. Daniel's knowledge of the dream and of its meaning is given to him in a vision by night, which is the method of divine illumination throughout the book, and may be regarded as a lower stage thereof than the communications to prophets of 'the word of the Lord.'

The passage falls into two parts: the image and the stone.

I. The Image.

It was a human form of strangely mingled materials, of giant size no doubt, and of majestic aspect. Barbarous enough it would have looked beside the marble lovelinesses of Greece, but it was quite like the coarser art which sought for impressiveness through size and costliness. Other people than Babylonian sculptors think that bigness is greatness, and dearness preciousness.

This image embodied what is now called a philosophy of history. It set forth the fruitful idea of a succession and unity in the rise and fall of conquerors and kingdoms. The four empires represented by it are diverse, and yet parts of a whole, and each following on the other. So the truth is taught that history is an organic whole, however unrelated its events may appear to a superficial eye. The writer of this book had learned lessons far in advance of his age, and not yet fully grasped by many so-called historians.

But, further, the human figure of the image sets

D

forth all these kingdoms as being purely the work of
men.   Not that the overruling divine providence is
ignored, but that the play of human passions, the lust
of conquest and the like, and the use of human means,
such as armies, are emphasised.

Again, the kingdoms are seen in their brilliancy, as
they would naturally appear to the thoughts of a
conqueror, whose highest notion of glory was earthly
dominion, and who was indifferent to the suffering
and blood through which he waded to a throne.   When
the same kingdoms are shown to Daniel in chapter vii.
they are represented by beasts.   Their cruelty and the
destruction of life which they caused were uppermost
in a prophet's view; their vulgar splendour dazzled a
king's sleeping eyes, because it had intoxicated his
waking thoughts.   Much worldly glory and many of
its aims appear as precious metal to dreamers, but
are seen by an illuminated sight to be bestial and
destructive.

Once more there is a steady process of deterioration
in the four kingdoms.   Gold is followed by silver, and
that by brass, and that by the strange combination of
iron and clay.   This may simply refer to the diminution
of worldly glory, but it may also mean deterioration,
morally and otherwise.   Is it not the teaching of
Scripture that, unless God interpose, society will
steadily slide downwards?   And has not the fact been
so, wherever the brake and lever of revelation have
not arrested the decline and effected elevation?   We
are told nowadays of evolution, as if the progress of
humanity were upwards; but if you withdraw the
influence of supernatural revelation, the evidence of
power in manhood to work itself clear of limitations
and lower forms is very ambiguous at the best—in

reference to morals, at all events. Evil is capable of development, as well as good; and perhaps Nebuchadnezzar's colossus is a truer representation of the course of humanity than the dreams of modern thinkers who see manhood becoming steadily better by its own effort, and think that the clay and iron have inherent power to pass into fine gold.

The question of the identification of these successive monarchies does not fall to be discussed here. But I may observe that the definite statement of verse 44 ('in the days of these kings') seems to date the rise of the everlasting kingdom of God in the period of the last of the four, and therefore that the old interpretation of the fourth kingdom as the Roman seems the most natural. The force of that remark may, no doubt, be weakened by the consideration that the Old Testament prophets' perspective of the future brought the coming of Messiah into immediate juxtaposition with the limits of their own vision; but still it has force.

The allocation of each part of the symbol is of less importance for us than the lessons to be drawn from it as a whole. But the singular amalgam of iron and clay in the fourth kingdom is worth notice. No sculptor or metallurgist could make a strong unity out of such materials, of which the combination could only be apparent and superficial. The fact to which it points is the artificial unity into which the great conquering empires of old crushed their unfortunate subject peoples, who were hammered, not fused, together. 'They shall mingle themselves with the seed of men' (ver. 43), may either refer to the attempts to bring about unity by marriages among different races, or to other vain efforts to the same end. To obliterate nationalities has alwa, **s** been the conquering despot's effort, from Nebuchadnezzar to the Czar of Russia, and it always fails. This is the weakness of these huge empires of antiquity, which have no internal cohesion, and tumble to pieces as soon as some external bond is loosened. There is only one kingdom which has no disintegrating forces lodged in it, because it unites men individually to its king, and so binds them to one another; and that is the kingdom which Nebuchadnezzar saw in its destructive aspect.

II. So we have now to think of the stone cut out without hands.

Three things are specified with regard to it: its origin, its duration, and its destructive energy. The origin is heavenly, in sharp contrast to the human origin of the kingdoms symbolised in the colossal man. That idea is twice expressed: once in plain words, 'the God of heaven shall set up a kingdom'; and once figuratively as being cut out of the mountain without hands. By the mountain we are probably to understand Zion, from which, according to many a prophecy, the Messiah King was to rule the earth (Ps. ii.; Isa. ii. 3).

The fulfilment of this prediction is found, not only in the supernatural birth of Jesus Christ, but in the spread of the gospel without any of the weapons and aids of human power. Twelve poor men spoke, and the world was shaken and the kingdoms remoulded. The seer had learned the omnipotence of ideas and the weakness of outward force. A thought from God is stronger than all armies, and outconquers conquerors. By the mystery of Christ's Incarnation, by the power of weakness in the preachers of the Cross, by the energies of the transforming Spirit, the God of heaven has set up the kingdom. 'It shall never be destroyed.' Its divine origin guarantees its perpetual duration. The kingdoms of man's founding, whether they be in the realm of thought or of outward dominion, 'have their day, and cease to be,' but the kingdom of Christ lasts as long as the eternal life of its King. He cannot die any more, and He cannot live discrowned. Other forms of human association perish, as new conditions come into play which antiquate them; but the kingdom of Jesus is as flexible as it is firm, and has power to adapt to itself all conditions in which men can live. It will outlast earth, it will fill eternity; for when He 'shall have delivered up the kingdom to His Father,' the kingdom, which the God of heaven set up, will still continue.

It 'shall not be left to other people.' By that, seems to be meant that this kingdom will not be like those of human origin, in which dominion passes from one race to another, but that Israel shall ever be the happy subjects and the dominant race. We must interpret the words of the spiritual Israel, and remember how to be Christ's subject is to belong to a nation who are kings and priests.

The destructive power is graphically represented. The stone, detached from the mountain, and apparently self-moved, dashes against the heterogeneous mass of iron and clay on which the colossus insecurely stands, and down it comes with a crash, breaking into a thousand fragments as it falls. 'Like the chaff of the summer threshingfloors' (Daniel ii. 35) is the *débris*, which is whirled out of sight by the wind. Christ and His kingdom have reshaped the world. These ancient, hideous kingdoms of blood and misery are impossible now. Christ and His gospel shattered the Roman empire, and cast Europe into another mould. They have destructive work to do yet, and as surely as the sun rises daily, will do it. The things that can be shaken will be shaken till they fall, and human society will never obtain its stable form till it is moulded throughout after the pattern of the kingdom of Christ.

The vision of our passage has no reference to the quickening power of the kingdom; but the best way in which it destroys is by transformation. It slays the old and lower forms of society by substituting the purer which flow from possession of the one Spirit. That highest glory of the work of Christ is but partially represented here, but there is a hint in Daniel ii. 35, which tells that the stone has a strange vitality, and can grow, and does grow, till it becomes an earth-filling mountain.

That issue is not reached yet; but 'the dream is certain.' The kingdom is concentrated in its King, and the life of Jesus, diffused through His servants, works to the increase of the empire, and will not cease till the kingdoms of the world are the kingdoms of our God and of His Christ. That stone has vital power, and if we build on it we receive, by wonderful impartation, a kindred derived life, and become 'living stones.' It is laid for a sure foundation. If a man stumble over it while it lies there to be built upon, he will lame and maim himself. But it will one day have motion given to it, and, falling from the height of heaven, when He comes to judge the world which He rules and has redeemed, it will grind to powder all who reject the rule of the everlasting King of men.

HARMLESS FIRES

'Then Nebuchadnezzar in his rage and fury commanded to bring Shadrach, Meshach, and Abed-nego. Then they brought these men before the king. 14. Nebuchadnezzar spake and said unto them, Is it true, O Shadrach, Meshach, and Abed-nego, do not ye serve my gods, nor worship the golden image which I have set up? 15. Now if ye be ready that at what time ye hear the sound of the cornet, flute, harp, sackbut, psaltery, and dulcimer, and all kinds of musick, ye fall down and worship the image which I have made; well: but if ye worship not, ye shall be cast the same hour into the midst of a burning fiery furnace; and who is that God that shall deliver you out of my hands? 16. Shadrach, Meshach, and Abed-nego, answered and said to the king, O Nebuchadnezzar, we are not careful to answer thee in this matter. 17. If it be so, our God whom we serve is able to deliver us from the burning fiery furnace, and He will deliver us out of thine hand, O king. 18. But if not, be it known unto thee, O king, that we will not serve thy gods, nor worship the golden image which thou hast set up. 19. Then was Nebuchadnezzar full of fury, and the form of his visage was changed against Shadrach, Meshach, and Abed-nego: therefore he spake, and commanded that they should heat the furnace one seven times more than it was wont to be heated. 20. And he commanded the most mighty men that were in his army to bind Shadrach, Meshach, and Abed-nego, and to cast them into the burning fiery furnace. 21. Then these men were bound in their coats, their hosen, and their hats, and their other garments, and were cast into the midst of the burning fiery furnace. 22. Therefore because the king's commandment was urgent, and the furnace exceeding hot, the flame of the fire slew those men that took up Shadrach, Meshach, and Abed-nego. 23. And these three men, Shadrach, Meshach, and Abed-nego, fell down bound into the midst of the burning fiery furnace. 24. Then Nebuchadnezzar the king was astonied, and rose up in haste, and spake, and said unto his counsellors, Did not we cast three men bound into the midst of the fire? They answered and said unto the king, True, O king. 25. He answered and said, Lo, I see four men loose, walking in the midst of the fire, and they have no hurt; and the form of the fourth is like the Son of God.'—DANIEL iii. 13-25.

THE way in which the 'Chaldeans' describe the three recusants, betrays their motive in accusing them. 'Certain Jews whom thou hast set over the affairs of the province of Babylon' could not but be envied and hated, since their promotion wounded both national pride and professional jealousy. The form of the accusation was skilfully calculated to rouse a despot's rage. 'They have not regarded thee' is the head and front of their offending. The inflammable temper of the king blazed up according to expectation, as is the way with tyrants. His passion of rage is twice mentioned (vs. 13, 19), and in one of the instances, is noted as distorting his features. What a picture of ungoverned fury as of

one who had never been thwarted! It is the true portrait of an Eastern despot.

Where was Daniel in this hour of danger? His
absence is not accounted for, and conjecture is useless;
but the fact that he has no share in the incident seems
to raise a presumption in favour of the disputed historical character of the Book, which, if it had been
fiction, could scarcely have left its hero out of so
brilliant an instance of faithfulness to Jehovah.

Nebuchadnezzar's vehement address to the three
culprits is very characteristic and instructive. Fixed
determination to enforce his mandate, anger which
breaks into threats that were by no means idle, and a
certain wish to build a bridge for the escape of servants who had done their work well, are curiously
mingled in it. His question, best rendered as in the
Revised Version, 'Is it of purpose . . . that ye' do so
and so? seems meant to suggest that they may repair
their fault by pleading inadvertence, accident, or the
like, and that He will accept the transparent excuse.
The renewed offer of an opportunity of worship does
not say what will happen should they obey; and the
omission makes the clause more emphatic, as insisting
on the act, and slurring over the self-evident result.

On the other hand, in the next clause the act is
slightly touched ('if ye worship not'); and all the
stress comes on the grim description of the consequence. This monarch, who has been accustomed
to bend men's wills like reeds, tries to shake these
three obstinate rebels by terror, and opens the door
of the furnace, as it were, to let them hear it roar. He
finishes with a flash of insolence which, if not blasphemy, at least betrays his belief that he was stronger
than any god of his conquered subject peoples.

But the main point to notice in this speech is the unconscious revelation of his real motive in demanding the act of worship. The crime of the three was not that they worshipped wrongly, but that they disobeyed Nebuchadnezzar. He speaks of 'my gods,' and of the 'image which I have set up.' Probably it was an image of the god of the Babylonian pantheon whom he took for his special patron, and was erected in commemoration of some victorious campaign.

At all events, the worship required was an act of obedience to him, and to refuse it was rebellion. Idolatry is tolerant of any private opinions about gods, and intolerant of any refusal to obey authority in worship. So the early Christians were thrown to the lions, not because they worshipped Jesus, but because they would not sacrifice at the Emperor's command. It is not only heathen rulers who have confounded the spheres of civil and religious obedience. Nonconformity in England was long identified with disloyalty; and in many so-called Christian countries to-day a man may think what he likes, and worship as he pleases in his chamber, if only he will decently comply with authority and pretend to unite in religious ceremonies, which those who appoint and practise them observe with tongue in cheek.

But we may draw another lesson from this truculent apostle of his god. He is not the only instance of apparent religious zeal which is at bottom nothing but masterfulness. 'You shall worship my god, not because he is God, but because he is mine.' That is the real meaning of a great deal which calls itself 'zeal for the Lord.' The zealot's own will, opinions, fancies, are crammed down other people's throats, and the insult in not thinking or worshipping as he does, is worse in his eyes than the offence against God.

The kind of furnace in which recusants are roasted has changed since Nebuchadnezzar's time, and what is called persecution for religion is out of fashion now. But every advance in the application of Christian principle to social and civil life brings a real martyrdom on its advocates. Every audacious refusal to bow to the habits or opinions of the majority, is visited by consequences which only the martyr spirit will endure. Despots have no monopoly of imperious intolerance. A democracy is more cruel and more impatient of singularity, and especially of religious singularity, than any despot.

England and America have no need to fear the old forms of religious persecution. In both, a man may profess and proclaim any kind of religion or of no religion. But in both, the advance guard of the Christian Church, which seeks to apply Christ's teachings more rigidly to individual and social life, has to face obloquy, ostracism, misrepresentation, from the world and the fossil church, for not serving their gods, nor worshipping the golden image which they have set up. Martyrs will be needed and persecutors will exist till the world is Christian.

How did the three confessors meet this rumble of thunder about their ears? The quiet determination of their reply is very striking and beautiful. It is perfectly loyal, and perfectly unshaken. 'We have no need to answer thee' (Revised Version). 'It is ill sitting at Rome and striving with the Pope.' Nebuchadnezzar's palace was not precisely the place to dispute with Nebuchadnezzar; and as his logic was only 'Do as I bid you, or burn,' the sole reply possible was, 'We will not do as you bid, and we will burn.' The 'If' which is immediately spoken is already in the minds of the speakers, when they say that *they* do not need to answer. They think that God will take up the taunt which ended the king's tirade. Beautifully they are silent, and refer the blusterer to God, whose voice they believe that He will hear in His deed. 'But Thou shalt answer, Lord, for me,' is the true temper of humble faith, dumb before power as a sheep before her shearers. and yet confident that the meek will not be left unvindicated. Let us leave ourselves in God's hands; and when conscience accuses, or the world maligns or threatens, let us be still, and feel that we have One to speak for us, and so we may hold our peace.

The rendering of verse 17 is doubtful, but the general meaning is clear. The brave speakers have hope that God will rebuke the king's taunt, and will prove Himself to be able to deliver out of his hand. So they repeat his very words with singular boldness, and contradict him to his face. They have no absolute certainty of deliverance, but whether it comes or not will make no manner of difference to them. They have absolute certainty as to duty; and so they look the furious tyrant right in the eyes, and quietly say, 'We will not serve thy gods.' Nothing like that had ever been heard in those halls.

Duty is sovereign. The obligation to resist all temptations to go against conscience is unaffected by consequences. There may be hope that God will not suffer us to be harmed, but whether He does or not should make no difference to our fixed resolve. That temper of lowly faith and inflexible faithfulness which these Hebrews showed in the supreme moment, when they took their lives in their hands, may be as nobly

illustrated in the small difficulties of our peaceful lives.
The same laws shape the curves of the tiny ripples in a
basin and of the Atlantic rollers. No man who cannot
say 'I will not' in the face of frowns and dangers, be
they what they may, and stick to it, will do his part.
He who has conquered regard for personal consequences, and does not let them deflect his course a '
hairsbreadth, is lord of the world.

How small Nebuchadnezzar was by the side of his
three victims! How empty his threats to men who
cared nothing whether they burned or not, so long as
they did not apostatise! What can the world do
against a man who says, 'It is all one to me whether
I live or die; I will not worship at your shrines?' The
fire of the furnace is but painted flames to such an one.

The savage punishment intended for the audacious
rebels is abundantly confirmed as common in Babylon
by the inscriptions, which may be seen quoted by many
commentators. The narrative is exceedingly graphic.
We see the furious king, with features inflamed with
passion. We hear his hoarse, angry orders to heat the
furnace seven times hotter, which he forgot would be a
mercy, as shortening the victims' agonies. We see the
swift execution of the commands, and the unresisting
martyrs bound as they stood, and dragged away by
the soldiers to the near furnace, the king following.
Its shape is a matter of doubt. Probably the three
were thrown in from above, and so the soldiers were
caught by the flames.

'And these three men . . . fell down bound into the
midst of the burning fiery furnace.' Their helplessness
and desperate condition are pathetically suggested by
that picture, which might well be supposed to be the
last of them that mortal eyes would see. Down into

the glowing mass, like chips of wood into Vesuvius,
they sank. The king sitting watching, to glut his fury
by the sight of their end, had some way of looking into
the core of the flames.

The story shifts its point of view with very picturesque abruptness after verse 23. The vaunting king
shall tell what he saw, and thereby convict himself of
insolent folly in challenging 'any god' to deliver out
of his hand. He alone seems to have seen the sight,
which he tells to his courtiers. The bonds were gone,
and the men walking free in the fire, as if it had been
their element. Three went in bound, four walk there
at large; and the fourth is 'like a son of the gods,'
by which expression Nebuchadnezzar can have meant
nothing more than he had learned from his religion;
namely, that the gods had offspring of superhuman
dignity. He calls the same person an angel in Daniel
iii. 28. He speaks there as the three would have
spoken, and here as Babylonian mythology spoke.

But the great lesson to be gathered from this miracle
of deliverance is simply that men who sacrifice themselves for God find in the sacrifice abundant blessing.
They may, or may not, be delivered from the external
danger. Peter was brought out of prison the night
before his intended martyrdom; James, the brother of
John, was slain with the sword, but God was equally
near to both, and both were equally delivered from
'Herod and from all the expectation of the people of
the Jews.' The disposal of the outward event is in His
hands, and is a comparatively small matter. But no
furnace into which a man goes because he will be true
to God, and will not yield up his conscience, is a tenth
part so hot as it seems, and it will do no real harm. The
fire burns bonds, but not Christ's servants, consuming

many things that entangled, and setting them free.
'I will walk at liberty : for I seek Thy precepts'—even
if we have to walk in the furnace. No trials faced in
obedience to God will be borne alone. 'When thou
passest through the waters, I will be with thee ; . . .
when thou walkest through the fire, thou shalt not be
burned.'

The form which Nebuchadnezzar saw amid the flame,
as invested with more than human majesty, may have
been but one of the ministering spirits sent forth to
minister to the martyrs—the embodiment of the divine
power which kept the flames from kindling upon them.
But we have Jesus for our Companion in all trials, and
His presence makes it possible for us to pass over hot
ploughshares with unblistered feet; to bathe our hands
in fire and not feel the pain ; to accept the sorest consequences of fidelity to Him, and count them as 'not
worthy to be compared with the glory which shall be
revealed,' and is made more glorious through these
light afflictions. A present Christ will never fail His
servants, and will make the furnace cool even when its
fire is fiercest.

MENE, TEKEL, PERES

'Then Daniel answered and said before the king, Let thy gifts be to thyself,
and give thy rewards to another; yet I will read the writing unto the king, and
make known to him the interpretation. 18. O thou king, the most high God gave
Nebuchadnezzar thy father a kingdom, and majesty, and glory, and honour:
19. And for the majesty that he gave him, all people, nations, and languages,
trembled and feared before him : whom he would he slew ; and whom he would
he kept alive ; and whom he would he set up; and whom he would he put
down. 20. But when his heart was lifted up, and his mind hardened in pride, he
was deposed from his kingly throne, and they took his glory from him : 21. And he
was driven from the sons of men ; and his heart was made like the beasts, and his
dwelling was with the wild asses : they fed him with grass like oxen, and his
body was wet with the dew of heaven ; till he knew that the most high God ruled
in the kingdom of men, and that he appointeth over it whomsoever he will.
22. And thou his son, O Belshazzar, hast not humbled thine heart, though thou
knewest all this ; 23. But hast lifted up thyself against the Lord of Heaven ; and
they have brought the vessels of his house before thee, and thou, and thy lords,

thy wives, and thy concubines, have drunk wine in them; and thou hast praised the gods of silver, and gold, of brass, iron, wood, and stone, which see not, nor hear, nor know: and the God in whose hand thy breath is, and whose are all thy ways, hast thou not glorified: 24. Then was the part of the hand sent from him; and this writing was written. 25. And this is the writing that was written, 'MENE, MENE, TEKEL, UPHARSIN.' 26. This is the interpretation of the thing: MENE; God hath numbered thy kingdom, and finished it. 27. TEKEL; Thou art weighed in the balances, and art found wanting. 28. PERES; Thy kingdom is divided, and given to the Medes and Persians. 29. Then commanded Belshazzar, and they clothed Daniel with scarlet, and put a chain of gold about his neck, and made a proclamation concerning him, that he should be the third ruler in the kingdom. 30. In that night was Belshazzar the king of the Chaldeans slain. 31. And Darius the Median took the kingdom, being about threescore and two years old.'— DANIEL v. 17-31.

BELSHAZZAR is now conceded to have been a historical personage, the son of the last monarch of Babylon, and the other name in the narrative which has been treated as erroneous—namely, Darius—has not been found to be mentioned elsewhere, but is not thereby proved to be a blunder. For why should it not be possible for Scripture to preserve a name that secular history has not yet been ascertained to record, and why must it always be assumed that, if Scripture and cuneiform or other documents differ, it is Scripture that must go to the wall?

We do not deal with the grim picture of the drunken orgy, turned into abject terror as 'the fingers of a man's hand' came forth out of empty air, and in the full blaze of 'the candlestick' wrote the illegible signs. There is something blood-curdling in the visibility of but a part of the hand and its busy writing. Whose was the body, and where was it? No wonder if the riotous mirth was frozen into awe, and the wine lost flavour. Nor need we do more than note the craven-hearted flattery addressed to Daniel by the king, who apparently had never heard of him till the queen spoke of him just before. We have to deal with the indictment, the sentence, and the execution.

I. The indictment. Daniel's tone is noticeably stern.

He has no reverential preface, no softening of his message. His words are as if cut with steel on the rock. He brushes aside the promises of vulgar decorations and honours with undisguised contempt, and goes straight to his work of rousing a torpid conscience.

Babylon was the embodiment and type of the godless world-power, and Belshazzar was the incarnation of the spirit which made Babylon. So Daniel's indictment gathers together the main forms of sin, which cleave to every godless national or individual life. And he begins with that feather-brained frivolity which will learn nothing by example. Nebuchadnezzar's fate might have taught his successors what came of God-forgetting arrogance, and attributing success to oneself; and his restoration might have been an object-lesson to teach that devout recognition of the Most High as sovereign was the beginning of a king's prosperity and sanity. But Belshazzar knew all this, and ignored it all. Was he singular in that? Is not the world full of instances of the ruin that attends godlessness, which yet do not check one godless man in his career? The wrecks lie thick on the shore, but their broken sides and gaunt skeletons are not warnings sufficient to keep a thousand other ships from steering right on to the shoals. Of these godless lives it is true, 'This their way is their folly; yet their posterity approve their sayings,' and their doings, and say and do them over again. Incapacity to learn by example is a mark of godless lives.

Further, Belshazzar 'lifted up' himself 'against the Lord of heaven,' and 'glorified not Him in whose hand was his breath and whose were all his ways.' The very essence of all sin is that assertion of self as Lord, as sufficient, as the director of one's path. To make myself my centre, to depend on myself, to enthrone my own will as sovereign, is to fly in the face of nature and fact, and is the mother of all sin. To live to self is to die while we live; to live to God is to live even while we die. Nations and individuals are ever tempted thus to ignore God, and rebelliously to say, 'Who is Lord over us?' or presumptuously to think themselves architects of their own fortunes, and sufficient for their own defence. Whoever yields to that temptation has let the 'prince of the devils' in, and the inferior evil spirits will follow. Positive acts are not needed; the negative omission to 'glorify' the God of our life binds sin on us.

Further, Belshazzar, the type of godlessness, had desecrated the sacrificial vessels by using them for his drunken carouse, and therein had done just what we do when we take the powers of heart and mind and will, which are meant to be filled with affections, thoughts, and purposes, that are 'an odour of a sweet smell, well-pleasing to God,' and desecrate them by pouring from them libations before creatures. Is not love profaned when it is lavished on men or women without one reference to God? Is not the intellect desecrated when its force is spent on finite objects of thought, and never a glance towards God? Is not the will prostituted from its high vocation when it is used to drive the wheels of a God-ignoring life?

The coin bears the image and superscription of the true king. It is treason to God to render it to any paltry 'Cæsar' of our own coronation. Belshazzar was an avowed idolater, but many of us are worshipping

E

gods 'which see not, nor hear, nor know' as really as
he did. We cannot but do so, if we are not worshipping
God; for men must have some person or thing which
they regard as their supreme good, to which the
current of their being sets, which, possessed, makes
them blessed; and that is our god, whether we call it
so or not.

Further, Belshazzar was carousing while the Medes
and Persians were ringing Babylon round, and his
hand should have been grasping a sword, not a wine-
cup. Drunkenness and lust, which sap manhood, are
notoriously stimulated by peril, as many a shipwreck
tells when desperate men break open the spirit casks,
and go down to their death intoxicated, and as many an
epidemic shows when morality is flung aside, and mad
vice rules and reels in the streets before it sinks down
to die. A nation or a man that has shaken off God will
not long keep sobriety or purity.

II. After the stern catalogue of sins comes the
tremendous sentence. Daniel speaks like an embodied
conscience, or like an avenging angel, with no word of
pity, and no effort to soften or dilute the awful truth.
The day for wrapping up grim facts in muffled words
was past. Now the only thing to be done was to bare
the sword, and let its sharp edge cut. The inscription,
as given in verse 25, is simply 'Numbered, numbered,
weighed and breakings.' The variation in verse 28
(Peres) is the singular of the noun used in the plural
in verse 25, with the omission of 'U,' which is merely
the copulative 'and.' The disjointed brevity adds to
the force of the words. Apparently, they were not
written in a character which 'the king's wise men'
could read, and probably were in Aramaic letters as
well as language, which would be familiar to Daniel.

Of course, a play on the word 'Peres' suggests the *Persian* as the agent of the *breaking*. Daniel simply supplied the personal application of the oracular writing. He fits the cap on the king's head. 'God hath numbered *thy* kingdom . . . *thou* art weighed . . . *thy* kingdom is divided' (broken).

These three fatal words carry in them the summing up of all divine judgment, and will be rung in the ears of all who bring it on themselves. Belshazzar is a type of the end of every godless world-power and of every such individual life. 'Numbered'—for God allows to each his definite time, and when its sum is complete, down falls the knife that cuts the threads. 'Weighed' —for 'after death the judgment,' and a godless life, when laid in the balance which His hand holds, is 'altogether lighter than vanity.' 'Breakings'—for not only will the godless life be torn away from its possessions with much laceration of heart and spirit, but the man himself will be broken like some earthen vessel coming into sharp collision with an express engine. Belshazzar saw the handwriting on the same night in which it was carried out in act; we see it long before, and we can read it. But some of us are mad enough to sit unconcerned at the table, and go on with the orgy, though the legible letters are gleaming plain on the wall.

III. The execution of the sentence need not occupy us long. Belshazzar so little realised the facts, that he issued his order to deck out Daniel in the tawdry pomp he had promised him, as if a man with such a message would be delighted with purple robes and gold chains, and made him third ruler of the kingdom which he had just declared was numbered and ended by God. The force of folly could no further go. No

wonder that the hardy invaders swept such an im-
becile from his throne without a struggle! His blood
was red among the lees of the wine-cups, and the
ominous writing could scarcely have faded from the
wall when the shouts of the assailants were heard,
the palace gates forced, and the half-drunken king,
alarmed too late, put to the sword. 'He that, being
often reproved, hardeneth his neck shall suddenly be
destroyed, and that without remedy.'

A TRIBUTE FROM ENEMIES

Then said these men, We shall not find any occasion against this Daniel, except
we find it against him concerning the law of his God.'—DANIEL vi. 5.

DANIEL was somewhere about ninety years old when
he was cast to the lions. He had been for many years
the real governor of the whole empire; and, of course,
in such a position had incurred much hatred and
jealousy. He was a foreigner and a worshipper of
another God, and therefore was all the more unpopular,
as a Brahmin would be in England if he were a Cabinet
Minister. He was capable and honest, and therefore
all the incompetent and all the knavish officials would
recognise in him their natural enemy. So, hostile
intrigues, which grow quickly in courts, especially in
Eastern courts, sprung up round him, and his subordinates laid their heads together in order to ruin
him. They say, in the words of my text, 'We cannot
find any holes to pick. There is only one way to put
him into antagonism to the law, and that is by making
a law which shall be in antagonism to God's law.' And
so they scheme to have the mad regulation enacted,
which, in the sequel of the story, we find was enforced.
These intriguers say, ' We shall not find any occasion

against this Daniel, except we find it against him concerning the law of his God.'

Now, then, if we look at that confession, wrung from
the lips of malicious observers, we may, I think, get
two or three lessons.

I. First, note the very unfavourable soil in which a
character of singular beauty and devout consecration
may be rooted and grow.

What sort of a place was that court where Daniel
was? Half shambles and half pigsty. Luxury, sen-
suality, lust, self-seeking, idolatry, ruthless cruelty,
and the like were the environment of this man. And
in the middle of these there grew up that fair flower of
a character, pure and stainless, by the acknowledgment
of enemies, and in which not even accusers could find a
speck or a spot. There are no circumstances in which
a man *must* have his garments spotted by the world.
However deep the filth through which he has to wade,
if God sent him there, and if he keeps hold of God's
hand, his purity will be more stainless by reason of the
impurity round him. There were saints in Cæsar's
household, and depend upon it, they were more saintly
saints just because they *were* in Cæsar's household.
You will always find that people who have any goodness
in them, and who live in conditions unusually opposed
to goodness, have a clearer faith, and a firmer grasp of
their Master, and a higher ideal of Christian life, just
because of the foulness in which they have to live. It
may sound a paradox, but it is a deep truth that unfavourable circumstances are the most favourable for
the development of Christian character. For that
development comes, not by what we draw from the
things around, but by what we draw from the soil in
which we are rooted, even God Himself, in whom the

roots find both anchorage and nutriment. And the more we are thrown back upon Him, and the less we find food for our best selves in the things about us, the more likely is our religion to be robust and thorough-going, and conscious ever of His presence. Resistance strengthens muscles, and the more there is need for that in our Christian lives, the manlier and the stronger and the better shall we probably be. Let no man or woman say, 'If only circumstances were more favour-able, oh, what a saint I could be; but how can I be one, with all these unfavourable conditions? How can a man keep the purity of his Christian life and the fervour of his Christian communion amidst the tricks and chicanery and small things of Manchester business? How can a woman find time to hold fellowship with God, when all day long she is distracted in her nursery with all these children hanging on her to look after? How can we, in our actual circumstances, reach the ideal of Christian character?'

Ah, brother, if the ideal's being realised depends on circumstances, it is a poor affair. It depends on you, and he that has vitality enough within him to keep hold of Jesus Christ, has thereby power enough within him to turn enemies into friends, and unfavourable circumstances into helps instead of hindrances. Your ship can sail wonderfully near to the wind if you trim the sails rightly, and keep a good, strong grip on the helm, and the blasts that blow all but in your face, may be made to carry you triumphantly into the haven of your desire. Remember Daniel, in that god-less court reeking with lust and cruelty, and learn that purity and holiness and communion with God do not depend on environment, but upon the inmost will of the man.

II. Notice the keen critics that all good men have to face.

In this man's case, of course, their eyesight was mended by the microscope of envy and malice. That is no doubt the case with some of us too. But whether that be so or no, however unobtrusive and quiet a Christian person's life may be, there will be some people standing close by who, if not actually watching for his fall, are at least by no means indisposed to make the worst of a slip, and to rejoice over an inconsistency.

We do not need to complain of that. It is perfectly reasonable and perfectly right. There will always be a tendency to judge men, who by any means profess that they are living by the highest law, with a judgment that has very little charity in it. And it is perfectly right that it should be so. Christian people need to be trained to be indifferent to men's opinions, but they also need to be reminded that they are bound, as the Apostle says, to 'provide things honest in the sight of all men.' It is a reasonable and right requirement that they should ' have a good report of them that are without.' Be content to be tried by a high standard, and do not wonder, and do not forget that there are keen eyes watching your conduct, in your home, in your relations to your friends, in your business, in your public life, which would weep no tears, but might gleam with malicious satisfaction, if they saw inconsistencies in you. Remember it, and shape your lives so that they may be disappointed.

If a minister falls into any kind of inconsistency or sin, if a professing Christian makes a bad failure in Manchester, what a talk there is, and what a pointing of fingers! We sometimes think it is hard; it is all right. It is just what should be meted out to us. Let us remember that unslumbering tribunal which sits in judgment upon all our professions, and is very ready to condemn, and very slow to acquit.

III. Notice, again, the unblemished record.

These men could find no fault, 'forasmuch as Daniel was faithful.' 'Neither was there any error'—of judgment, that is,—'or fault'—dereliction of duty, that is,—'found in him.' They were very poor judges of his religion, and they did not try to judge that; but they were very good judges of his conduct as prime minister, and they did judge that. The world is a very poor critic of my Christianity, but it is a very sufficient one of my conduct. It may not know much about the inward emotions of the Christian life, and the experiences in which the Christian heart expatiates and loves to dwell, but it knows what short lengths, and light weights, and bad tempers, and dishonesty, and selfishness are. And it is by our conduct, in the things that they and we do together, that worldly men judge what we are in the solitary depths where we dwell in communion with God. It is useless for Christians to be talking, as so many of them are fond of doing, about their spiritual experiences and their religious joy, and all the other sweet and sacred things which belong to the silent life of the spirit in God, unless, side by side with these, there is the doing of the common deeds which the world is actually able to appraise in such a fashion as to extort, even from them, the confession, 'We find no occasion against this man.'

You remember the pregnant, quaint old saying, 'If a Christian man is a shoeblack, he ought to be the best shoeblack in the parish.' If we call ourselves Christians, we are bound, by the very name, to live in such a fashion as that men shall have no doubt of the

reality of our profession and of the depth of our fellowship with Christ. It is by our common conduct that
they judge us. And the 'Christian Endeavourer' needs
to remember, whether he or she be old or young, that
the best sign of the reality of the endeavour is the doing
of common things with absolute rightness, because they
are done wholly for Christ's sake.

It is a sharp test, and I wonder how many of us
would like to go out into the world, and say to all the
irreligious people who know us, ' Now come and tell me
what the faults are that you have seen in me.' There
would be a considerable response to the invitation, and
perhaps some of us would learn to know ourselves
rather better than we have been able to do. ' We shall
not find any occasion in *this* Daniel '—I wonder if they
would find it in *that* Daniel—' except we find it concerning the law of his God.' There is a record for a
man!

IV. Lastly, note obedient disobedience.

The plot goes on the calculation that, whatever
happens, this man may be trusted to do what his God
tells him, no matter who tells him not to do it. And
so on that calculation the law, surely as mad a one as
any Eastern despot ever hatched, is passed that, for a
given space of time, nobody within the dominions of
this king, Darius, is to make any petition or request of
any man or god, save of the king only. It was one of
the long series of laws that have been passed in order
to be broken, and being broken, might be an instrument
to destroy the men that broke it. It was passed with
no intention of getting obedience, but only with the
intention of slaying one faithful man, and the plot
worked according to calculation.

What did it matter to Daniel what was forbidden or

commanded? He needed to pray to God, and nothing shall hinder him from doing that. And so, obediently disobedient, he brushes the preposterous law of the poor, shadowy Darius on one side, in order that he may keep the law of his God.

Now I do not need to remind you how obedience to God has in the past often had to be maintained by disobedience to law. I need not speak of martyrs, nor of the great principle laid down so clearly by the apostle Peter, 'We ought to obey God rather than man.' Nor need I remind you that if a man, for conscience sake, refuses to render active obedience to an unrighteous law, and unresistingly accepts the appointed penalty, he is not properly regarded as a law-breaker.

If earthly authorities command what is clearly contrary to God's law, a Christian is absolved from obedience, and cannot be loyal unless he is a rebel. That is how our forefathers read constitutional obligations. That is how the noble men on the other side of the Atlantic, fifty years ago, read their constitutional obligations in reference to that devilish institution of slavery. And in the last resort—God forbid that we should need to act on the principle—Christian men are set free from allegiance when the authority over them commands what is contrary to the will and the law of God.

But all that does not touch us. But I will tell you what does touch us. Obedience to God needs always to be sustained—in some cases more markedly, in some cases less so—but always in some measure, by disobedience to the maxims and habits of most men round about us. If they say 'Do this,' and Jesus Christ says 'Don't,' then they may talk as much as they like, but

we are bound to turn a deaf ear to their exhortations
and threats.

> 'He is a slave that dare not be
> In the right with two or three,

as that peaceful Quaker poet of America sings.

And for us, in our little lives, the motto, 'This did not
I, because of the fear of the Lord,' is absolutely essential
to all noble Christian conduct.   Unless you are prepared
to be in the minority, and now and then to be called
'narrow,' 'fanatic,' and to be laughed at by men because
you will not do what they do, but abstain and resist,
then there is little chance of your ever making much
of your Christian profession.

These people calculated upon Daniel, and they had a
right to calculate upon him.   Could the world calculate
upon us, that we would rather go to the lions' den than
conform to what God and our consciences told us to be
a sin?   If not, we have not yet learned what it means
to be a disciple.   The commandment comes to us
absolutely, as it came to the servants in the first
miracle, 'Whatsoever He saith unto you '—that, and
that only—'whatsoever He saith unto you, do it.'

FAITH STOPPING THE MOUTHS OF LIONS

'Then the king commanded, and they brought Daniel, and cast him into the den
of lions.   Now the king spake and said unto Daniel, Thy God whom thou servest
continually, He will deliver thee.   17. And a stone was brought, and laid upon the
mouth of the den; and the king sealed it with his own signet, and with the signet
of his lords; that the purpose might not be changed concerning Daniel.   18. Then
the king went to his palace, and passed the night fasting: neither were instruments of musick brought before him : and his sleep went from him.   19. Then the
king arose very early in the morning, and went in haste unto the den of lions.   20.
And when he came to the den, he cried with a lamentable voice unto Daniel: and
the king spake and said to Daniel, O Daniel, servant of the living God, is thy God,
whom thou servest continually, able to deliver thee from the lions? 21. Then said
Daniel unto the king, O king, live for ever.   22. My God hath sent His angel, and
hath shut the lions' mouths, that they have not hurt me: forasmuch as before
Him innocency was found in me; and also before thee, O king, have I done no

hurt. 23. Then was the king exceeding glad for him, and commanded that they should take Daniel up out of the den. So Daniel was taken up out of the den, and no manner of hurt was found upon him, because he believed in his God. 24. And the king commanded, and they brought those men which had accused Daniel, and they cast them into the den of lions, them, their children, and their wives; and the lions had the mastery of them, and brake all their bones in pieces or ever they came at the bottom of the den. 25. Then king Darius wrote unto all people, nations, and languages, that dwell in all the earth; Peace be multiplied unto you. 26. I make a decree, That in every dominion of my kingdom men tremble and fear before the God of Daniel: for He is the living God, and stedfast for ever, and His kingdom that which shall not be destroyed, and His dominion shall be even unto the end. 27. He delivereth and rescueth, and He worketh signs and wonders in heaven and in earth, who hath delivered Daniel from the power of the lions. 28. So this Daniel prospered in the reign of Darius, and in the reign of Cyrus the Persian.'—DANIEL vi. 16-28.

DANIEL was verging on ninety when this great test of his faithfulness was presented to him. He had been honoured and trusted through all the changes in the kingdom, and, when the Medo-Persian conquest came, the new monarch naturally found in him, as a foreigner, a more reliable minister than in native officials. 'Envy doth merit as its shade pursue,' and the crafty trick by which his subordinates tried to procure his fall, was their answer to Darius's scheme of making him prime minister. Our passage begins in the middle of the story, but the earlier part will come into consideration in the course of our remarks.

I. We note, first, the steadfast, silent confessor and the weak king. Darius is a great deal more conspicuous in the narrative than Daniel. The victim of injustice is silent. He does not seem to have been called on to deny or defend the indictment. His deed was patent, and the breach of the law flagrant. He, too, was 'like a sheep before the shearers,' dumb. His silence meant, among other things, a quiet, patient, fixed resolve to bear all, and not to deny his God. Weak men bluster. Heroic endurance has generally little to say. Without resistance, or a word, the old man, an hour ago the foremost in the realm, is hauled off and flung into the pit or den. It is useless and

needless to ask its form. The entrance was sealed
with two seals, one the king's, one the conspirators',
that neither party might steal a march on the other.
Fellows in iniquity do not trust each other. So, down
in the dark there, with the glittering eyeballs of the
brutes round him, and their growls in his ears, the old
man sits all night long, with peace in his heart, and looking up trustfully, through the hole in the roof, to his
Protector's stars, shining their silent message of cheer.

The passage dwells on the pitiable weakness and
consequent unrest of the king. He had not yielded
Daniel to his fate without a struggle, which the
previous narrative describes in strong language. 'Sore
displeased,' he 'set his heart' on delivering him, and
'laboured' to do so. The curious obstacle, limiting
even his power, is a rare specimen of conservatism in
its purest form. So wise were our ancestors, that
nothing of theirs shall ever be touched. Infallible
legislators can make immutable laws; the rest of us
must be content to learn by blundering, and to grow
by changing. The man who says, 'I never alter my
opinions,' condemns himself as either too foolish or too
proud to learn.

But probably, if the question had been about a law
that was inconvenient to Darius himself, or to these
advocates of the constitution as it has always been,
some way of getting round it would have been found
out. If the king had been bold enough to assert himself, he could have walked through the cobweb. But
this is one of the miseries of yielding to evil counsels,
that one step taken calls for another. 'In for a penny,
in for a pound.' Therefore let us all take heed of
small compliances, and be sure that we can never say
about any doubtful course, 'Thus far will I go, and no

farther.' Darius was his servants' servant when once
he had put his name to the arrogant decree. He did
not know the incidence of his act, and we do not know
that of ours; therefore let us take heed of the quality
of actions and motives, since we are wholly incapable
of estimating the sweep of their consequences.

Darius's conduct to Daniel was like Herod's to John
the Baptist and Pilate's to Jesus. In all the cases the
judges were convinced of the victim's innocence, and
would have saved him; but fear of others biassed
justice, and from selfish motives, they let fierce hatred
have its way. Such judges are murderers. From all
come the old lessons, never too threadbare to be dinned
into the ears, especially of the young, that to be weak
is, in a world so full of temptation, the same as to be
wicked, and that he who has a sidelong eye to his
supposed interest, will never see the path of duty
plainly.

What a feeble excuse to his own conscience was
Darius's parting word to Daniel! 'Thy God, whom
thou servest continually, He will deliver thee!' And
was flinging him to the lions the right way to treat a
man who served God continually? Or, what right had
Darius to expect that any god would interfere to stop
the consequences of his act, which he thus himself condemned? We are often tempted to think, as he did,
that a divine intervention will come in between our
evil deeds and their natural results. We should be
wiser if we did not do the things that, by our own confession, need God to avert their issues.

But that weak parting word witnessed to the impression made by the life-long consistency of Daniel.
He must be a good man who gets such a testimony
from those who are harming him. The busy minister

of state had done his political work so as to extort
that tribute from one who had no sympathy with his
religion. Do we do ours in that fashion ? How many
of our statesmen 'serve God continually' and obviously
in their public life ?

What a contrast between the night passed in the
lions' den and the palace! 'Stone walls do not a
prison make, nor iron bars a cage,' and soft beds and
luxurious delights of sense bring no ease to troubled
consciences. Daniel is more at rest, though his 'soul
is among lions,' than Darius in his palace. Peter sleeps
soundly, though the coming morning is to be his last.
Better to be the victim than the doer of injustice!

The verdict of nightly thoughts on daily acts is
usually true, and if our deeds do not bear thinking of
'on our beds,' the sooner we cancel them by penitence
and reversed conduct, the better. But weak men are
often prone to swift and shallow regrets, which do not
influence their future any more than a stone thrown
into the sea makes a permanent gap. Why should
Darius have waited for morning, if his penitence had
moved him to a firm resolution to undo the evil done?
He had better have sprung from his bed, and gone
with his guards to open the den in the dark. Feeble
lamentations are out of place when it is still time
to act.

The hurried rush to the den in the morning twilight,
and the 'lamentable voice,' so unlike royal impassive-
ness, indicate the agitation of an impulsive nature,
accustomed to let the feeling of the moment sway it
unchecked. Absolute power tends to make that type
of man. The question thrown into the den seems to
imply that its interior was not seen. If so, the half-
belief in Daniel's survival is remarkable. It indicates,

as before, the impression of steadfast devoutness made
by the old man's life, and also a belief that his God
was possibly a true and potent divinity.

Such a belief was quite natural, but it does not mean
that Darius was prepared to accept Daniel's God as his
god. His religion was probably elastic and hospitable
enough to admit that other nations might have other
gods. But his thoughts about this 'living God' are a
strange medley. He is not sure whether He is stronger
than the royal lions, and he does not seem to feel that
if a god delivers, his own act in surrendering a favoured
servant of such a god looks very black. A half-belief
blinds men to the opposition between their ways and
God's, and to the certain issue of their going in one
direction and God in another. If Daniel be delivered,
what will become of Darius? But, like most men, he
is illogical, and that question does not seem to have
occurred to him. Surely this man may sit for a
portrait of a weak, passionate nature, in the feebleness of his resistance to evil, the half hopes that
wrong would be kept from turning out so badly as it
promised, the childish moanings over wickedness that
might still have been mended, and the incapacity to
take in the grave, personal consequences of his crime.

II. We next note the great deliverance. The king
does not see Daniel, and waits in sickening doubt
whether any sound but the brutes' snarl at the disturber
of their feast will be heard. There must have been a
sigh of relief when the calm accents were audible from
the unseen depth. And what dignity, respect, faith,
and innocence are in them! Even in such circumstances the usual form of reverential salutation to the
king is remembered. That night's work might have
made a sullen rebel of Daniel, and small blame to him

if he had had no very amiable feelings to Darius; but he had learned faithfulness in a good school, and no trace of returning evil for evil was in his words or tones.

The formal greeting was much more than a form, when it came up from among the lions. It heaped coals of fire on the king's head, let us hope, and taught him, if he needed the lesson, that Daniel's disobedience had not been disloyalty. The more religion compels us to disregard the authority and practices of others, the more scrupulously attentive should we be to demonstrate that we cherish all due regard to them, and wish them well. How simply, and as if he saw nothing in it to wonder at, he tells the fact of his deliverance! 'My God has sent His angel, and hath shut the lions' mouths.' He had not been able to say, as the king did before the den was opened, 'Thy God will deliver thee'; but he had gone down into it, knowing that He was able, and leaving himself in God's care. So it was no surprise to him that he was safe. Thankfulness, but not astonishment, filled his heart. So faith takes God's gifts, however great and beyond natural possibility they may be; for the greatest of them are less than the Love which faith knows to move all things, and whatsoever faith receives is just like Him.

Daniel did not say, as Darius did, that he served God continually, but he did declare his own innocency in God's sight and unimpeachable fidelity to the king. His reference is probably mainly to his official conduct; but the characteristic tone of the Old Testament saint is audible, which ventured on professions of uprightness, accordant with an earlier stage of revelation and religious consciousness, but scarcely congruous

with the deeper and more inward sense of sin produced
by the full revelation in Christ. But if the tone of the
latter part of verse 22 is somewhat strange to us, the
historian's summary in verse 23 gives the eternal truth
of the matter: 'No manner of hurt was found upon
him, because he had trusted in his God.' That is the
basis of the reference in Hebrews xi. 33: 'Through
faith . . . stopped the mouths of lions.'

Simple trust in God brings His angel to our help, and
the deliverance, which is ultimately to be ascribed to
His hand muzzling the gaping beasts of prey, may also
be ascribed to the faith which sets His hand in motion.
The true cause is God, but the indispensable condition
without which God will not act, and with which He
cannot but act, is our trust. Therefore all the great
things which it is said to do are due, not to anything
in it, but wholly to that of which it lays hold. A foot
or two of lead pipe is worth little, but if it is the
channel through which water flows into a city, it is
priceless.

Faith may or may not bring external deliverances,
such as it brought to Daniel; but the good cheer which
this story brings us does not depend on these. When
Paul lay in Rome, shortly before his martyrdom, the
experience of Daniel was in his mind, as he thankfully
wrote to Timothy, 'I was delivered out of the mouth of
the lion.' He adds a hope which contrasts strangely, at
first sight, with the clear expectation of a speedy and
violent death, expressed a moment or two before ('I
am already being offered, and the time of my departure is come') when he says, 'The Lord will deliver
me from every evil work'; but he had learned that it
was possible to pass through the evil and yet to be
delivered from it, and that a man might be thrown

to the lions and devoured by them, and yet be truly shielded from all harm from them. So he adds, 'And will save me unto His heavenly kingdom,' thereby teaching us that the true deliverance is that which carries us into, or something nearer towards, the eternal home. Thus understood, the miracle of Daniel's deliverance is continually repeated to all who partake of Daniel's faith, 'Thou hast made the Most High thy habitation . . . thou shalt tread upon the lion and adder.'

The savage vengeance on the conspirators and the proclamation of Darius must be left untouched. The one is a ghastly example of retributive judgment, in which, as sometimes is the case even now, men fall into the pit they have digged for others, and it shows the barbarous cruelty of that gorgeous civilisation. The other is an example of how far a man may go in perceiving and acknowledging the truth without its influencing his heart. The decree enforces recognition of Daniel's God, in language which even prophets do not surpass; but it is all lip-reverence, as evanescent as superficial. It takes more than a fright caused by a miracle to make a man a true servant of the living God.

The final verse of the passage implies Daniel's restoration to rank, and gives a beautiful, simple picture of the old man's closing days, which had begun so long before, in such a different world as Nebuchadnezzar's reign, and closed in Cyrus's, enriched with all that should accompany old age—honour, obedience, troops of friends. 'When a man's ways please the Lord, He maketh even his enemies to be at peace with him.'

A NEW YEAR'S MESSAGE

'But go thou thy way till the end be: for thou shalt rest, and stand in thy lot at the end of the days.'—DANIEL xii. 13.

DANIEL had been receiving partial insight into the future by the visions recorded in previous chapters. He sought for clearer knowledge, and was told that the book of the future was sealed and closed, so that no further enlightenment was possible for him. But duty was clear, whatever might be dark; and there were some things in the future certain, whatever might be problematic. So he is bidden back to the common paths of life, and is enjoined to pursue his patient course with an eye on the end to which it conducts, and to leave the unknown future to unfold itself as it may.

I do not need, I suppose, to point the application. Anticipations of what may be before us have, no doubt, been more or less in the minds of all of us in the last few days. The cast of them will have been very different, according to age and present circumstances. But bright or dark, hopes or dreads, they reveal nothing. Sometimes we think we see a little way ahead, and then swirling mists hide all.

So I think that the words of my text may help us not only to apprehend the true task of the moment, but to discriminate between the things in the unknown future that are hidden and those that stand clear. There are three points, then, in this message—the journey, the pilgrim's resting-place, and the final home. 'Go thou thy way till the end be: for thou shalt rest, and stand in thy lot at the end of the days.' Let us, then, look at these three points briefly.

I. The journey.

84

That is a threadbare metaphor for life. But threadbare as it is, its significance is inexhaustible. But before I deal with it, note that very significant 'but' with which my text begins. The Prophet has been asking for a little more light to shine on the dark unknown that stretches before him. And his request is negatived —'*But* go thou thy way.' In the connection that means, 'Do not waste your time in dreaming about, or peering into, what you can never see, but fill the present with strenuous service.' 'Go thou thy way.' Never mind the far-off issues; the step before you is clear, and that is all that concerns you. Plod along the path, and leave to-morrow to take care of itself. There is a piece of plain practical wisdom, none the less necessary for us to lay to heart because it is so obvious and commonplace.

And then, if we turn to the emblem with which the continuity of daily life and daily work is set forth here, as the path along which we travel, how much wells up in the shape of suggestion, familiar, it may be, but very needful and wholesome for us all to lay to heart!

The figure implies perpetual change. The landscape glides past us, and we travel on through it. How impossible it would be for us older people to go back to the feelings, to the beliefs, to the tone and the temper with which we used to look at life thirty or forty years ago! Strangely and solemnly, like the silent motion of some gliding scene in a theatre, bit by bit, inch by inch, change comes over all surroundings, and, saddest of all, in some aspects, over ourselves.

> 'We all are changed, by still degrees,
> All but the basis of the soul.'

And it is foolish for us ever to forget that we live in a state of things in which constant alteration is the law, as surely as, when the train whizzes through the country, the same landscape never meets the eye twice, as the traveller looks through the windows. Let us, then, accept the fact that nothing abides with us, and so not be bewildered nor swept away from our moorings, nor led to vain regrets and paralysing retrospects when the changes that must come do come, sometimes slowly and imperceptibly, sometimes with stunning suddenness, like a bolt out of the blue. If life is truly represented under the figure of a journey, nothing is more certain than that we sleep in a fresh hospice every night, and leave behind us every day scenes that we shall never traverse again. What madness, then, to be putting out eager and desperate hands to clutch what must be left, and so to contradict the very law under which we live!

Then another of the well-worn commonplaces which are so believed by us all that we never think about them, and therefore need to be urged, as I am trying, poorly enough, to do now—another of the commonplaces that spring from this image is that life is continuous. Geologists used to be divided into two schools, one of whom explained everything by invoking great convulsions, the other by appealing to the uniform action of laws. There are no convulsions in life. To-morrow is the child of to-day, and yesterday was the father of this day. What we are, springs from what we have been, and settles what we shall be. The road leads somewhither, and we follow it step by step. As the old nursery rhyme has it—

> 'One foot up and one foot down,
> That's the way to London town.'

We make our characters by the continual repetition of small actions. Let no man think of his life as if it were a

heap of unconnected points. It is a chain of links that
are forged together inseparably. Let no man say, ' I
do this thing, and there shall be no evil consequences
impressed upon my life as results of it.' It cannot
be. 'To-morrow *shall be* as this day, and much more
abundant." We shall to-morrow be more of everything
that we are to-day, unless by some strong effort of
repentance and change we break the fatal continuity,
and make a new beginning by God's grace. But let
us lay to heart this, as a very solemn truth which lifts
up into mystical and unspeakable importance the things
that men idly call trifles, that life is one continuous
whole, a march towards a definite end.

And therefore we ought to see to it that the direction
in which our life runs is one that conscience and God
can approve. And, since the rapidity with which a
body falls increases as it falls, the more needful that
we give the right direction and impulses to the life.
It will be a dreadful thing if our downward course
acquires strength as it travels, and being slow at first,
gains in celerity, and accrues to itself mass and weight,
like an avalanche started from an Alpine summit, which
is but one or two bits of snow and ice at first, and falls
at last into the ravine, tons of white destruction. The
lives of many of us are like it.

Further, the metaphor suggests that no life takes its
fitting course unless there is continuous effort. There
will be crises when we have to run with panting breath
and strained muscles. There will be long stretches
of level commonplace where speed is not needed, but
'pegging away' is, and the one duty is persistent con-
tinuousness in a course. But whether the task of the
moment is to 'run and not be weary,' or to 'walk and
not faint,' crises and commonplace stretches of land

alike require continuous effort, if we are to ' run with patience the race that is set before us.'

Mark the emphasis of my text, ' Go thy way *till* the end.' You, my contemporaries, you older men! do not fancy that in the deepest aspect any life has ever a period in it in which a man may ' take it easy.' You may do that in regard to outward things, and it is the hope and the reward of faithfulness in youth and middle age that, when the grey hairs come to be upon us, we may slack off a little in regard to outward activity. But in regard to all the deepest things of life, no man may ever lessen his diligence until he has attained the goal.

Some of you will remember how, in a stormy October night, many years ago, the *Royal Charter* went down when three hours from Liverpool, and the passengers had met in the saloon and voted a testimonial to the captain because he had brought them across the ocean in safety. Until the anchor is down and we are inside the harbour, we may be shipwrecked, if we are careless in our navigation. ' Go thou thy way *until the end.*' And remember, you older people, that until that end is reached you have to use all your power, and to labour as earnestly, and guard yourself as carefully, as at any period before.

And not only ' *till* the end,' but ' go thou thy way *to* the end.' That is to say, let the thought that the road has a termination be ever present with us all. Now, there is a great deal of the so-called devout contemplation of death which is anything but wholesome. People were never meant to be always looking forward to that close. Men may think of ' the end ' in a hundred different connections. One man may say, ' Let us eat and drink, for to-morrow we die.' Another man may say, 'I have only a little while to master this science, to make a name for myself, to win wealth. Let me bend all my efforts in a fierce determination—made the fiercer because of the thought of the brevity of life—to win the end.' The mere contemplation of the shortness of our days may be an ally of immorality, of selfishness, of meanness, of earthly ambitions, or it may lay a cooling hand on fevered brows, and lessen the pulsations of hearts that throb for earth.

But whilst it is not wholesome to be always thinking of death, it is more unwholesome still never to let the contemplation of that end come into our calculations of the future, and to shape our lives in an obstinate blindness to what is the one certain fact which rises up through the whirling mists of the unknown future, like some black cliff from the clouds that wreath around it. Is it not strange that the surest thing is the thing that we forget most of all? It sometimes seems to me as if the sky rained down opiates upon people, as if all mankind were in a conspiracy of lunacy, because they, with one accord, ignore the most prominent and forget the only certain fact about their future; and in all their calculations do *not* 'so number their days' as to 'apply' their 'hearts unto wisdom.' 'Go thou thy way until the end,' and let thy way be marked out with a constant eye towards the end.

II. Note, again, the resting-place.

'Go thou thy way, for thou shalt rest.' Now, I suppose, to most careful readers that clearly is intended as a gracious, and what they call a euphemistic way of speaking about death. 'Thou shalt rest'; well, that is a thought that takes away a great deal of the grimness and the terror with which men generally invest the close. It is a thought, of course, the force of which is very different in different stages and conditions of life. To you young people, eager, perhaps ambitious, full of the consciousness of inward power, happy, and, in all human probability, with the greater portion of your lives before you in which to do what you desire, the thought of 'rest' comes with a very faint appeal. And yet I do not suppose that there is any one of us who has not some burden that is hard to carry, or who has not learned what weariness means.

But to us older people, who have tasted disappointments, who have known the pressure of grinding toil for a great many years, whose hearts have been gnawed by harassments and anxieties of different kinds, whose lives are apparently drawing nearer their end than the present moment is to their beginning, the thought, 'Thou shalt rest,' comes with a very different appeal from that which it makes to these others.

.' There remaineth a rest for the people of God,
And I have had trouble enough for one,'

says our great modern poet; and therein he echoes the deepest thoughts of most of this congregation. That rest is the cessation of toil, but the continuance of activity—the cessation of toil, and anxiety, and harassment, and care, and so the darkness is made beautiful when we think that God draws the curtain, as a careful mother does in her child's chamber, that the light may not disturb the slumberer.

But, dear friends, that final cessation of earthly work has a double character. 'Thou shalt rest' was said to this man of God. But what of people whom death takes away from the only sort of work that they are fit to do? It will be no rest to long for the occupations which you never can have any more. And if you have been living for this wretched present, to be condemned to have nothing to do any more in it and with it will be torture, and not repose. Ask yourselves how you would like to be taken out of your shop, or your mill, or your study, or your laboratory, or your counting-house, and never be allowed to go into it again. Some of you know how wearisome a holiday is when you cannot get to your daily work. You will get a very long holiday after you are dead. And if the hungering after the withdrawn occupation persists, there will be very little pleasure in rest. There is only one way by which we can make that inevitable end a blessing, and turn death into the opening of the gate of our resting-place; and that is by setting our heart's desires and our spirit's trust on Jesus Christ, who is the 'Lord both of the dead and of the living.' If we do that, even that last enemy will come to us as Christ's representative, with Christ's own word upon his lip, ' Come unto Me, ye that are weary and are heavy laden, and I'—because He has given Me the power—'*I* will give you rest.'

> ' Sleep, full of rest, from head to foot;
> Lie still, dry dust, secure of change.'

III. That leads me to the last thought, the home.

' Thou shalt stand in thy lot at the end of the days.' ' Stand'—that is Daniel's way of preaching, what he has been preaching in several other parts of his book, the doctrine of the resurrection. ' Thou shalt stand in *thy lot.*' That is a reference to the ancient partition of the land of Canaan amongst the tribes, where each man got his own portion, and sat under his own vine and fig-tree. And so there emerge from these symbolical words thoughts upon which, at this stage of my sermon, I can barely touch. First comes the thought that, however sweet and blessed that reposeful state may be, humanity has not attained its perfec-

tion until once again the perfected spirit is mated with,
and enclosed within, its congenial servant, a perfect
body. 'Corporeity is the end of man.' Body, soul, and
spirit partake of the redemption of God.

But then, apart from that, on which I must not dwell,
my text suggests one or two thoughts. God is the true
inheritance. Each man has his own portion of the
common possession, or, to put it into plainer words,
in that perfect land each individual has precisely so
much of God as he is capable of possessing. 'Thou
shalt stand in thy lot,' and what determines the lot is
how we wend our way till that other end, the end of
life. 'The end of the days' is a period far beyond the
end of the life of Daniel. And as the course that
terminated in repose has been, so the possession of
'the portion of the inheritance of the saints in light'
shall be, for which that course has made men meet.
Destiny is character worked out. A man will be where
he is fit for, and have what he is fit for. Time is the
lackey of eternity. His life here settles how much of
God a man shall be able to hold, when he stands in his
lot at the 'end of the days,' and his allotted portion,
as it stretches around him, will be but the issue and
the outcome of his life here on earth.

Therefore, dear brethren, tremendous importance
attaches to each fugitive moment. Therefore each act
that we do is weighted with eternal consequences. If
we will put our trust in Him, 'in whom also we obtain
the inheritance,' and will travel on life's common way
in cheerful godliness, we may front all the uncertainties
of the unknown future, sure of two things—that we
shall rest, and that we shall stand in our lot. We shall
all go where we have fitted ourselves, by God's grace,
to go; get what we have fitted ourselves to possess;

and be what we have made ourselves. To the Christian man the word comes, 'Thou shalt stand in thy lot.' And the other word that was spoken about one sinner, will be fulfilled in all whose lives have been unfitting them for heaven: 'Judas by transgression fell, that he might go to his own place.' He, too, stands in his lot. Now settle which lot is **yours.**

HOSEA

THE VALLEY OF ACHOR

'I will give her . . . the valley of Achor for a door of hope.'—HOSEA ii. 15.

THE Prophet Hosea is remarkable for the frequent use
which he makes of events in the former history of his
people. Their past seems to him a mirror in which
they may read their future. He believes that 'which
is to be hath already been,' the great principles of the
divine government living on through all the ages, and
issuing in similar acts when the circumstances are
similar. So he foretells that there will yet be once
more a captivity and a bondage, that the old story of
the wilderness will be repeated once more. In that
wilderness God will speak to the heart of Israel. Its
barrenness shall be changed into the fruitfulness of
vineyards, where the purpling clusters hang ripe for
the thirsty travellers. And not only will the sorrows
that He sends thus become sources of refreshment, but
the gloomy gorge through which they journey—the
valley of Achor—will be a door of hope.

One word is enough to explain the allusion. You
remember that after the capture of Jericho by Joshua,
the people were baffled in their first attempt to press
up through the narrow defile that led from the plain of
Jordan to the highlands of Canaan. Their defeat was
caused by the covetousness of Achan, who for the sake

of some miserable spoil which he found in a tent, broke
God's laws, and drew down shame on Israel's ranks.
When the swift, terrible punishment on him had
purged the camp, victory again followed their assault,
and Achan lying stiff and stark below his cairn, they
pressed on up the glen to their task of conquest. The
rugged valley, where that defeat and that sharp act of
justice took place, was named in memory thereof, the
valley of *Achor*, that is, *trouble*; and our Prophet's
promise is that as then, so for all future ages, the
complicity of God's people with an evil world will work
weakness and defeat, but that, if they will be taught by
their trouble and will purge themselves of the accursed
thing, then the disasters will make a way for hope to
come to them again. The figure which conveys this is
very expressive. The narrow gorge stretches before
us, with its dark overhanging cliffs that almost shut
out the sky; the path is rough and set with sharp
pebbles; it is narrow, winding, steep; often it seems
to be barred by some huge rock that juts across it, and
there is barely room for the broken ledge yielding
slippery footing between the beetling crag above and
the steep slope beneath that dips so quickly to the
black torrent below. All is gloomy, damp, hard; and
if we look upwards the glen becomes more savage as it
rises, and armed foes hold the very throat of the pass.
But, however long, however barren, however rugged,
however black, however trackless, we may see if we
will, a bright form descending the rocky way with
radiant eyes and calm lips, God's messenger, Hope;
and the rough rocks are like the doorway through
which she comes near to us in our weary struggle.
For us all, dear friends, it is true. In all our difficulties
and sorrows, be they great or small; in our business

perplexities; in the losses that rob our homes of their light; in the petty annoyances that diffuse their irritation through so much of our days; it is within our power to turn them all into occasions for a firmer grasp of God, and so to make them openings by which a happier hope may flow into our souls.

But the promise, like all God's promises, has its well-defined conditions. Achan has to be killed and put safe out of the way first, or no shining Hope will stand out against the black walls of the defile. The tastes which knit us to the perishable world, the yearnings for Babylonish garments and wedges of gold, must be coerced and subdued. Swift, sharp, unrelenting justice must be done on the lust of the flesh, and the lust of the eye, and the pride of life, if our trials are ever to become *doors of hope*. There is no natural tendency in the mere fact of sorrow and pain to make God's love more discernible, or to make our hope any firmer. All depends on how we use the trial, or as I say—first stone Achan, and then hope!

So, the trouble which detaches us from earth gives us new hope. Sometimes the effect of our sorrows and annoyances and difficulties is to rivet us more firmly to earth. The eye has a curious power, which they call persistence of vision, of retaining the impression made upon it, and therefore of seeming to see the object for a definite time after it has really been withdrawn. If you whirl a bit of blazing stick round, you will see a circle of fire though there is only a point moving rapidly in the circle. The eye has its memory like the soul. And the soul has its power of persistence like the eye, and that power is sometimes kindled into activity by the fact of loss. We often see our departed joys, and gaze upon them all the more eagerly for their departure. The loss of dear ones should stamp their image on our hearts, and set it as in a golden glory. But it sometimes does more than that; it sometimes makes us put the present with its duties impatiently away from us. Vain regret, absorbed brooding over what is gone, a sorrow kept gaping long after it should have been healed, like a grave-mound off which desperate love has pulled turf and flowers, in the vain attempt to clasp the cold hand below—in a word, the trouble that does not withdraw us from the present will never be a door of hope, but rather a grim gate for despair to come in at.

The trouble which knits us to God gives us new hope. That bright form which comes down the narrow valley is His messenger and herald—sent before His face. All the light of hope is the reflection on our hearts of the light of God. Her silver beams, which shed quietness over the darkness of earth, come only from that great Sun. If our hope is to grow out of our sorrow, it must be because our sorrow drives us to God. It is only when we by faith stand in His grace, and live in the conscious fellowship of peace with Him, that we rejoice in hope. If we would see Hope drawing near to us, we must fix our eyes not on Jericho that lies behind among its palm-trees, though it has memories of conquests, and attractions of fertility and repose, nor on the corpse that lies below that pile of stones, nor on the narrow way and the strong enemy in front there; but higher up, on the blue sky that spreads peaceful above the highest summits of the pass, and from the heavens we shall see the angel coming to us. Sorrow forsakes its own nature, and leads in its own opposite, when sorrow helps us to see God. It clears away the thick trees, and lets the sunlight into the forest shades, and then in

G

time corn will grow. Hope is but the brightness that
goes before God's face, and if we would see it we must
look at Him.

The trouble which we bear rightly with God's help,
gives new hope. If we have made our sorrow an
occasion for learning, by living experience, somewhat
more of His exquisitely varied and ever ready power
to aid and bless, then it will teach us firmer confidence
in these inexhaustible resources which we have thus
once more proved. 'Tribulation worketh patience, and
patience experience, and experience hope.' That is the
order. You cannot put patience and experience into
a parenthesis, and omitting them, bring hope out of
tribulation. But if, in my sorrow, I have been able to
keep quiet because I have had hold of God's hand, and
if in that unstruggling submission I have found that
from His hand I have been upheld, and had strength
above mine own infused into me, then my memory will
give the threads with which Hope weaves her bright
web. I build upon two things—God's unchangeableness,
and His help already received; and upon these strong
foundations I may wisely and safely rear a palace of
Hope, which shall never prove a castle in the air. The
past, when it is God's past, is the surest pledge for the
future. Because He has been with us in six troubles,
therefore we may be sure that in seven He will not
forsake us. I said that the light of hope was the
brightness from the face of God. I may say again,
that the light of hope which fills our sky is like that
which, on happy summer nights, lives till morning in
the calm west, and with its colourless, tranquil beauty,
tells of a yesterday of unclouded splendour, and prophesies a to-morrow yet more abundant. The glow
from a sun that is set, the experience of past deliver-

ances, is the truest light of hope to light our way through the night of life.

One of the psalms gives us, in different form, a metaphor and a promise substantially the same as that of this text. 'Blessed are the men who, passing through the valley of weeping, make it a well.' They gather their tears, as it were, into the cisterns by the wayside, and draw refreshment and strength from their very sorrows, and then, when thus we in our wise husbandry have irrigated the soil with the gathered results of our sorrows, the heavens bend over us, and weep their gracious tears, and 'the rain also covereth it with blessings.' 'No chastisement for the present seemeth to be joyous, but grievous; nevertheless, afterward it yieldeth the peaceable fruit of righteousness.'

Then, dear friends, let us set ourselves with our loins girt to the road. Never mind how hard it may be to climb. The slope of the valley of trouble is ever upwards. Never mind how dark is the shadow of death which stretches athwart it. If there were no sun there would be no shadow; presently the sun will be right overhead, and there will be no shadow then. Never mind how black it may look ahead, or how frowning the rocks. From between their narrowest gorge you may see, if you will, the guide whom God has sent you, and that Angel of Hope will light up all the darkness, and will only fade away when she is lost in the sevenfold brightness of that upper land, whereof our 'God Himself is Sun and Moon'—the true Canaan, to whose everlasting mountains the steep way of life has climbed at last through valleys of trouble, and of weeping, and of the shadow of death.

'LET HIM ALONE'

'Ephraim is joined to idols: let him alone.'—HOSEA iv. 17.

THE tribe of Ephraim was the most important member
of the kingdom of Israel; consequently its name was
not unnaturally sometimes used in a wider application
for the whole of the kingdom, of which it was the
principal part. Being the 'predominant partner,' its
name was used alone for that of the whole firm, just
as in our own empire, we often say 'England,' meaning
thereby the three kingdoms: England, Scotland, and
Ireland. So 'Ephraim' here does not mean the single
tribe, but the whole kingdom of Israel.

Now Hosea himself was a Northerner, a subject of
that kingdom; and its iniquities and idolatries weighed
heavily on his heart, and were ripped up and brought
to light with burning eloquence in his prophesies. The
words of my text have often, and terribly, been mis-
understood. And I wish now to try to bring out their
true meaning and bearing. They have a message for
us quite as much as they had for the people who originally received them.

I. I must begin by explaining what, in my judgment,
this text does not mean.

First, it is not what it is often taken to be, a threatening of God's abandoning of the idolatrous nation. I dare
say we have all heard grim sermons from this text,
which have taken that view of it, and have tried to
frighten men into believing now, by telling them that,
perhaps, if they do not, God will never move on their
hearts, or deal with them any more, but withdraw His
grace, and leave them to insensibility. There is not a

word of that sort in the text. Plainly enough it is not
so, for this vehement utterance of the Prophet is not a
declaration as to God, and what He is going to do, but
it is a commandment to some men, telling them what
they are to do. 'Let him alone' does not mean the
same thing as '*I* will let him alone'; and if people
had only read with a little more care, they would have
been delivered from perpetrating a libel on the divine
lovingkindness and forbearance.

It is clear enough, too, that such a meaning as that
which has been forced upon the words of my text, and
is the common use of it, I believe, in many evangelical
circles, cannot be its real meaning, because the very
fact that Hosea was prophesying to call Ephraim from
his sin showed that God had *not* let Ephraim alone, but
was wooing him by His prophet, and seeking to win
him back by the words of his mouth. God was doing
all that He could do, rising early and sending His
messenger and calling to Ephraim: 'Turn ye! Turn
ye! why will ye die?' For Hosea, in the very act of
pleading with Israel on God's behalf, to have declared
that God had abandoned it, and ceased to plead, would
have been a palpable absurdity and contradiction.

But beyond considerations of the context, other
reasons conclusively negative such an interpretation
of this text. I, for my part, do not believe that there
are any bounds or end to God's forbearing pleading
with men in this life. I take, as true, the great words
of the old Psalm, in their simplest sense—'His mercy
endureth for ever'; and I fall back upon the other
words which a penitent had learned to be true by
reflecting on the greatness of his own sin: 'With
Him are multitudes of redemptions'; and I turn from
psalmists and prophets to the Master who showed us

God's heart, and knew what He spake when He laid it down as the law and the measure of human forgiveness which was moulded upon the pattern of the divine, that it should be 'seventy times seven'— the multiplication of both the perfect numbers into themselves—than which there can be no grander expression for absolute innumerableness and unfailing continuance.

No, no! men may say to God, 'Speak no more to us'; or they may get so far away from Him, as that they only hear God's pleading voice, dim and faint, like a voice in a dream. But surely the history of His progressive revelation shows us that, rather than such abandonment of the worst, the law of the divine dealing is that the deafer the man, the more piercing the voice beseeching and warning. The attraction of gravitation decreases as distance increases, but the further away we are from Him, the stronger is the attraction which issues from Him, and would draw us to Himself.

Clear away, then, altogether out of your minds any notion that there is here declared what, in my judgment, is not declared anywhere in the Bible, and never occurs in the divine dealings with men. Be sure that He never ceases to seek to draw the most obstinate, idolatrous, and rebellious heart to Himself. That divine charity 'suffereth long, and is kind' . . . 'hopeth all things, and beareth all things.'

Again, let me point out that the words of my text do not enjoin the cessation of the efforts of Christian people for the recovery of the most deeply sunken in sin. 'Let him alone' is a commandment, and it is a commandment to God's Church, but it is not a com-

mandment to despair of any that they may be brought
into the fold, or to give up efforts to that end. If
our Father in heaven never ceases to bear in His
heart His prodigal children, it does not become those
prodigals, who have come back, to think that any
of their brethren are too far away to be drawn by
their loving proclamation of the Father's heart of
love.

There is the glory of our Gospel, that, taking far
sadder, graver views of what sin and alienation from
God are, than the world's philosophers and philan-
thropists do, it surpasses them just as much as in the
superb confidence with which it sets itself to the cure
of the disease as in the unflinching clearness with which
it diagnoses the disease as fatal, if it be not dealt with
by the all-healing Gospel. All other methods for the
restoration and elevation of mankind are compelled to
recognise that there is an obstinate residuum that will
not and cannot be reached by their efforts. It used
to be said that some old cannon-balls, that had been
brought from some of the battlefields of the Peninsula,
resisted all attempts to melt them down; so there are
'cannon-balls,' as it were, amongst the obstinate evil-
doers, and the degraded and 'dangerous' classes, which
mark the despair of our modern reformers and civilisers
and elevators, for no fire in their furnaces can melt
down their hardness. No; but there is the furnace of
the Lord in Jerusalem, and the fire of God in Zion,
which can melt them down, and has done so a hundred
and a thousand times, and is as able to do it again to-
day as it ever was. Despair of no human soul. That
boundless confidence in the power of the Gospel is
the duty of the Christian Church. 'The damsel is
not dead, but sleepeth!' They laughed Him to scorn,

knowing that she was dead. But He put out His hand, and said unto her 'Talitha cumi, I say unto thee, Arise!' When we stand on one side of the bed with your social reformers on the other, and say 'The damsel is not dead, but sleepeth,' they laugh us to scorn, and bid us try our Gospel upon these people in our slums, or on those heathens in the New Hebrides. We have the right to answer, 'We have tried it, and man after man, and woman after woman have risen from the sick-bed, like Peter's wife's mother; and the fever has left them, and they have ministered unto Him. There are no people in the world about whom Christians need despair, none that Christ's Gospel cannot redeem. Whatever my text means, it does not mean cowardly and unbelieving doubt as to the power of the Gospel on the most degraded and sinful.

II. So, the text enjoins on the Christian Church separation from an idolatrous world.

'Ephraim is joined to idols.' Do you 'let him alone.' Now, there has been much harm done by misreading the force of the injunction of separation from the world. There is a great deal of union and association with the most godless people in our circle, which is inevitable. Family bonds, business connections, civic obligations—all these require that the Church shall not withdraw from the world. There is the wide common ground of Politics and Art and Literature, and a hundred other interests, on which it does Christian men no good, and the world much harm, if the former withdraw to themselves, and on the plea of superior sanctity, leave these great departments of interest and influence to be occupied only by non-Christians.

Then, besides these thoughts of necessary union and association upon common ground, there is the other consideration that absolute separation would defeat the very purpose for which Christian people are here. 'Ye are the salt of the earth,' said Christ. Yes, and if you keep the meat on one plate and the salt on another, what good will the salt be? It has to be rubbed in particle by particle, and brought into contact over all the surface, and down into the depths of the meat that it is to preserve from putrefaction. And no Christian churches or individuals do their duty, and fulfil their function on earth, unless they are thus closely associated and intermingled with the world that they should be trying to leaven and save. A cloistered solitude, or a proud standing apart from the ordinary movements of the community, or a neglect, on the plea of our higher duties, of the duties of the citizen of a free country—these are not the ways to fulfil the exhortation of my text. 'Let the dead bury their dead,' said Christ; but He did not mean that His Church was to stand apart from the world, and let it go its own way. It is a bad thing for both when little Christian côteries gather themselves together, and talk about their own goodness and religion, and leave the world to perish. Clotted blood is death; circulated, it is life.

But, whilst all this is perfectly true—and there are associations that we must not break if we are to do our work as Christian people—it is also true that it is possible, in the closest unions with men who do not share our faith, to do the same thing that they are doing, with a difference which separates us from them, even whilst we are united with them. They tell us that, however dense any material substance may seem to be, there is always a film of air between contiguous particles. And there should be a film between us and our Christless friends and companions and partners, not perceptible perhaps to a superficial observer, but most real. If we do our common work as a religious duty, and in the exercise of all our daily occupations 'set the Lord always before' us, however closely we may be associated with people who do not so live, they will know the difference; never fear! And you will know the difference, and will not be identified with them, but separate in a wholesome fashion from them.

And, dear brethren, if I may go a step further, I would venture to say that it seems to me that our Christian communities want few things more in this day than the reiteration of the old saying, 'Have no fellowship with the unfruitful works of darkness, but rather reprove them.' There is so much in this time to break down the separation between him that believeth in Christ and him that doth not; narrowness has come to be thought such an enormous wickedness, and liberality is so lauded by all sorts of superficial people, that Christian men need to be summoned back to their standard. 'Being let go, they went to their own company'—there is a natural affinity which should, and will, if our faith is vital, draw us to those who, on the gravest and solemnest things, have the same thoughts, the same hopes, the same faith. I do not urge you, God knows, to be bigoted and narrow, and shut yourselves up in your faith, and leave the world to go to the devil; but I do not wish, either, that Christian people should fling themselves into the arms and nestle in the hearts of persons who do not share with them 'like precious faith.'

I am sure that there are many Christian people, old
and young, who are suffering in their religious life
because they are neglecting this commandment of my
text. 'Let him alone.' There can be no deep affection, and, most of all—if I may venture on such
ground—no wedded love worth the name, where there
is not unanimity in regard to the deepest matters. It
does not say much for the religion of a professing
Christian who finds his heart's friends and his chosen
companions in people that have no sympathy with
the religion which he professes. It does not say
much for you if it is so with you, for the Christian,
whom you like least, is nearer you in the depths of
your true self than is the non-Christian whom you
love most.

Be sure, too, that if we mix ourselves up with
Ephraim, we shall find ourselves grovelling beside
him before his idols ere long. Godlessness is infec-
tious. Many a young woman, a professing Christian,
has married a godless man in the fond hope that she
might win him. It is a great deal more frequently
the case that he perverts her than that she converts
him. Do not let us knit ourselves in these close
bonds with the worshippers of idols, lest we 'learn
their ways, and get a snare into our souls.' 'Be not
unequally yoked with unbelievers. What fellowship
hath light with darkness? Wherefore, come out
from among them and be ye separate, saith the
Lord. Touch not the unclean thing, and I will
be a Father unto you, and ye shall be My sons and
My daughters.'

'PHYSICIANS OF NO VALUE'

'When Ephraim saw his sickness, and Judah saw his wound, then went Ephraim to Assyria, and sent to king Jareb: but he is not able to heal you, neither shall he cure you of your wound.'—HOSEA v. 13 (R.V.).

THE long tragedy which ended in the destruction of the Northern Kingdom by Assyrian invasion was already beginning to develop in Hosea's time. The mistaken politics of the kings of Israel led them to seek an ally where they should have dreaded an enemy. As Hosea puts it in figurative fashion, Ephraim's discovery of his 'sickness' sent him in the vain quest for help to the apparent source of the 'sickness,' that is to Assyria, whose king in the text is described by a name which is not his real name, but is a significant epithet, as the margin puts it, 'a king that should contend'; and who, of course, was not able to heal nor to cure the wounds. which he had inflicted. Ephraim's suicidal folly is but one illustration of a universal madness which drives men to seek for the healing of their misery, and the alleviation of their discomfort, in the repetition of the very acts which brought these about. The attempt to get relief in such a fashion, of course, fails; for as the verse before our text emphatically proclaims, it is God who has been 'as a moth unto Ephraim,' gnawing away his strength : and it is only He who can heal, since in reality it is He, and not the quarrelsome king of Assyria, who has inflicted the sickness.

Thus understood, the text carries wide lessons, and may serve us as a starting-point for considering man's discovery of his 'sickness,' man's mad way of seeking healing, God's way of giving it.

I. First, then, man's discovery of his sickness.

The greater part of most lives is spent in mechanical, unreflecting repetition of daily duties and pleasures. We are all apt to live on the surface, and it requires an effort, which we are too indolent to make except under the impulse of some arresting motive, to descend into the depths of our own souls, and there to face the solemn facts of our own personality. The last place with which most of us are familiar, is our innermost self. Men are dimly conscious that things within are not well with them; but it is only one here and there that says so distinctly to himself, and takes the further step of thoroughly investigating the cause. But that superficial life is at the mercy of a thousand accidents, each one of which may break through the thin film, and lay bare the black depths.

But there is another aspect of this discovery of sickness, far graver than the mere consciousness of unrest. Ephraim does not see his sickness unless he sees his sin. The greater part of every life is spent without that deep, all-pervading sense of discord between itself and God. Small and recurrent faults may evoke recurring remonstrances of conscience, but that is a very different thing from the deep tones and the clear voice of condemnation in respect to one's whole life and character which sounds in a heart that has learned how 'deceitful and desperately wicked' it is. Such a conviction may flash upon a man at any moment, and from a hundred causes. A sorrow, a sunset-sky, a grave, a sermon, may produce it.

But even when we have come to recognise clearly our unrest, we have gone but part of the way, we have become conscious of a symptom, not of the disease. Why is it that man is alone among the creatures in that discontent with externals, and that dissatisfaction

with himself? 'Foxes have holes, and the birds of the
air have roosting-places': why is it that amongst all
God's happy creatures, and God's shining stars, men
stand 'strangers in a strange land,' and are cursed with
a restlessness which has not 'where to lay its head'? The
consciousness of unrest is but the agitation of the limbs
which indicates disease. That disease is the twitching
paralysis of sin. Like 'the pestilence that walketh in
darkness,' it has a fell power of concealing itself, and
the man whose sins are the greatest is always the least
conscious of them. He dwells in a region where the
malaria is so all-pervading that the inhabitants do not
know what the sweetness of an unpoisoned atmosphere
is. If there is a 'worst man' in the world, we may be
very sure that no conscience is less troubled than his is.

So the question may well be urged on those so terribly
numerous amongst us, whose very unconsciousness of
their true condition is the most fatal symptom of their
fatal disease. What is the worth of a peace which is
only secured by ignoring realities, and which can be
shattered into fragments by anything that compels a
man to see himself as he is? In such a fool's paradise
thousands of us live. 'Use and wont,' the continual
occupation with the trifles of our daily lives, the fleeting satisfactions of our animal nature, the shallow
wisdom which bids us 'let sleeping dogs lie,' all conspire
to mask, to many consciences, their unrest and their
sin. We abstain from lifting the curtain behind which
the serpent lies coiled in our hearts, because we dread
to see its loathly length, and to rouse it to lift its
malignant head, and to strike with its forked tongue.
But sooner or later—may it not be too late—we shall
be set face to face with the dark recess, and discover
the foul reptile that has all the while been coiled there.

II. Man's mad way of seeking healing.

Can there be a more absurd course of action than
that recorded in our text? 'When Ephraim saw his
sickness, then went Ephraim to Assyria.' The Northern
Kingdom sought for the healing of their national
calamities from the very cause of their national
calamities, and in repetition of their national sin. A
hopeful policy, and one which speedily ended in the only
possible result! But that insanity was but a sample
of the infatuation which besets us all. When we are
conscious of our unrest, are we not all tempted to seek
to conceal it with what has made it? Take examples
from the grosser forms of animal indulgence. The
drunkard's vulgar proverb recommending 'a hair of the
dog that bit you,' is but a coarse expression of a common
fault. He is wretched until 'another glass' steadies, for
a moment, his trembling hand, and gives a brief stimulus
to his nerves. They say that the Styrian peasants, who
habitually eat large quantities of arsenic, show symp-
toms of poison if they leave it off suddenly. These are
but samples, in the physical region, of a tendency which
runs through all life, and leads men to drown thought
by plunging into the thick of the worldly absorptions
that really cause their unrest. The least persistent of
men is strangely obstinate in his adherence to old
ways, in spite of all experience of their crooked
slipperiness. We wonder at the peasants who have
their cottages and vineyards on the slopes of Vesuvius,
and who build them, and plant them, over and over
again after each destructive eruption. The tragedy
of Israel is repeated in many of our lives; and the
summing up of the abortive efforts of one of its
kings to recover power by following the gods that
had betrayed him, might be the epitaph of the

infatuated men who see their sickness and seek to
heal it by renewed devotion to the idols who occasioned
it : 'They were the ruin of him and of all Israel.' The
experience of the woman who had ' spent all her living
on physicians, and was nothing the better, but rather
the worse,' sums up the sad story of many a life.

But again the sense of sin sometimes seeks to conceal
itself by repetition of sin. When the dormant snake
begins to stir, it is lulled to sleep again by absorption
of occupations, or by an obstinate refusal to look inwards, and often by plunging once more into the sin
which has brought about the sickness. To seek thus for
ease from the stings of conscience, is like trying to silence
a buzzing in the head by standing beside Niagara thun-
dering in our ears. They used to beat the drums when
a martyr died, in order to drown his testimony ; and so
foolish men seek to silence the voice of conscience by
letting passions shout their loudest. It needs no words
to demonstrate the incurable folly of such conduct; but
alas, it takes many words far stronger than mine to
press home the folly upon men. The condition of such
a half-awakened conscience is very critical if it is
soothed by any means by which it is weakened and
its possessor worsened. In the sickness of the soul
homœopathic treatment is a delusion. Ephraim may
go to Assyria, but there is no healing of him there.

III. God's way of giving true healing.

Ephraim thought that, because the wounds were
inflicted by Assyria, it was the source to which to
apply for bandages and balm. If it had realised that
Assyria was but the battle-axe wherewith the hand
of God struck it, it would have learned that from
God alone could come healing and health. The unrest
which betrays the presence in our souls of a deep-

seated sin, is a divine messenger. We terribly misin-
terpret the true source of all that disturbs us when we
attribute it only to the occasions which bring it about;
for the one purpose of all our restlessness is to drive
us nearer to God, and to wrench us away from our
Assyria. The true issue of Ephraim's sickness would
have been the penitent cry, 'Come, let us return to the
Lord our God, for He hath smitten, and He will bind
us up.' It is in the consciousness of loving nearness to
Him that all our unrest is soothed, and the heaving
ocean in our hearts becomes as a summer's sea and
'birds of peace sit brooding on the charmed waves.' It
is in that same consciousness that conscience ceases to
condemn, and loses its sting. The prophet from whom
our text is taken ends his wonderful ministry, that had
been full of fiery denunciations and dark prophecies,
with words that are only surpassed in their tenderness
and the outpouring of the heart of God, by the fuller
revelation in Jesus Christ: 'O Israel, return unto the
Lord thy God. Take with you words, and return unto
the Lord, and say unto Him: Assyria shall not save us,
for in Thee the fatherless findeth mercy.' The divine
answer which he was commissioned to bring to the
penitent Israel—'I will heal their backslidings, I will
love them freely; if Mine anger is turned away from
Me'—is, in all its wealth of forgiving love but an
imperfect prophecy of the great Physician, from the
hem of whose garment flowed out power to one who
'had spent all her living on physicians and could not
be healed of any,' and who confirmed to her the power
which she had thought to steal from Him unawares
by the gracious words which bound her to Him for
ever—'Daughter, thy faith hath made thee whole; go
in peace.'

H

'FRUIT WHICH IS DEATH'

'Israel is an empty vine, he bringeth forth fruit unto himself: according to the multitude of his fruit he hath increased the altars; according to the goodness of his land they have made goodly images. 2. Their heart is divided; now shall they be found faulty: He shall break down their altars, He shall spoil their images. 3. For now they shall say, We have no king, because we feared not the Lord; what then should a king do to us? 4. They have spoken words, swearing falsely in making a covenant: thus judgment springeth up as hemlock in the furrows of the field. 5. The inhabitants of Samaria shall fear because of the calves of Beth-aven: for the people thereof shall mourn over it, and the priests thereof that rejoiced on it, for the glory thereof, because it is departed from it. 6. It shall be also carried unto Assyria for a present to king Jareb: Ephraim shall receive shame, and Israel shall be ashamed of his own counsel. 7. As for Samaria, her king is cut off as the foam upon the water. 8. The high places also of Aven, the sin of Israel, shall be destroyed: the thorn and the thistle shall come up on their altars; and they shall say to the mountains, Cover us; and to the hills, Fall on us. 9. O Israel, thou hast sinned from the days of Gibeah: there they stood: the battle in Gibeah against the children of iniquity did not overtake them. 10. It is in my desire that I should chastise them; and the people shall be gathered against them, when they shall bind themselves in their two furrows. 11. And Ephraim is as an heifer that is taught, and loveth to tread out the corn; but I passed over upon her fair neck: I will make Ephraim to ride; Judah shall plow, and Jacob shall break his clods. 12. Sow to yourselves in righteousness, reap in mercy; break up your fallow ground: for it is time to seek the Lord, till He come and rain righteousness upon you. 13. Ye have plowed wickedness, ye have reaped iniquity; ye have eaten the fruit of lies: because thou didst trust in thy way, in the multitude of thy mighty men. ·14. Therefore shall a tumult arise among thy people, and all thy fortresses shall be spoiled, as Shalman spoiled Beth-arbel in the day of battle: the mother was dashed in pieces upon her children. 15. So shall Beth-el do unto you because of your great wickedness: in a morning shall the king of Israel utterly be cut off.'—HOSEA x. 1-15.

THE prophecy of this chapter has two themes—Israel's sin, and its punishment. These recur again and again. Reiteration, not progress of thought, characterises Hosea's fiery stream of inspired eloquence. Conviction of sin and prediction of judgment are his message. We trace a fourfold repetition of it here, and further note that in each case there is a double reference to Israel's sin as consisting in the rebellion which set up a king and in the schism which established the calf worship; while there is also a double phase of the punishment corresponding to these, in the annihilation of the kingdom and the destruction of the idols.

The first section may be taken to be verses 1-3. The

image of a luxuriant vine laden with fruit is as old as Jacob's blessing of the tribes (Gen. xlix. 22), where it is applied to Joseph, whose descendants were the strength of the Northern Kingdom. Hosea has already used it, and here it is employed to set forth picturesquely the material prosperity of Israel. Probably the period referred to is the successful reign of Jeroboam II. But prosperity increased sin. The more fruit or material wealth, the more altars; the better the harvests, the more the obelisks or pillars to gods, falsely supposed to be the authors of the blessings. The words are as condensed as a proverb, and are as true to-day as ever. Israel had attributed its prosperity to Baal (Hosea ii. 8). The misuse of worldly wealth and the tendency of success to draw us away from God, and to blind to the true source of all blessing, are as rife now as then.

The root of the evil was, as always, a heart divided —that is, between God and Baal—or, perhaps, 'smooth'; that is, dissimulating and insincere. In reality, Baal alone possesses the heart which its owner would share between him and Jehovah. 'All in all, or not at all,' is the law. Whether Baals or calves were set beside God, He was equally deposed.

Then, with a swift turn, Hosea proclaims the impending judgment, setting himself and the people as if already in the future. He hears the first peal of the storm, and echoes it in that abrupt 'now.' The first burst of the judgment shatters dreams of innocence, and the cowering wretches see their sin by the lurid light. That discovery awaits every man whose heart has been 'divided.' To the gazers and to himself masks drop, and the true character stands out with appalling clearness. What will that light show us to be? An unnamed hand overthrows altars and pillars. No need to say whose it is. One half of Israel's sin is crushed at a blow, and the destruction of the other follows immediately.

They themselves abjure their allegiance; for they have found out that their king is a king Log, and can do them no good. A king, set up in opposition to God's will, cannot save. The ruin of their projects teaches godless men at last that they have been fools to take their own way; for all defences, recourses, and protectors, chosen in defiance of God, prove powerless when the strain comes. The annihilation of one half of their sin sickens them of the other. The calves and the monarchy stood or fell together. It is a dismal thing to have to bear the brunt of chastisement for what we see to have been a blunder as well as a crime. But such is the fate of those who seek other gods and another king.

In verse 4 Hosea recurs to Israel's crime, and appends a description of the chastisement, substantially the same as before, but more detailed, which continues till verse 8. The sin now is contemplated in its effects on human relations. Before, it was regarded in relation to God. But men who are wrong with Him cannot be right with one another. Morality is rooted in religion, and if we lie to God, we shall not be true to our brother. Hence, passing over all other sins for the present, Hosea fixes upon one, the prevalence of which strikes at the very foundation of society. What can be done with a community in which lying has become a national characteristic, and that even in formal agreements? Honey-combed with falsehood, it is only fit for burning.

Sin is bound by an iron link to penalty. Therefore, says Hosea, God's judgment springs up, like a bitter plant (the precise name of which is unknown) in the furrows, where the farmer did not know that its seeds lay. They little dreamed what they were sowing when they scattered abroad their lies, but this is the fruit of these. 'Whatsoever a man soweth, that shall he also reap'; and whatever other crop we may hope to gather from our sins, we shall gather that bitter one which we did not expect. The inevitable connection of sin and judgment, the bitterness of its results, the unexpectedness of them, are all here, and to be laid to heart by us.

Then verses 5 and 6 dilate with keen irony on the fate of the first half of Israel's sin—the calf. It was thought a god, but its worshippers shall be in a fright for it. 'Calves,' says Hosea, though there was but one at Beth-el; and he uses the feminine, as some think, depreciatingly. 'Beth-aven' or the 'house of vanity,' he says, instead of Beth-el, 'the house of God.' A fine god whose worshippers had to be alarmed for its safety! 'Its people'—what a contrast to the name they might have borne, 'My people'! God disowns them, and says, 'They belong to it, not to Me.' The idolatrous priests of the calf worship will tremble when that image, which had been shamefully their 'glory,' is carried off to Assyria, and given as a present to 'king Jareb'—a name for the king of Assyria meaning the fighting or quarrelsome king. The captivity of the god is the shame of the worshippers. To be 'ashamed of their own counsel' is the certain fate of all who depart from God; for, sooner or later, experience will demonstrate to the blindest that their refuges of lies can neither save themselves nor those who trust in them. But shame is one thing and repentance another; and many a man will say, 'I have been a great fool, and my clever

policy has all crumbled to pieces,' who will only therefore change his idols, and not return to God.

Verse 7 recurs to the political punishment of the civil
rebellion. The image for the disappearance of the king
is striking, whether we render 'foam' or 'chip,' but the
former has special beauty. In the one case we see the
unsubstantial bubble,

> 'A moment white, then melts for ever';

and in the other, the helpless twig swept down by the
stream. Either brings vividly before us the powerless-
ness of Israel against the roaring torrent of Assyrian
power; and the figure may be widened out to teach
what is sure to become of all man-made and self-chosen
refuges when the floods of God's judgments sweep over
the world. The captivity of the idol and the burst
bubble of the monarchy bid us all make Jehovah our
God and King. The vacant shrine and empty throne
are followed by utter and long-continued desolation.
Thorns and thistles have time to grow on the altars,
and no hand cuts them down. What of the men thus
stripped of all in which they had trusted? Desperate,
they implore the mountains to fall on them, as prefer-
ring to die, and the hills to cover them, as willing to be
crushed, if only they may be hidden. That awful cry
is heard again in our Lord's predictions of judgment,
and in the Apocalypse. Therefore this prophecy fore-
shadows, in the destruction of Israel's confidences and
in their shame and despair, a more dreadful coming
day, in which we shall be concerned.

Verses 9 to 11 again give the sin and its punishment.
'The days of Gibeah' recall the hideous story of lust
and crime which was the low-water mark of the law-
less days of old. That crime had been avenged by

merciless war. But its taint had lived on, and the
Israel of Hosea's day 'stood,' obstinately persistent,
just where the Benjamites had been then, and set
themselves in dogged resistance, as these had done,
'that the battle against the children of unrighteous-
ness might not touch them.'

Stiff-necked setting oneself against God's merciful
fighting with evil lasts for a little while, but verse 10
tells how soon and easily it is annihilated. God's 'desire'
brushes away all defences, and the obstinate sinners
are like children, who are whipped when their father
wills, let them struggle as they may. The instruments
of chastisement are foreign armies, and the chastisement itself is described with a striking figure as 'bind-
ing them to their two transgressions'; that is, the
double sin which is the keynote of the chapter.
Punishment is yoking men to their sins, and making
them drag the burden like bullocks in harness. What
sort of load are we getting together for ourselves?
When we have to drag the consequences of our doings
behind us, how shall we feel?

The figure sets the Prophet's imagination going, and
he turns it another way, comparing Israel to a heifer,
broken in, and liking the easy work of threshing, in
which the unmuzzled ox could eat its fill, but now set
to harder tasks in the fields. Judah, too, is to share in
the punishment. If men will not serve God in and
because of prosperous ease, He will try what toil and
privation will do. Abused blessings are withdrawn,
and the abundance of the threshing-floor is changed
for dragging a heavy plough or harrow.

Verse 12 still deals with the figure suggested in the
close of the previous verse. It is the only break in the
clouds in this chapter. It is a call to amendment,

accompanied by a promise of acceptance. If we 'sow
for righteousness'—that is, if our efforts are directed
to embodying it in our lives—we 'shall reap according
to mercy.' That is true universally, whether it is taken
to mean God's mercy to us, or ours to others. The aim
after righteousness ever secures the divine favour, and
usually ensures the measure which we mete being
measured to us again.

But sowing is not all; thorns must be grubbed up.
We must not only turn over a new leaf, but tear out
the old one. The old man must be slain if the new
man is to live. The call to amend finds its warrant in
the assurance that there is still time to seek the Lord,
and that, for all His threatenings, He is ready to rain
blessings upon the seekers. The unwearying patience
of God, the possibility of the worst sinner's repentance,
the conditional nature of the threatenings, the possibility of breaking the bond between sin and sorrow,
the yet deeper thought that righteousness must come
from above, are all condensed in this brief gospel before
the Gospel.

But that bright gleam passes, and the old theme
recurs. Once more we have sin and punishment exhibited in their organic connection in verses 13 and
14. Israel's past had been just the opposite of sowing righteousness and reaping mercy. Wickedness
ploughed in, iniquity will surely be its fruit. Sin
begets sin, and is its own punishment. What fruit
have we of doing wrong? 'Lies'; that is, unfulfilled
expectations of unrealised satisfaction. No man gets
the good that he aimed at in sinning, or he gets something more that spoils it. At last the deceitfulness of
sin will be found out, but we may be sure of it now.
The root of all Israel's sin was the root of ours; namely,

trust in self, and consequent neglect of God. The first half of verse 13 is an exhaustive analysis of the experience of every sinful life; the second, a penetrating disclosure of the foundation of it.

Then the whole closes with the repeated threatening, dual as before, and illustrated by the forgotten horrors of some dreadful siege, one of the 'unhappy, far-off things,' fallen silent now. A significant variation occurs in the final threatening, in which Beth-el is set forth as the cause, rather than as the object, of the destruction. 'They were the ruin of him and of all Israel.' Our vices are made the whips to scourge us. Our idols bring us no help, but are the causes of our misery.

The Prophet ends with the same double reference which prevails throughout, when he once more declares the annihilation of the monarchy, which, rather than a particular person, is meant by 'the king.' 'In the morning' is enigmatical. It may mean 'prematurely,' or 'suddenly,' or 'in a time of apparent prosperity,' or, more probably, the Prophet stands in vision in that future day of the Lord, and points to 'the king' as the first victim. The force of the prophecy does not depend on the meaning of this detail. The teaching of the whole is the certainty that suffering dogs sin, but yet does so by no iron, impersonal law, but according to the will of God, who will rain righteousness even on the sinner, being penitent, and will endow with righteousness from above every lowly soul that seeks for it.

DESTRUCTION AND HELP

'O Israel, thou hast destroyed thyself; but in Me is thine help.'—HOSEA xiii. 9 (A.V.).
'It is thy destruction, O Israel, that thou art against Me, against thy Help' (R.V.).

THESE words are obscure by reason of their brevity.
Literally they might be rendered, 'Thy destruction for,
in, or against Me ; in, or against thy Help.' Obviously,
some words must be supplied to bring out any sense.
Our Authorised Version has chosen the supplement 'is,'
which fails to observe the second occurrence with 'thy
Help' of the preposition, and is somewhat lax in
rendering the 'for' of the second clause by the neutral
'but.' It is probably better to read, as the Revised
Version, with most modern interpreters, 'Thou art
against Me, against thy Help,' and to find in the second
clause the explanation, or analysis, of the destruction
announced in the first. So we have here the wail of
the parental love of God over the ruin which Israel
has brought on itself, and that parental love is setting
forth Israel's true condition, in the hope that they
may discern it. Thus, even the rebuke holds enclosed
a promise and a hope. Since God is their help, to
depart from Him has been ruin, and the return to Him
will be life. Hosea, or rather the Spirit that spake
through Hosea, blended wonderful tenderness with unflinching decision in rebuke, and unwavering certainty
in foretelling evil with unfaltering hope in the promise
of possible blessing. His words are set in the same
key as the still more wonderfully tender ones that
Jesus uttered as He looked across the valley from
Olivet to the gleaming city on the other side, and

122

wailed, 'O Jerusalem, Jerusalem, how often would I have gathered thy children together, as a hen gathereth her chickens under her wings, and ye would not! Therefore your house is left unto you desolate.'

We may note here

I. The loving discovery of ruin.

It is strange that men should need to be told, and that with all emphasis, the evil case in which they are; and stranger still that they should resent the discovery and reject it. This pathetic pleading is the voice of a divine Father trying to convince His son of misery and danger; and the obscurity of the text is as if that voice was choked with sobs, and could only speak in broken syllables the tragical word in which all the evil of Israel's sin is gathered up—'his destruction,' or 'corruption.' It gathers up in one terrible picture the essential nature of sin and the death of the soul, which is its wages—inward misery and unrest, outward sorrows, the decay of mental and moral powers, the spreading taint which eats its way through the whole personality of a man who has sinned, and pauses not till it has reduced his corpse to putrefaction. All these, and a hundred more effects of sin, are crowded together in that one word 'thy destruction.'

It is strange that it needs God's voice, and that in its most piercing tones, to convince men of ruin brought by sin. A mortifying limb is painless. There is no consciousness in the drugged sleep which becomes heavier and heavier till it ends in death. There is no surer sign of the reality and extent of the corruption brought about by sin, than man's ignorance of it. There is no more tragical proof that a man is 'wretched, and miserable, and blind, and naked' than his vehement affirmation, 'I am rich, and have gotten riches, and have need of nothing,' and his self-complacent rejection of the counsel to 'buy refined gold, and white garments, and eye-salve to anoint his eyes.' So obstinately unconscious are we of our ruin that even God's voice, whether uttered in definite words, or speaking in sharp sorrows and punitive acts, but too often fails to pierce the thick layer of self-complacency in which we wrap ourselves, and to pierce the heart with the arrow of conviction. Indeed we may say that the whole process of divine education of a soul, conducted through many channels of providences, has for its end mainly this—to convince His wandering children that to be against Him, against their Help, is their destruction.

But, perhaps, the strangest of all is the attitude which we often take up of resenting the love that would reveal our ruin. It is stupid of the ox to kick against its driver's goad; but that is wise in comparison with the action of the man who is angry with God because He warns that departure from Him is ruin. Many of us treat Christianity as if it had made the mischief which it reveals, and would fain mend; and we all need to be reminded that it is cruel kindness to conceal unpleasant truths, and that the Gospel is no more to be blamed for the destruction which it declares than is the signal-man with his red flag responsible for the broken-down viaduct to which the train is rushing that he tries to save.

II. The loving appeal to conscience as to the cause.

Israel's destruction arose from the fact of Israel having turned against God, its Help. Sin is suicide. God is our Help, and only Help. His will is love and blessing. His only relation to our sin is to hate it, and fight against it. In conflict of love with lovelessness one

of His chiefest weapons is to drive home to our consciousness the conviction of our sin. When He is
driven to punish, it is our wrongdoing that forces Him
to what Isaiah calls, 'His strange act.' The Heavenly
Father is impelled by His love not to spare the rod,
lest the sparing spoil the child. An earthly father
suffers more punishment than he inflicts upon the
little rebel whom, unwillingly and with tears, he may
chastise; and God's love is more tender, as it is more
wise, than that of the fathers of our flesh who corrected
us. 'He doth not willingly afflict nor is soon angry';
and of all the mercies which He bestows upon us, none
is more laden with His love than the discipline by
which He would make us know, through our painful
experience, that it is 'an evil and bitter thing to forsake the Lord, and that His fear is not in us.' In its
essence and depth, separation from God is death to the
creature that wrenches itself away from the source of
life; and all the weariness and pains of a godless life
are, if we take them as He meant them, the very
angels of His presence.

Just as the sole reason for our sorrows lies in our
wrongdoing, the sole cause of our wrongdoing is in
ourselves. It is because 'Israel is against Me' that
Israel's destruction rushes down upon it. It could
have defended its hankering after Assyria and idols,
by wise talk about political exigencies and the wisdom
of trying to turn possibly powerful enemies into
powerful allies, and the folly of a little nation, on a
narrow strip of territory between the desert and the
sea, fancying itself able to sustain itself uncrushed between the upper millstone of Assyria on the north,
and the under one, Egypt, on the south. But circumstances are never the cause, though they may afford

the excuse of rebellion against our Helper, God; and
all the modern talk about environments and the like,
is merely a cloak cast round, but too scanty to conceal
the ugly fact of the alienated will.   All the excuses for
sin, which either modern scientific jargon about 'laws,'
or hyper-Calvinistic talk about 'divine decrees,' alleges,
are alike shattered against the plain fact of conscience,
which proclaims to every evil-doer, 'Thou art the
man!' We shall get no further and no deeper than
the truth of our text: 'It is thy destruction that thou
art against Me.'

The pleading God has from the beginning spoken
words as tender as they are stern, and as stern as they
are tender. His voice to the sons of men has from of
old asked the unanswerable question, 'Why should ye
be stricken any more?' and has answered it, so far as
answer is possible, by the fact, which is as mysterious
as it is undeniable, 'Ye will revolt more and more.'
God calls upon man to judge between Him and His
vineyard, and asks, 'What could have been done more
to My vineyard that I have not done unto it? Wherefore, when I looked that it should bring forth grapes,
brought it forth wild grapes?' The fault lay not in the
vine-dresser, but in some evil influence that had found
its way into the life and sap of the vine, and bore fruits
in an unnatural product, which could not have been
traced to the vine-dresser's action. So God stands, as
with clean hands, declaring that 'He is pure from the
blood of all men; that He has no pleasure in the death
of the wicked'; and His word to the men on whom
falls the whole weight of His destroying power is,
'Thou hast procured this unto thyself.'

III. The loving forbearance which still offers
restoration.

He still claims to be Israel's Help. Separation from Him has all but destroyed the rebellious; but it has not in the smallest degree affected the fulness of His power, nor the fervency of His desire to help. However earth may be shaken by storms, or swathed in mist that darkens all things and shuts out heaven, the sun is still in its tabernacle and pouring down its rays through the cloudless blue that is above the enfolding cloud. Our text has wrapped up in it the broad gospel that all our self-inflicted destruction may be arrested, and all the evil which brought it about swept away. God is ready to prove Himself our true and only Helper in that, as our prophet says, 'He will ransom us from the power of the grave'; and, even when death has laid its cold hand upon us, will redeem us from it, and destroy the destruction which had fixed its talons in us. All the guilt is ours; all the help is His; His work is to conquer and cast out our sins, to heal our sicknesses, to soothe our sorrows. And He has Himself vindicated His great name of our Help when He has revealed Himself as 'the God and Father of our Lord and Saviour Jesus Christ.'

ISRAEL RETURNING

'O Israel, return unto the Lord thy God; for thou hast fallen by thine iniquity. 2. Take with you words, and turn to the Lord: say unto Him, Take away all iniquity, and receive us graciously: so will we render the calves of our lips. 3. Asshur shall not save us; we will not ride upon horses: neither will we say any more to the work of our hands, Ye are our gods: for in thee the fatherless findeth mercy. 4. I will heal their backsliding, I will love them freely: for mine anger is turned away from Him. 5. I will be as the dew unto Israel: He shall grow as the lily, and cast forth His roots as Lebanon. 6. His branches shall spread, and His beauty shall be as the olive-tree, and His smell as Lebanon. 7. They that dwell under His shadow shall return; they shall revive as the corn, and grow as the vine: the scent thereof shall be as the wine of Lebanon. 8. Ephraim shall say, What have I to do any more with idols? I have heard Him, and observed Him:

I am like a green fir-tree. From me is thy fruit found. 9. Who is wise, and He shall understand these things? prudent, and He shall know them? for the ways of the Lord are right, and the just shall walk in them: but the transgressors shall fall therein.'—HOSEA xiv. 1-9.

HOSEA is eminently the prophet of divine love and of human repentance. Both streams of thought are at their fullest in this great chapter. In verses 1 to 3 the very essence of true return to God is set forth in the prayer which Israel is exhorted to offer, while in verses 4 to 8 the forgiving love of God and its blessed results are portrayed with equal poetical beauty and spiritual force. Verse 9 closes the chapter and the book with a kind of epilogue.

I. The summons to repentance.

'Israel,' of course, here means the Northern Kingdom, with which Hosea's prophecies are chiefly occupied. 'Thou hast fallen by thine iniquity'—that is the lesson taught by all its history, and in a deeper sense it is the lesson of all experience. Sin brings ruin for nations and individuals, and the plain teachings of each man's own life exhort each to 'return unto the Lord.' We have all proved the vanity and misery of departing from Him; surely, if we are not drawn by His love, we might be driven by our own unrest, to go back to God.

The Prophet anticipates the clear accents of the New Testament call to repentance in his expansion of what he meant by returning. He has nothing to say about sacrifices, nor about self-reliant efforts at moral improvement. 'Take with you *words*,' not 'the blood of bulls and goats.' Confession is better than sacrifice. What words are they which will avail? Hosea teaches the penitent's prayer. It must begin with the petition for forgiveness, which implies recognition of the peti-tioner's sin. The cry, 'Take away all iniquity,' does not specify sins, but masses the whole black catalogue into one word. However varied the forms of our transgressions, they are in principle one, and it is best to bind them all into one ugly heap, and lay it at God's feet. We have to confess not only *sins*, but *sin*, and the taking away of it includes divine cleansing from its power, as well as divine forgiveness of its guilt. Hosea bids Israel ask that God would take away all iniquity; John pointed to 'the Lamb of God, which taketh away the sin of the world.' But beyond forgiveness and cleansing, the penitent heart will seek that God would 'accept the good' in it, which springs up by His grace, when the evil has been washed from it, like flowers that burst from soil off which the matted undergrowth of poisonous jungle has been cleared. Mere negative absence of 'evil' is not all that we should desire or exhibit; there must be positive good; and however sinful may have been the past, we are not too bold when we ask and expect that we may be made able to produce 'good,' which shall be fragrant as sweet incense to God.

Petitions are followed by vows. On the one hand, the experience of forgiveness and cleansing will put a new song in our mouths, and instead of animal sacrifices, we shall render the praise which is better than 'calves' laid on the altar. Perhaps the Septuagint rendering of that difficult phrase 'the calves of our lips,' which is given in Hebrews xiii. 15, 'the fruit of our lips,' is preferable. In either case, the same thought appears—that the penitent's experience of forgiving and restoring love makes 'the tongue of the dumb sing,' and it will bind men's hearts more closely to God than anything besides can do, so that their old inclinations to false reliances and idolatries drop away

from them. The old fable tells us that the storm made
the traveller wrap his cloak closer round him, but the
sunshine made him throw it off. Judgments often
make men cling more closely to their sins, but forgiving
mercy makes them 'cast off the works of darkness.'
The men who had experienced that in God, the Israel,
which by its sins had brought down the punishment
of His repudiation of being its father (i. 9), had found
mercy, would no longer feel temptation to turn to
Assyria for help, nor to seek protection from Egypt's
cavalry, nor to debase their manhood by calling stocks
and stones, the work of their own hands, their gods.
What earthly sweetness will tempt, or what earthly
danger will affright, the heart that is feeling the bliss
of union with God? Would Judas's thirty pieces of
silver attract the disciple reclining on Jesus' bosom?
We are most firmly bound to God, not by our resolves,
but by our experience of His all-sufficient mercy. Fill
the heart with that wine of the kingdom, and bitter
or poisonous draughts will find no entrance into
the cup.

II. God's welcoming answer.

The very abruptness of its introduction, without any
explanation as to the speaker, suggests how swiftly
and joyfully the Father hastens to meet the returning
prodigal while he is yet afar off. Like pent-up waters
rushing forth as soon as a barrier is taken away, God's
love pours itself out immediately. His answer ever
gives more than the penitent asks—robe and ring and
shoes, and a feast to him who dared not expect more
than a place among the hired servants. He gives not
by drops, but in floods, answering the prayer for the
taking away of iniquity by the promise to heal backsliding, going beyond desires and hopes in the gift of

love which asks for no recompense, is drawn forth by
no desert, but wells up from the depths of God's heart.
and strengthens the new, tremulous trust of the penitent
by the assurance that every trace of anger is effaced
from God's heart.

The blessings consequent on the gift of God's love
are described in lovely imagery, drawn, like Hosea's
other abundant similes, from nature, and especially
from trees and flowers. The source of all fruitfulness
is a divine influence, which comes silently and refreshing as the 'dew,' or, rather, as the 'night mist,' a
phenomenon occurring in Palestine in summer, and
being, accurately, rolling masses of vapour brought
from the Mediterranean, which counteract the dry
heat and keep vegetation alive. The influences which
refresh and fructify our souls must fall in many a
silent hour of meditation and communion. They will
effloresce into manifold shapes of beauty and fruitfulness, of which the Prophet signalises three. The lily
may stand for beauty of purity, though botanists differ
as to the particular flower meant. Christians should
present to the world 'whatsoever things are lovely,'
and see to it that their goodness is attractive. But the
fragrant, pure lily has but shallow roots, and beauty is
not all that a character needs in this world of struggle
and effort. So there are to be both the lily's blossom
and roots like Lebanon. The image may refer to the
firm buttresses of the widespread foot-hills, from which
the sovereign summits of the great mountain range
rise, or, as is rather suggested by the accompanying
similes from the vegetable world, it may refer to the
cedars growing there. Their roots are anchored deep
and stretch far underground; therefore they rear
towering heads, and spread broad shelves of dark

foliage, safe from any blast. Our lives must be deep
rooted in God if they are to be strong. Roots generally
spread beneath the soil about as far as branches extend
above it. There should be at least as much underground, 'hid with Christ in God,' as is visible to the
world.

But beauty and strength are not all. So Hosea
thinks of yet another of the characteristic growths of
Palestine, the olive, which is not strikingly beautiful
in form, with its strangely gnarled, contorted stem, its
feeble branches, and its small, pointed, pale leaves, but
has the beauty of fruitfulness, and is green when other
trees are bare. Such 'beauty' should be ours, and will
be if the 'dew' falls on us.

In verse 7 there are difficulties, both as to the
application of the 'his,' and as to the reading and
rendering of some of the words. But the general drift
is clear.· It prolongs the tones of the foregoing verses,
keeping to the same class of images, and expressing
fruitfulness, abundant as the corn and precious as the
grape, and fragrance like the 'bouquet' of the choicest
wine.

Verse 8 offers great difficulties on any interpretation.
The supplement 'shall say' is questionable, and it is
doubtful whether Ephraim is the speaker at all, and
whether, if so, he speaks all the four clauses, and who
speaks any or all of them, if not he. To the present
writer, it seems best to take the supplement as right,
and possible to regard the whole verse as spoken by
Ephraim, though perhaps the last clause is meant to
be God's utterance. The meaning will then come out
as follows. The penitent Israel again speaks, after the
gracious promises preceding. The tribal name is, as
usual in Hosea, equivalent to Israel, whose penitent

cry we heard at the beginning of the passage. Now we
hear his glad response to God's abundant answer.
'What have I to do any more with idols?' He had
vowed (verse 3) to have no more to do with them, and
the resolve is deepened by the rich grace held forth to
him. Hosea had lamented Ephraim's mad adherence
to 'his idols' (iv. 17), but now the union is dissolved,
and by penitence and reception of God's grace, he
is joined to the Lord, and parted from them. His
renunciation of idolatry is based, in the second clause,
on his experience of what God can do, and on his
having heard God's gracious voice of pardon and
promise. If a man hears God, he will not be drawn to
worship at any idol's shrine.

Further, in the third clause, Ephraim is joyfully
conscious of the change that has passed on him, in
accordance with the great promises just spoken, and
with grateful astonishment that such verdure should
have burst out from the dry and rotten stump of his
own sinful nature, exclaims, 'I am like a green fir-tree.'
That is another reason why he will have no more to
do with idols. They could never have made his sapless
nature break into leafage. But what of the fourth
clause—'From Me is thy fruit found'? Can we understand that to mean that Ephraim still speaks, keeping
up the image of the previous clause, and declaring that
all the new fruitfulness which he finds in himself he
recognises to be God's, both in the sense that, in reality,
it is produced by Him, and that it belongs to Him? He
comes seeking fruit, and He finds it. All our good is
His, and we shall be happy, productive, and wise, in
proportion as we offer all our works to Him, and feel
that, after all, they are not ours, but the works of that
Spirit which dwells in penitent and believing hearts.

Some have thought that this last clause must be taken as spoken by God; but, even if so taken, it conveys substantially the same thought as to the divine origin of man's fruitfulness.

The last verse is rather a general reflection summing up the whole than an integral part of this wonderful representation of penitence, pardon, and fruitfulness. It declares the great truth that the knowledge of the pardoning mercy of God, and of the ways by which He weans men from sin and makes them fruitful of good, makes us truly wise. That knowledge is more than intellectual apprehension; it is experience. Providence has its mysteries, but they who keep near to God, and are 'just' because they do, will find the opportunity of free, unfettered activity in God's ways, and transgressors will stumble therein. Therefore wisdom and safety lie in penitence and confession, which will ever be met by gracious pardon and showers of blessing that will cause our hearts, which sin has made desert, to rejoice and blossom like the rose.

THE DEW AND THE PLANTS

' I will be as the dew unto Israel: he shall grow as the lily, and cast forth his roots as Lebanon. 6. His branches shall spread, and his beauty shall be as the olive-tree . . .'—HOSEA xiv. 5, 6.

LIKE his brethren, Hosea was a poet as well as a prophet. His little prophecy is full of similes and illustrations drawn from natural objects; scarcely any of them from cities or from the ways of men; almost all of them from Nature, as seen in the open country, which he evidently loved, and where he had looked upon things with a clear and meditative eye. This whole chapter is full of emblems drawn from the vegetable world. The lily, the cedar, the olive, are in my text. And there follow, in the subsequent verses, the corn, and the vine, and the green fir-tree.

The words which I have read, no doubt originally had simply a reference to the numerical increase of the people and their restoration to their land, but they may be taken by us quite fairly as having a very much deeper and more blessed reference than that. For they describe the uniform condition of all spiritual life and growth, 'I will be as the dew unto Israel'; and then they set forth some of the manifold aspects of that growth, and the consequences of receiving that heavenly dew, under the various metaphors to which I have referred. It is in that higher signification that I wish to look at them now.

I. The first thought that comes out of the words is that for all life and growth of the spirit there must be a bedewing from God.

'I will be as the dew unto Israel.' Now, scholars tell us that the kind of moisture that is meant in these words is not what we call dew, of which, as a matter of fact, there falls, in Palestine, little or none at the season of the year referred to in my text, but that the word really means the heavy night-clouds that come upon the wings of the south-west wind, to diffuse moisture and freshness over the parched plains, in the very height and fierceness of summer. The metaphor of my text becomes more beautiful and striking, if we note that, in the previous chapter, where the Prophet was in his threatening mood, he predicts that 'an east wind shall come, the wind of the Lord shall come up from the wilderness'—the burning sirocco, with death upon its wings—'and his spring shall become dry, and his fountain shall be dried up.' We have then to

imagine the land gaping and parched, the hot air
having, as with invisible tongue of flame, licked
streams and pools dry, and having shrunken fountains
and springs. Then, all at once there comes down upon
the baking ground and on the faded, drooping flowers
that lie languid and prostrate on the ground in the
darkness, borne on the wings of the wind, from the
depths of the great unfathomed sea, an unseen
moisture. You cannot call it rain, so gently does
it diffuse itself; it is liker a mist, but it brings life
and freshness, and everything is changed. The dew,
or the night mist, as it might more properly be
rendered, was evidently a good deal in Hosea's mind;
you may remember that he uses the image again in a
remarkably different aspect, where he speaks of men's
goodness as being like 'a morning cloud, and the early
dew that passes away.'

The natural object which yields the emblem was all
inadequate to set forth the divine gift which is compared to it, because as soon as the sun has risen, with
burning heat, it scatters the beneficent clouds, and the
'sunbeams like swords' threaten to slay the tender
green shoots. But this mist from God that comes
down to water the earth is never dried up. It is not
transient. It may be ours, and live in our hearts.
Dear brethren, the prose of this sweet old promise is
'If I depart, I will send Him unto you.' If we are
Christian people, we have the perpetual dew of that
divine Spirit, which falls on our leaves and penetrates
to our roots, and communicates life, freshness, and
power, and makes growth possible—more than possible,
certain—for us. 'I'—Myself through My Son, and in
My Spirit—'I will be'—an unconditional assurance—
'as the dew unto Israel.'

Yes! That promise is in its depth and fulness applicable only to the Christian Israel, and it remains true to-day and for ever. Do we see it fulfilled? One looks round upon our congregations, and into one's own heart, and we behold the parable of Gideon's fleece acted over again—some places soaked with the refreshing moisture, and some as hard as a rock and as dry as tinder and ready to catch fire from any spark from the devil's forge and be consumed in the everlasting burnings some day. It will do us good to ask ourselves why it is that, with a promise like this for every Christian soul to build upon, there are so few Christian souls that have anything like realised its fulness and its depth. Let us be quite sure of this—God has nothing to do with the failure of His promise, and let us take all the blame to ourselves.

'I will be as the dew unto Israel.' Who was Israel? The man that wrestled all night in prayer with God, and took hold of the angel and prevailed and wept and made supplication to Him. So Hosea tells us; and as he says in the passage where he describes the Angel's wrestling with Jacob at Peniel, 'there He spake with us'—when He spake, He spake with him who first bore the name. Be you Israel, and God will surely be your dew; and life and growth will be possible. That is the first lesson of this great promise.

II. The second is, that a soul thus bedewed by God will spring into purity and beauty.

We go back to Hosea's vegetable metaphors. 'He shall grow as the lily' is his first promise. If I were addressing a congregation of botanists, I should have something to say about what kind of a plant is meant, but that is quite beside the mark for my present purpose. It is sufficient to notice that in this

metaphor the emphasis is laid upon the two attributes which I have named—beauty and purity. The
figure teaches us that ugly Christianity is not Christ's
Christianity. Some of us older people remember that
it used to be a favourite phrase to describe unattrac-
tive saints that they had ' grace grafted on a crab stick.'
There are a great many Christian people whom one
would compare to any other plant rather than a lily.
Thorns and thistles and briers are a good deal more
like what some of them appear to the world. But we
are bound, if we are Christian people, by our obligations
to God, and by our obligations to men, to try to make
Christianity look as beautiful in people's eyes as we
can. That is what Paul said, ' Adorn the teaching ';
make it look well, inasmuch as it has made you look
attractive to men's eyes. Men have a fairly accurate
notion of beauty and goodness, whether they have any
goodness or any beauty in their own characters or not.
Do you remember the words : ' Whatsoever things are
lovely, whatsoever things are of good report, whatsoever things are venerable . . . if there be any praise '—
from men—' think on these things '? If we do not keep
that as the guiding star of our lives, then we have
failed in one very distinct duty of Christian people—
namely, to grow more like a lily, and to be graceful in
the lowest sense of that word, as well as *grace full* in
the highest sense of it. We shall not be so in the
lower, unless we are so in the higher. It may be a
very modest kind of beauty, very humble, and not at
all like the flaring reds and yellows of the gorgeous
flowers that the world admires. These are often like
a great sunflower, with a disc as big as a cheese. But
the Christian beauty will be modest and unobtrusive
and shy, like the violet half buried in the hedge-bank,

and unnoticed by careless eyes, accustomed to see beauty only in gaudy, flaring blooms. But unless you, as a Christian, are in your character arrayed in the 'beauty of holiness,' and the holiness of beauty, you are not quite the Christian that Jesus Christ wants you to be ; setting forth all the gracious and sweet and refining influences of the Gospel in your daily life and conduct. That is the second lesson of our text.

III. The third is, that a God-bedewed soul that has been made fair and pure by communion with God, ought also to be strong.

He 'shall cast forth his roots like Lebanon.' Now I take it that simile does not refer to the roots of that giant range that slope away down under the depths of the Mediterranean. That is a beautiful emblem, but it is not in line with the other images in the context. As these are all dependent on the promise of the dew, and represent different phases of the results of its fulfil- ment, it is natural to expect thus much uniformity in their variety, that they shall all be drawn from plant- life. If so, we must suppose a condensed metaphor here, and take 'Lebanon' to mean the forest which another prophet calls 'the glory of Lebanon.' The characteristic tree in these, as we all know, was the cedar.

It is named in Hebrew by a word which is connected with that for 'strength.' It stands as the very type and emblem of stability and vigour. Think of its firm roots by which it is anchored deep in the soil. Think of the shelves of massive dark foliage. Think of its un- changed steadfastness in storm. Think of its towering height; and thus arriving at the meaning of the emblem, let us translate it into practice in our own lives. 'He shall cast forth his roots as Lebanon.' Beauty? Yes!

Purity? Yes! And braided in with them, if I may so say, the strength which can say 'No!' which can resist, which can persist, which can overcome; power drawn from communion with God. 'Strength and beauty' should blend in the worshippers, as they do in the 'sanctuary' in God Himself. There is nothing admirable in mere force; there is often something sickly and feeble, and therefore contemptible in mere beauty. Many of us will cultivate the complacent and the amiable sides of the Christian life, and be wanting in the manly 'thews that throw the world,' and can fight to the death. But we have to try and bring these two excellences of character together, and it needs an immense deal of grace and wisdom and imitation of Jesus Christ, and a close clasp of His hand, to enable us to do that. Speak we of strength? He is the type of strength. Of beauty? He is the perfection of beauty. And it is only as we keep close to Him that our lives will be all fair with the reflected loveliness of His, and strong with the communicated power of His grace—'strong in the Lord, and in the power of His might.'

Brethren, if we are to set forth anything, in our daily lives, of this strength, remember that our lives must be rooted in, as well as bedewed by, God. Hosea's emblems, beautiful and instructive as they are, do not reach to the deep truth set forth in still holier and sweeter words; 'I am the Vine, ye are the branches.' The union of Christ and His people is closer than that between dew and plant. Our growth results from the communication of His own life to us. Therefore is the command stringent and obedience to it blessed, 'Abide in Me, for apart from Me ye can do'—and are—'nothing.'

Let us remember that the loftier the top of the tree

and the wider the spread of its shelves of dark foliage, if it is steadfastly to stand, unmoved by the loud winds when they call, the deeper must its roots strike into the firm earth. If your life is to be a fair temple-palace worthy of God's dwelling in, if it is to be impregnable to assault, there must be quite as much masonry underground as above, as is the case in great old buildings and palaces. And such a life must be a life 'hid with Christ in God,' then it will be strong. When we strike our roots deep into Him, our branch also shall not wither, and our leaf shall be green, and all that we do shall prosper. The wicked are not so. They are like chaff — rootless, fruitless, lifeless, which the wind driveth away.

IV. Lastly, the God-bedewed soul, beautiful, pure, strong, will bear fruit.

That is the last lesson from these metaphors. 'His beauty shall be as the olive-tree.' Anybody that has ever seen a grove of olives knows that their beauty is not such as strikes the eye. If it was not for the blue sky overhead, that rays down glorifying light, they would not be much to look at or talk about. The tree has a gnarled, grotesque trunk which divides into insignificant branches, bearing leaves mean in shape, harsh in texture, with a silvery underside. It gives but a quivering shade and has no massiveness, nor symmetry. Ay! but there are olives on the branches. And so the beauty of the humble tree is in what it grows for man's good. After all, it is the outcome in fruitfulness which is the main thing about us. God's meaning, in all His gifts of dew, and beauty, and purity, and strength, is that we should be of some use in the world.

The olive is crushed into oil, and the oil is used for

smoothing and suppling joints and flesh, for nourishing and sustaining the body as food, for illuminating
darkness as oil in the lamp. And these three things
are the three things for which we Christian people
have received all our dew, and all our beauty, and all
our strength—that we may give other people light,
that we may be the means of conveying to other
people nourishment, that we may move gently in the
world as lubricating, sweetening, soothing influences,
and not irritating and provoking, and leading to strife
and alienation. *The* question after all is, Does anybody
gather fruit off *us*, and would anybody call *us* 'trees
of righteousness, the planting of the Lord, that He
may be glorified'? That is lesson four from this text.
May we all open our hearts for the dew from heaven,
and then use it to produce in ourselves beauty, purity,
strength, and fruitfulness!

AMOS

A PAIR OF FRIENDS

'Can two walk together, except they be agreed?'—AMOS iii. 8.

THEY do not need to be agreed about everything. They must, however, wish to keep each other's company, and they must be going by the same road to the same place. The application of the parable is very plain, though there are differences of opinion as to the bearing of the whole context which need not concern us now. The 'two,' whom the Prophet would fain see walking together, are God and Israel, and his question suggests not only the companionship and communion with God which are the highest form of religion and the aim of all forms and ceremonies of worship, but also the inexorable condition on which alone that height of communion can be secured and sustained. Two *may* walk together, though the one be God in heaven and the other be I on earth. But they have to be agreed thus far, at any rate, that both shall wish to be together, and both be going the same road.

I. So I ask you to look, first, at that possible blessed companionship which may cheer a life.

There are three phrases in the Old Testament, very like each other, and yet presenting different facets or aspects of the same great truth. Sometimes we read about 'walking before God,' as Abraham was bid to do. That means ordering the daily life under the continual

sense that we are 'ever in the great Taskmaster's eye.'
Then there is 'walking after God,' and that means
conforming the will and active efforts to the rule that
He has laid down, setting our steps firm on the paths
that He has prepared that we should walk in them,
and accepting His providences. But also, high above
both these conceptions of a devout life is the one which
is suggested by my text, and which, as you remember,
was realised in the case of the patriarch Enoch—
'walking with God.' For to walk before Him may
have with it some tremor, and may be undertaken in
the spirit of the slave who would be glad to get away
from the jealous eye that rebukes his slothfulness;
and 'walking after Him' may be a painful and partial
effort to keep His distant figure in sight; but to 'walk
with Him' implies a constant, quiet sense of His
Divine Presence which forbids that I should ever be
lonely, which guides and defends, which floods my
soul and fills my life, and in which, as the companions
pace along side by side, words may be spoken by either,
or blessed silence may be eloquent of perfect trust and
rest.

But, dear brother, far above us as such experience
seems to sound, such a life is a possibility for every
one of us. We *may* be able to say, as truly as our
Lord said it, 'I am not alone, for the Father is with
me.' It is possible that the dreariest solitude of a soul,
such as is not realised when the body is removed from
men, but is felt most in the crowded city where there
is none that loves or fathoms and sympathises, may be
turned into blessed fellowship with Him. Yes, but
that solitude will not be so turned unless it is first
painfully felt. As Daniel said, 'I was left alone, and I
saw the great vision.' We need to feel in our deepest

hearts that loneliness on earth before we walk with
God.

If we are so walking, it is no piece of fanaticism to
say that there will be mutual communications. Do you
not believe that God knows His way into the spirits
that He has endowed with conscious life? Do you
not believe that He speaks now to people as truly as
He did to prophets and Apostles of old? as truly; though
the results of His speech to us of to-day be not of the
same authority for others as the words that He spoke
to a Paul or a John. The belief in God's communications as for ever sounding in the depths of the Christian
spirit does not at all obliterate the distinction between
the kind of inspiration which produced the New Testament and that which is realised by all believing and
obedient souls. High above all our experience of hearing the words of God in our hearts stands that of those
holy men of old who heard God's message whispered in
their ears, that they might proclaim it on the house-
tops to all the world through all generations. But
though they and we are on a different level, and God
spoke to them for a different purpose, He speaks in
our spirits, if we will comply with the conditions, as
truly as He did in theirs. As really as it was ever true
that the Lord spoke to Abraham, or Isaiah, or Paul,
it is true that He now speaks to the man who walks
with Him. Frank speech on both sides beguiles many
a weary mile, when lovers or friends foot it side by
side; and this pair of friends of whom our text speaks
have mutual intercourse. God speaks with His servant
now, as of old, 'as a man speaketh with his friend';
and we on our parts, if we are truly walking with Him,
shall feel it natural to speak frankly to God. As two
friends on the road will interchange remarks about

K

trifles, and if they love each other, the remarks about
the trifles will be weighted with love, so we can tell
our smallest affairs to God; and if we have Him for
our Pilgrim-Companion, we do not need to lock up any
troubles or concerns of any sort, big or little, in our
hearts, but may speak them all to our Friend who goes
with us.

The two *may* walk together. That is the end of all
religion. What are creeds for? What are services and
sacraments for? What is theology for? What is
Christ's redeeming act for? All culminate in this true,
constant fellowship between men and God. And unless,
in some measure, that result is arrived at in our cases,
our religion, let it be as orthodox as you like, our faith
in the redemption of Jesus Christ, let it be as real as
you will, our attendances on services and sacraments,
let them be as punctilious and regular as may be, are
all 'sounding brass and tinkling cymbal.' Get side by
side with God; that is the purpose of all these, and
fellowship with Him is the climax of all religion.

It is also the secret of all blessedness, the only thing
that will make a life absolutely sovereign over sorrow,
and fixedly unperturbed by all tempests, and invulner-
able to all 'the slings and arrows of outrageous fortune.'
Hold fast by God, and you have an amulet against
every evil, and a shield against every foe, and a mighty
power that will calm and satisfy your whole being.
Nothing else, nothing else will do so. As Augustine
said, 'O God! Thou hast made us for Thyself, and in
Thyself only are we at rest.' If the Shepherd is with
us we will fear no evil.

II. Now, a word, in the next place, as to the sadly
incomplete reality, in much Christian experience, which
contrasts with this possibility.

I am afraid that very, very few so-called Christian people habitually feel, as they might do, the depth and blessedness of this communion. And sure I am that only a very small percentage of us have anything like the continuity of companionship which my text suggests as possible. There may be, and therefore there should be, running unbroken through a Christian life one long, bright line of communion with God and happy inspiration from the sense of His presence with us. Is it a line in *my* life, or is there but a dot here, and a dot there, and long breaks between? The long, embarrassed pauses in a conversation between two who do not know much of, or care much for, each other are only too like what occurs in many professing Christians' intercourse with God. Their communion is like those time-worn inscriptions that archæologists dig up, with a word clearly cut and then a great gap, and then a letter or two, and then another gap, and then a little bit more legible, and then the stone broken, and all the rest gone. Did you ever read the meteorological reports in the newspapers and observe a record like this, 'Twenty minutes' sunshine out of a possible eight hours'? Do you not think that such a state of affairs is a little like the experience of a great many Christian people in regard to their communion with God? It is broken at the best, and imperfect at the completest, and shallow at the deepest. O, dear brethren! rise to the height of your possibilities, and live as close to God as He lets you live, and nothing will much trouble you.

III. And now, lastly, a word about the simple explanation of the failure to realise this continual presence.

'Can two walk together except they be agreed?' Certainly not. Our fathers, in a sterner and more religious age than ours, used to be greatly troubled how to account for a state of Christian experience which they supposed to be due to God's withdrawing of the sense of His presence from His children. Whether there is any such withdrawal or not, I am quite certain that that is not the cause of the interrupted communion between God and the average Christian man.

I make all allowance for the ups and downs and changing moods which necessarily affect us in this present life, and I make all allowance, too, for the pressure of imperative duties and distracting cares which interfere with our communion, though, if we were as strong as we might be, they would not wile us away from, but drive us to, our Father in heaven. But when all such allowances have been made, I come back to my text as *the* explanation of interrupted communion. The two are *not* agreed; and that is why they are not walking together. The consciousness of God's presence with us is a very delicate thing. It is like a very sensitive thermometer, which will drop when an iceberg is a league off over the sea, and scarcely visible. We do not wish His company, or we are not in harmony with His thoughts, or we are not going His road, and therefore, of course, we part. At bottom there is only one thing that separates a soul from God, and that is sin—sin of some sort, like tiny grains of dust that get between two polished plates in an engine that ought to move smoothly and closely against each other. The obstruction may be invisible, and yet be powerful enough to cause friction, which hinders the working of the engine and throws everything out of gear. A light cloud that we cannot see may come between us and a star, and we shall only know it is there, because the star is *not* visibly there. Similarly, many a Christian, quite unconsciously, has something

or other in his habits, or in his conduct, or in his affections, which would reveal itself to him, if he would
look, as being wrong, because it blots out God.

Let us remember that very little divergence will, if
the two paths are prolonged far enough, part their
other ends by a world. Our way may go off from the
ways of the Lord at a very acute angle. There may be
scarcely any consciousness of parting company at the
beginning. Let the man travel on upon it far enough,
and the two will be so far apart that he cannot see
God or hear Him speak. Take care of the little diver-
gences which are habitual, for their accumulated
results will be complete separation. There must be
absolute surrender if there is to be uninterrupted
fellowship.

Such, then, is the direction in which we are to look
for the reasons for our low and broken experiences of
communion with God. Oh, dear friends! when we do
as we sometimes do, wake with a start, like a child
that all at once starts from sleep and finds that its
mother is gone—when we wake with a start to feel
that we are alone, then do not let us be afraid to go
straight back. Only be sure that we leave behind us
the sin that parted us.

You remember how Peter signalised himself on the
lake, on the occasion of the second miraculous draught
of fishes, when he floundered through the water and
clasped Christ's feet. He did not say then, 'Depart
from Me, for I am a sinful man, O Lord!' He had
said that before on a similar occasion, when he felt
his sin less, but now he knew that the best place for
the denier was with his head on Christ's bosom. So,
if we have parted from our Friend, there should be
no time lost ere we go back. May it be true of us

that we walk with God, so that at last the great
promise may be fulfilled about us, 'that we shall walk
with Him in white,' being by His love accounted
'worthy,' and so 'follow,' and keep company with, 'the
Lamb whithersoever He goeth!'

SMITTEN IN VAIN

'Come to Beth-el, and transgress; at Gilgal multiply transgression; and bring
your sacrifices every morning, and your tithes after three years: 5. And offer a
sacrifice of thanksgiving with leaven, and proclaim and publish the free offerings;
for this liketh you, O ye children of Israel, saith the Lord God. 6. And I also have
given you cleanness of teeth in all your cities, and want of bread in all your
places: yet have ye not returned unto Me, saith the Lord. 7. And also I have
withholden the rain from you, when there were yet three months to the harvest:
and I caused it to rain upon one city, and caused it not to rain upon another city:
one piece was rained upon, and the piece whereupon it rained not withered. 8. So
two or three cities wandered unto one city, to drink water; but they were not
satisfied: yet have ye not returned unto Me, saith the Lord. 9. I have smitten you
with blasting and mildew: when your gardens, and your vineyards, and your fig-
trees, and your olive-trees increased, the palmerworm devoured them: yet have ye
not returned unto Me, saith the Lord. 10. I have sent among you the pestilence,
after the manner of Egypt: your young men have I slain with the sword, and
have taken-away your horses; and I have made the stink of your camps to come
up unto your nostrils: yet have ye not returned unto Me, saith the Lord. 11. I
have overthrown some of you, as God overthrew Sodom and Gomorrah, and ye
were as a firebrand plucked out of the burning: yet have ye not returned unto
Me, saith the Lord. 12. Therefore thus will I do unto thee, O Israel: and because
I will do this unto thee, prepare to meet thy God, O Israel. 13. For, lo, He that
formeth the mountains, and createth the wind, and declareth unto man what is
his thought, that maketh the morning darkness, and treadeth upon the high
places of the earth, The Lord, The God of hosts, is His name.' - AMOS iv. 4-13.

THE reign of Jeroboam II. was one of brilliant military
success and of profound moral degradation. Amos
was a simple, hardy shepherd from the southern
wilds of Judah, and his prophecies are redolent of his
early life, both in their homely imagery and in the
wholesome indignation and contempt for the silken-
robed vice of Israel. No sterner picture of an utterly
rotten social state was ever drawn than this book gives
of the luxury, licentiousness, and oppressiveness of
the ruling classes. This passage deals rather with the
religious declension underlying the moral filth, and

sets forth the self-willed idolatry of the people (vs. 4, 5),
their obstinate resistance to God's merciful chastisement (vs. 6-11), and the heavier impending judgment
(vs. 12, 13).

I. Indignant irony flashes in that permission or
command to persevere in the calf worship. The seeming command is the strongest prohibition. There can
be no worse thing befall a man than that he should be
left to go on frowardly in the way of his heart. The
real meaning is sufficiently emphasised by that second
verb, 'and *transgress.*' 'Flock to one temple after
another, and heap altars with sacrifices which you
were never bid to offer, but understand that what you
do is not worship, but sin.' That is a smiting sentence
to pass upon elaborate ceremonial. The word literally
means treason or rebellion, and by it Amos at one blow
shatters the whole fabric. Note, too, that the offering
of tithes was not called for by Mosaic law, 'every
three days' (Revised Version), and that the use of
leaven in burnt offerings was prohibited by it, and
also that to call for freewill offerings was to turn
spontaneousness into something like compulsion, and to
bring ostentation into worship. All these characteristics spoiled the apparent religiousness, over and
above the initial evil of disobedience, and warrant
Amos's crushing equation, 'Your worship $=$ rebellion.'
All are driven home by the last words of verse 5, 'So
ye love it.' The reason for all this prodigal ostentatious
worship was to please themselves, not to obey God.
That tainted everything, and always does.

The lessons of this burst of sarcasm are plain. The
subtle influence of self creeps in even in worship, and
makes it hollow, unreal, and powerless to bless the
worshipper. Obedience is better than costly gifts. The

beginning and end of all worship, which is not at the
same time 'transgression,' is the submission of tastes,
will, and the whole self.   Again, men will lavish gifts
far more freely in apparent religious service, which is
but the worship of their reflected selves, than in true
service of God.   Again, the purity of willing offerings
is marred when they are given in response to a loud
call, or, when given, are proclaimed with acclamations.
Let us not suppose that all the brunt of Amos's indignation fell only on these old devotees.   The principles
involved in it have a sharp edge, turned to a great
deal which is allowed and fostered among ourselves.

II. The blaze of indignation changes in the second
part of the passage into wounded tenderness, as the
Prophet speaks in the name of God, and recounts the
dreary monotony of failure attending all God's loving
attempts to arrest Israel's departure by the mercy of
judgment.   Mark the sad cadence of the fivefold
refrain, 'Ye have not returned unto Me, saith the
Lord.'   The 'unto' implies reaching the object to
which we turn, and is not the less forcible but more
usual word found in this phrase, which simply means
'towards' and indicates direction, without saying
anything as to how far the return has gone.   So there
may have been partial moments of bethinking themselves, when the chastisement was on Israel; but there
had been no thorough 'turning,' which had landed
them at the side of God.   Many a man turns *towards*
God, who, for lack of resolved perseverance, never so
turns as to get *to* God.   The repeated complaint of the
inefficacy of chastisements has in it a tone of sorrow
and of wonder which does not belong only to the
Prophet.   If we remember who it was who was
'grieved at the blindness of their heart,' and who

'wondered at their unbelief,' we shall not fear to recognise here the attribution of the same emotions to the heart of God.

To Amos, famine, drought, blasting, locusts, pestilence, and probably earthquake, were five messengers of God, and Amos was taught by God. If we looked deeper, we should see more clearly. The true view of the relation of all material things and events to God is this which the herdsman of Tekoa proclaimed. These messengers were not 'miracles,' but they were God's messengers all the same. Behind all phenomena stands a personal will, and they are nearer the secret of the universe who see God working in it all, than they who see all forces except the One which is the only true force. 'I give cleanness of teeth. I have withholden the rain. I have smitten. I have sent the pestilence. I have overthrown some of you.' To the Prophet's eye the world is all aflame with a present God. Let no scientific views, important and illuminating as these may be, hide from us the deeper truth, which lies beyond their region. The child who says 'God,' has got nearer the centre than the scientist who says 'Force.'

But Amos had another principle, that God sent physical calamities because of moral delinquencies and for moral and religious ends. These disasters were meant to bring Israel back to God, and were at once punishments and reformatory methods. No doubt the connection between sin and material evils was closer under the Old Testament than now. But if we may not argue as Amos did, in reference to such calamities as drought, and failures of harvests, and the like, as these affect communities, we may, at all events, affirm that, in the case of the individual, he is a wise man who regards all outward evil as having a possible bearing on his bettering spiritually. 'If a drought comes, learn to look to your irrigation, and don't cut down your forests so wantonly,' say the wise men nowadays; 'if pestilence breaks out, see to your drainage.' By all means. These things, too, are God's commandments, and we have no right to interpret the consequences of infraction of physical laws as being meant to punish nations for their breach of moral and religious ones. If we were prophets, we might, but not else. But still, is God so poor that He can have but one purpose in a providence? Every sorrow, of whatever sort, is meant to produce all the good effects which it naturally tends to produce; and since every experience of pain and loss and grief naturally tends to wean us from earth, and to drive us to find in God what earth can never yield, all our sorrows are His messengers to draw us back to Him. Amos' lesson as to the purpose of trials is not antiquated.

But he has still another to teach us; namely, the awful power which we have of resisting God's efforts to draw us back. 'Our wills are ours, we know not how,' but alas! it is too often not 'to make them Thine.' This is the true tragedy of the world that God calls, and we do refuse, even as it is the deepest mystery of sinful manhood that God calls and we can refuse. What infinite pathos and grieved love, thrown back upon itself, is in that refrain, 'Ye have not returned unto Me!' How its recurrence speaks of the longsuffering which multiplied means as others failed, and of the divine charity, which 'suffered long, was not soon angry, and hoped all things!' How vividly it gives the impression of the obstinacy that to all effort opposed insensibility, and clung the more closely and

insanely to the idolatry which was its crime and its
ruin! The very same temper is deep in us all. Israel
holds up the mirror in which we may see ourselves.
If blows do not break iron, they harden it. A wasted
sorrow—that is, a sorrow which does not drive us to
God—leaves us less impressible than it found us.

III. Again the mood changes, and the issue of pro-
tracted resistance is prophesied (vs. 12, 13). 'Therefore' sums up the instances of refusal to be warned,
and presents them as the cause of the coming evil.
The higher the dam is piled, the deeper the water that
is gathered behind it, and the surer and more destructive the flood when it bursts. Long-delayed judgments are severe in proportion as they are slow.
Note the awful vagueness of threatening in that
emphatic 'thus,' as if the Prophet had the event before
his eyes. There is no need to specify, for there can be
but one result from such obstinacy. The 'terror of
the Lord' is more moving by reason of the dimness
which wraps it. The contact of divine power with
human rebellion can only end in one way, and that
is too terrible for speech. Conscience can translate
'thus.' The thunder-cloud is all the more dreadful for
the vagueness of its outline, where its livid hues melt
into formless black. What bolts lurk in its gloom?

The certainty of judgment is the basis of a call to
repentance, which may avert it. The meeting with God
for which Israel is besought to prepare, was, of course,
not judgment after death, but the impending destruction of the Northern Kingdom. But Amos's prophetic
call is not misapplied when directed to that final day
of the Lord. Common-sense teaches preparation for a
certain future, and Amos's trumpet-note is deepened
and re-echoed by Jesus: 'Be ye ready also, for . . . the

Son of man cometh.' Note, too, that Israel's peculiar
relation to God is the very ground of the certainty of
its punishment, and of the appeal for repentance.
Just because He is 'thy God,' will He assuredly come to
judge, and you may assuredly prepare, by repentance,
to meet Him. The conditions of meeting the Judge,
and being 'found of Him in peace,' are that we should
be 'without spot, and blameless'; and the conditions
of being so spotless and uncensurable are, what they
were in Amos's day, repentance and trust. Only we
have Jesus as the brightness of the Father's glory to
trust in, and His all-sufficient work to trust to, for
pardon and purifying.

The magnificent proclamation of the name of the
Lord which closes the passage, is meant as at once a
guarantee of His judgment and an enforcement of the
call to be ready to meet Him. He in creation forms
the solid; changeless mountains and the viewless,
passing wind. The most stable and the most mobile
are His work. He reads men's hearts, and can tell
them their thoughts afar off. He is the Author of all
changes, both in the physical and the moral world,
bringing the daily wonder of sunrise and the nightly
shroud of darkness, and with like alternation blending
joy and sorrow in men's lives. He treads 'on the high
places of the earth,' making all created elevations the
path of His feet, and crushing down whatever exalts
itself. Thus, in creation almighty, in knowledge
omniscient, in providence changing all things and
Himself the same, subjugating all, and levelling a path
for His purposes across every opposition, He manifests
His name, as the living, eternal Jehovah, the God of
the Covenant, and therefore of judgment on its
breakers, and as the Commander and God of the

embattled forces of the universe. Is this a God whose coming to judge is to be lightly dealt with? Is not this a God whom it is wise for us to be ready to meet?

THE SINS OF SOCIETY

'For thus saith the Lord unto the house of Israel, Seek ye Me, and ye shall live: 5. But seek not Beth-el, nor enter into Gilgal, and pass not to Beer-sheba: for Gilgal shall surely go into captivity, and Beth-el shall come to nought. 6. Seek the Lord, and ye shall live; lest He break out like fire in the house of Joseph, and devour it, and there be none to quench it in Beth-el. 7. Ye who turn judgment to wormwood, and leave off righteousness in the earth, 8. Seek Him that maketh the seven stars and Orion, and turneth the shadow of death into the morning, and maketh the day dark with night: that calleth for the waters of the sea, and poureth them out upon the face of the earth: The Lord is His name: 9. That strengtheneth the spoiled against the strong, so that the spoiled shall come against the fortress. 10. They hate him that rebuketh in the gate, and they abhor him that speaketh uprightly. 11. Forasmuch therefore as your treading is upon the poor, and ye take from him burdens of wheat: ye have built houses of hewn stone, but ye shall not dwell in them; ye have planted pleasant vineyards, but ye shall not drink wine of them. 12. For I know your manifold transgressions and your mighty sins: they afflict the just, they take a bribe, and they turn aside the poor in the gate from their right. 13. Therefore the prudent shall keep silence in that time; for it is an evil time. 14. Seek good, and not evil, that ye may live: and so the Lord, the God of hosts, shall be with you, as ye have spoken. 15. Hate the evil, and love the good, and establish judgment in the gate: it may be that the Lord God of hosts will be gracious unto the remnant of Joseph.'—AMOS v. 4-15.

THE reign of Jeroboam II. in which Amos prophesied, was a period of great prosperity and of great corruption. Amos, born in the Southern Kingdom, and accustomed to the simple life of a shepherd, blazed up in indignation at the signs of misused wealth and selfish luxury that he saw everywhere, in what was to him almost a foreign country. If one fancies a godly Scottish Highlander sent to the West end of London, or a Bible-reading New England farmer's man sent to New York's 'upper ten,' one will have some notion of this prophet, the impressions made, and the task laid on him. He has a message to our state of society which, in many particulars, resembles that which he had to rebuke.

There seems to be a slight dislocation in the order of the verses of the passage, for verse 7 comes in awkwardly, breaking the connection between verses 6 and 8, and itself cut off from verse 10, to which it belongs. If we remove the intruding verse to a position after verse 9, the whole passage is orderly and falls into three coherent parts: an exhortation to seek Jehovah, enforced by various considerations (vs. 4-9); a vehement denunciation of social vices (vs. 7, 10-13); and a renewed exhortation to seek God by doing right to man (vs. 14, 15).

Amos's first call to Israel is but the echo of God's to men, always and everywhere. All circumstances, all inward experiences, joy and sorrow, prosperity and disaster, our longings and our fears, they all cry aloud to us to seek His face. That loving invitation is ever sounding in our ears. And the promise which Amos gave, though it may have meant on his lips the continuance of national life only, yet had, even on his lips, a deeper meaning, which we now cannot but hear in it. For, just as to 'seek the Lord' means more to us than it did to Israel, so the consequent life has greatened, widened, deepened into life eternal. But Amos's narrower, more external promise is true still, and there is no surer way of promoting true well-being than seeking God. 'With Thee is the fountain of life,' in all senses of the word, from the lowest purely physical to the highest, and it is only they who go thither to draw that will carry away their pitchers full of the sparkling blessing. The fundamental principle of Amos's teaching is an eternal truth, that to seek God is to find Him, and to find Him is life.

But Amos further teaches us that such seeking is

not real nor able to find, unless it is accompanied
with turning away from all sinful quests after vanities.   We must give up seeking Bethel, Gilgal, or
Beersheba, seats of the calf worship, if we are to
seek God to purpose.   The sin of the Northern
Kingdom was that it wanted to worship Jehovah
under the symbol of the calves, thus trying to unite
two discrepant things.   And is not a great deal of
our Christianity of much the same quality?   Too
many of us are doing just what Elijah told the crowds
on Carmel that they were doing, trying to 'shuffle
along on both knees.'   We would seek God, but we
would like to have an occasional visit to Bethel.   It
cannot be done.   There must be detachment, if there
is to be any real attachment.   And the certain
transiency of all creatural objects is a good reason
for not fastening ourselves to them, lest we should
share their fate.   'Gilgal shall go into captivity, and
Bethel shall come to nought,' therefore let us join
ourselves to the Eternal Love and we shall abide, as it
abides, for ever.

The exhortation is next enforced by presenting the
consequences of neglecting it.   To seek Him is life,
not to seek Him incurs the danger of finding Him
in unwelcome ways.   That is for ever true.   We do
not get away from God by forgetting Him, but we
run the risk of finding in Him, not the fire which
vitalises, purifies, melts, and gladdens, but that which
consumes.   The fire is one, but its effects are twofold.   God is for us either that fire into which it
is blessedness to be baptized, or that by which it is
death to be burned up.   And what can Bethel, or
calves, or all the world do to quench it or pluck us
out of it?

Once more the exhortation is urged, if we link verse
8 with verse 6, and supply 'Seek ye' at its beginning.
Here the enforcement is drawn from the considerations of God's workings in nature and history. The
shepherd from Tekoa had often gazed up at the silent
splendours of the Pleiades and Orion, as he kept watch
over his flocks by night, and had seen the thick darkness on the wide uplands thinning away as the morning stole up over the mountains across the Dead Sea,
and the day dying as he gathered his sheep together.
He had cowered under the torrential rains which swept
across his exposed homeland, and had heard God's voice
summoning the obedient waters of the sea, that He
might pour them down in rain.   But the moral
government of the world also calls on men to seek
Jehovah. 'He causeth destruction to flash forth on
the strong, so that destruction cometh upon the fortress.' High things attract the lightning. Godless
strength is sure, sooner or later, to be smitten down,
and no fortress is so impregnable that He cannot
capture and overthrow it. Surely wisdom bids us seek
Him that does all these wonders, and make Him our
defence and our high tower.

The second part gives a vivid picture of the vices
characteristic of a prosperous state of society which
is godless, and therefore selfishly luxurious. First,
civil justice is corrupted, turned into bitterness, and
prostrated to the ground. Then bold denouncers of
national sins are violently hated. Do we not know
that phase of an ungodly and rich society? What
do the newspapers say about Christians who try to
be social reformers? Are the epithets flung at them
liker bouquets or rotten eggs? 'Fanatics and fad-
dists' are the mildest of them. Then the poor are

trodden down and have to give large parts of their
scanty harvests to the rich. Have capital and labour
just proportions of their joint earnings? Would a
sermon on verse 11 be welcome in the suburbs of
industrial centres, where the employers have their
'houses of hewn stone'? Such houses, side by side
with the poor men's huts, struck the eye of the shepherd from Tekoa as the height of sinful luxury, and
still more sinful disproportion in the social condition
of the two classes. What would he have said if he had
lived in England or America? Justice, too, was bought
and sold. A murderer could buy himself off, while the
poor man, who could not pay, lost his case. We do not
bribe judges, but (legal) justice is an expensive luxury
still, and counsel's fees put it out of the reach of poor
men.

One of the worst features of such a state of society
as Amos saw is that men are afraid to speak out in
condemnation of it, and the ill weeds grow apace
for want of a scythe. Amos puts a certain sad
emphasis on 'prudent,' as if he was feeling how little
he could be called so, and yet there is a touch of
scorn in him too. The man who is over-careful of
his skin or his reputation will hold his tongue; even
good men may become so accustomed to the glaring
corruptions of society in the midst of which they
have always lived, that they do not feel any call to
rebuke or wage war against them; but the brave
man, the man who takes his ideals from Christ, and
judges society by its conformity with Christ's standard, will not keep silence, and the more he feels
that 'It is an evil time' the more will he feel that
he cannot but speak out, whatever comes of his protest. What masquerades as prudence is very often

L

sinful cowardice, and such silence is treason against Christ.

The third part repeats the exhortation to 'seek,' with a notable difference. It is now 'good' that is to be sought, and 'evil' that is to be turned from. These correspond respectively to 'Jehovah,' and 'Bethel, Gilgal, and Beersheba,' in former verses. That is to say, morality is the garb of religion, and religion is the only true source of morality. If we are not seeking the things that are lovely and of good report, our professions of seeking God are false; and we shall never earnestly and successfully seek good and hate evil unless we have begun by seeking and finding God, and holding Him in our heart of hearts. Modern social reformers, who fancy that they can sweeten society without religion, might do worse than go to school to Amos.

Notable, too, is the lowered tone of confidence in the beneficial result of obeying the Prophet's call. In the earlier exhortation the promise had been absolute. 'Seek ye Me, and ye *shall* live'; now it has cooled to 'it may be.' Is Amos faltering? No; but while it is always true that blessed life is found by the seeker after God, because He finds the very source of life, it is not always true that the consequences of past turnings from Him are diverted by repentance. 'It may be' that these have to be endured, but even they become tokens of Jehovah's graciousness, and the purified 'remnant of Joseph' will possess the true life more abundantly because they have been exercised thereby.

THE CARCASS AND THE EAGLES

' Woe to them that are at ease in Zion, and trust in the mountain of Samaria, which are named chief of the nations, to whom the house of Israel came! 2. Pass ye unto Calneh, and see; and from thence go ye to Hamath the great; then go down to Gath of the Philistines: be they better than these kingdoms ? or their border greater than your border? 3. Ye that put far away the evil day, and cause the seat of violence to come near; 4. That lie upon beds of ivory, and stretch themselves upon their couches, and eat the lambs out of the flock, and the calves out of the midst of the stall; 5. That chant to the sound of the viol, and invent to themselves instruments of musick, like David; 6. That drink wine in bowls, and anoint themselves with the chief ointments: but they are not grieved for the affliction of Joseph. 7. Therefore now shall they go captive with the first that go captive, and the banquet of them that stretched themselves shall be removed. 8. The Lord God hath sworn by Himself, saith the Lord the God of hosts, I abhor the excellency of Jacob, and hate his palaces: therefore will I deliver up the city with all that is therein.'—AMOS vi. 1-8.

AMOS prophesied during the reign of Jeroboam, the son of Joash. Jeroboam's reign was a time of great prosperity for Israel. Moab, Gilead, and part of Syria were reconquered, and the usual effects of conquest, increased luxury and vainglory, followed. Amos was not an Israelite born, for he came from Tekoa, away down south, in the wild country west of the Dead Sea, where he had been a simple herdsman till the divine call sent him into the midst of the corrupt civilisation of the Northern Kingdom. The first words of his prophecy give its whole spirit: 'The Lord will roar from Zion.' The word rendered 'roar' is the term specially used for the terrible cry with which a lion leaps on its surprised prey (Amos iii. 4, 8). It is from Zion, the seat of God's Temple, that the 'roar' proceeds, and Amos's prophecy is but the echo of it in Israel.

The prophecy of judgment in this passage is directed against the sins of the upper classes in Samaria. They are described in verse 1 as the 'notable men . . . to whom the house of Israel come,' which, in modern language, is just 'conspicuous citizens,' who set the fashion, and are looked to as authorities and leaders, whether in political or commercial or social life. The word by which they are designated is used in Numbers i. 17: ' Which are *expressed* by name.' The word ' carried back the thoughts of the degenerate aristocracy of Israel to the faith and zeal of their forefathers ' (Pusey, *Minor Prophets*, on this verse). Israel, Amos calls ' The first of the nations.' It is singular that such a title should be given to the nation against whose corruption his one business is to testify, but probably there is keen irony in the word. It takes Israel at its own estimate, and then goes on to show how rotten, and therefore short-lived, was the prosperity which had swollen national pride to such a pitch. The chiefs of the foremost nation in the world should surely be something better than the heartless debauchees whom the Prophet proceeds to paint. Anglo-Saxons on both sides of the Atlantic, who are by no means deficient in this same complacent estimate of their own superiority to all other peoples, may take note. The same thought is prominent in the description of these notables as ' at ease.' They are living in a fool's paradise, shutting their eyes to the thunder-clouds that begin to rise slowly above the horizon, and keeping each other in countenance in laughing at Amos and his gloomy forecasts. They ' trusted in the mountain of Samaria,' which, they thought, made the city impregnable to assault. No doubt they thought that the Prophet's talk about doing right and trusting in Jehovah was very fanatical and unpractical, just as many in England and America think that their nations are exalted, not by righteousness, but by armies, navies, and dollars or sovereigns.

Verse 2 is very obscure to us from our ignorance

of the facts underlying its allusions. In fact, it has been explained in exactly opposite ways, being taken by some to enumerate three instances of prosperous communities, which yet are not more prosperous than Israel, and by others to enumerate three instances of God's judgments falling on places which, though strong, had been conquered. In the former explanation, God's favour to Israel is made the ground of an implied appeal to their gratitude; in the latter, His judgments on other nations are made the ground of an appeal to their fear, lest like destruction should fall on them.

But the main points of the passage are the photograph of the crimes which are bringing the judgment of God, and the solemn divine oath to inflict the judgment. The crimes rebuked are not the false worship of the calves, though in other parts of his prophecy Amos lashes that with terrible invectives, nor foul breaches of morality, though these were not wanting in Israel, but the vices peculiar to selfish, luxurious upper classes in all times and countries, who forget the obligations of wealth, and think only of its possibilities of self-indulgence. French *noblesse* before the Revolution, and English peers and commercial magnates, and American millionaires, would yield examples of the same sin. The hardy shepherd from Tekoa had learned 'plain living and high thinking' before he was a prophet, and would look with wondering and disgusted eyes at the wicked waste which he saw in Samaria. He begins with scourging the reckless security already referred to. These notables in Israel were 'at ease' because they 'put far away the evil day,' by refusing to believe that it was at hand, and paying no heed to prophets' warnings, as their fellows do still and always, and as we all are tempted to do. They who see and declare the certain end of national or personal sins are usually jeered at as pessimists, fanatics, alarmists, bad patriots, or personal ill-wishers, and the men whom they try to warn fancy that they hinder the coming of a day of retribution by disbelieving in its coming. Incredulity is no lightning-conductor to keep off the flash, and, listened to or not, the low growls of the thunder are coming nearer.

With one hand these sinners tried to push away the evil day, while with the other they drew near to themselves that which made its coming certain—'the seat of violence,' or, rather, 'the sitting,' or 'session.' Violence, or wrongdoing, is enthroned by them, and where men enthrone iniquity, God's day of vengeance is not far off.

Then follows a graphic picture of the senseless, corrupting luxury of the Samaritan magnates, on which the Tekoan shepherd pours his scorn, but which is simplicity itself, and almost asceticism, before what he would see if he came to London or New York. To him it seemed effeminate to loll on a divan at meals, and possibly it was a custom imported from abroad. It is noted that 'the older custom in Israel was to sit while eating.' The woodwork of the divans, inlaid with ivory, had caught his eye in some of his peeps into the great houses, and he inveighs against them very much as one of the Pilgrim Fathers might do if he could see the furniture in the drawing-rooms of some of his descendants. There is no harm in pretty things, but the æsthetic craze does sometimes indicate and increase selfish heartlessness as to the poverty and misery, which have not only no ivory on their divans, but no divans at all. Thus stretched in unmanly indolence on their cushions, they feast on delicacies. 'Lambs out of the flock' and 'calves out of the stall' seem to mean animals too young to be used as food. These gourmands, like their successors, prided themselves on having dainties out of season, because they were more costly then. And their feasts had the adornment of music, which the shepherd, who knew only the pastoral pipe that gathered his sheep, refers to with contempt. He uses a very rare word of uncertain meaning, which is probably best rendered in some such way as the Revised Version does: 'They sing idle songs.' To him their elaborate performances seemed like empty babble. Worse than that, they 'devise musical instruments like David.' But how unlike him in the use they make of art! What a descent from the praises of God to the 'idle songs' fit for the hot dining-halls and the guests there! Amos was indignant at the profanation of art, and thought it best used in the service of God. What would he have said if he had been 'fastened into a front-row box,' and treated to a modern opera?

The revellers 'drink wine in bowls,' by which larger vessels than generally employed are intended. They drank to excess, or as we might say, by bucketfuls. So the dainty feast, with its artistic refinement and music, ends at last in a brutal carouse, and the heads anointed with the most costly unguents drop in drunken slumber. A similar picture of Samaritan manners is drawn by Isaiah (chap. xxviii.), and obviously drunkenness was one of the besetting sins of the capital.

But the darkest hue in the dark picture has yet to be added: 'They are not grieved for the affliction (literally, the 'breach,' or 'wound') of Joseph.' The tribe of Ephraim, Joseph's son, being the principal tribe of the Northern Kingdom, Joseph is often employed as a

synonym for Israel. All these pieces of luxury, corrupting and effeminate as they are, might be permitted, but
heartless indifference to the miseries groaning at the
door of the banqueting-hall goes with them. 'The
classes' are indifferent to the condition of 'the masses.'
Put Amos into modern English, and he is denouncing
the heartlessness of wealth, refinement, art, and culture,
which has no ear for the complaining of the poor, and
no eyes to see either the sorrows and sins around it, or
the lowering cloud that is ready to burst in tempest.

The inevitable issue is certain, because of the very
nature of God. It is outlined with keen irony. Amos
sees in imagination the long procession of sad captives,
and marching in the front ranks, the self-indulgent
Sybarites, whose pre-eminence is now only the melancholy prerogative of going first in the fettered train.
What has become of their revelry? It is gone, like the
imaginary banquets of dreams, and instead of luxurious
lolling on silken couches, there is the weary tramp of
the captive exiles. Such result must be, since God is
what He is. He has sworn 'by Himself'; His being and
character are the pledge that it will be so as Amos has
declared. How can such a God as He is do otherwise
than hate the pride of such a selfish, heartless, God-
forgetting aristocracy? How can He do otherwise than
deliver up the city? God has not changed, and though
His mills grind slowly, they do grind still; and it is as
true for England and America, as it was for Samaria,
that a wealthy and leisurely upper class, which cares
only for material luxury glossed over by art, which has
condescended to be its servant, is bringing near the evil
day which it hugs itself into believing will never come.

RIPE FOR GATHERING

'Thus hath the Lord God shewed unto me: and behold a basket of summer fruit.
2. And He said, Amos, what seest thou? And I said, A basket of summer fruit.
Then said the Lord unto me, The end is come upon My people of Israel; I will not
again pass by them any more. 3. And the songs of the temple shall be howlings
in that day, saith the Lord God: there shall be many dead bodies in every place;
they shall cast them forth with silence. 4. Hear this, O ye that swallow up the
needy, even to make the poor of the land to fail, 5. Saying, When will the new
moon be gone, that we may sell corn? and the sabbath, that we may set forth
wheat, making the ephah small, and the shekel great, and falsifying the balances
by deceit? 6. That we may buy the poor for silver, and the needy for a pair of
shoes; yea, and sell the refuse of the wheat? 7. The Lord hath sworn by the
excellency of Jacob, Surely I will never forget any of their works. 8. Shall not the
land tremble for this, and every one mourn that dwelleth therein? and it shall rise
up wholly as a flood; and it shall be cast out and drowned, as by the flood of Egypt.
9. And it shall come to pass in that day, saith the Lord God, that I will cause the
sun to go down at noon, and I will darken the earth in the clear day: 10. And I
will turn your feasts into mourning, and all your songs into lamentation; and I
will bring up sackcloth upon all loins, and baldness upon every head; and I will
make it as the mourning of an only son, and the end thereof as a bitter day.
11. Behold, the days come, saith the Lord God, that I will send a famine in the
land, not a famine of bread, nor a thirst for water, but of hearing the words of the
Lord: 12. And they shall wander from sea to sea, and from the north even to
the east, they shall run to and fro to seek the word of the Lord, and shall not find
it. 13. In that day shall the fair virgins and young men faint for thirst. 14. They
that swear by the sin of Samaria, and say, Thy God, O Dan, liveth: and, The
manner of Beer-sheba liveth; even they shall fall, and never rise up again.'—
AMOS viii. 1-14.

THERE are three visions in the former chapter, each
beginning as verse 1. This one is therefore intended
to be taken as the continuation of these, and it is in
substance a repetition of the third, only with more
detail and emphasis. An insolent attempt, by the
priest of Beth-el, to silence the Prophet, and the fiery
answer which he got for his pains, come between. The
stream of Amos's prophecy flows on, uninterrupted
by the boulder which had tried to dam it up. Some
courage was needed to treat Amaziah and his blasphem-
ous bluster as a mere parenthesis.

We have first to note the vision and its interpretation.
It is such as a countryman, 'a dresser of sycamore trees,'
would naturally have. Experience supplies forms and

material for the imagination, and moulds into which God-given revelations run. The point of the vision is rather obscured by the rendering 'summer fruit.' 'Ripe fruit' would be better, since the emblem represents the Northern Kingdom as ripe for the dreadful ingathering of judgment. The word for this (*qayits*) and that for 'the end' (*qets*) are alike in sound, but the play of words cannot be reproduced, except by some clumsy device, such as 'the end ripens,' or 'the time of ripeness comes.' The figure is frequent in other prophecies of judgment, as, for instance, in Revelation xiv. 14-20.

Observe the repetition, from the preceding vision, of 'I will not pass by them any more.' The first two visions had threatened judgments, which had been averted by the Prophet's intercession; but the third, and now the fourth, declare that the time for prolonged impunity is passed. Just as the mellow ripeness of the fruit fixes the time of gathering it, so there comes a stage in national and individual corruption, when there is nothing to be done but to smite. That period is not reached because God changes, but because men get deeper in sin. Because 'the harvest is ripe,' the long-delayed command, 'Put in thy sickle,' is given to the angel of judgment, and the clusters of those black grapes, whose juice in the wine-press of the wrath of God is blood, are cut down and cast in. It is a solemn lesson, applying to each soul as well as to communities. By neglect of God's voice, and persistence in our own evil ways, we can make ourselves such that we are ripe for judgment, and can compel long-suffering to strike. Which are we ripening for—the harvest when the wheat shall be gathered into Christ's barns, or that when the tares shall be bound in bundles for burning?

The tragedy of that fruit-gathering is described with extraordinary grimness and force in the abrupt language of verse 3. The merry songs sung in the palace (this rendering seems more appropriate here than 'temple') will be broken off, and the singers' voices will quaver into shrill shrieks, so suddenly will the judgment be. Then comes a picture as abrupt in its condensed terribleness as anything in Tacitus— 'Many the corpses; everywhere they fling them; hush!' We see the ghastly masses of dead ('corpse' is in the singular, as if a collective noun), so numerous that no burial-places could hold them; and no ceremonial attended them, but they were rudely flung anywhere by anybody (no nominative is given), with no accustomed voice of mourning, but in gloomy silence. It is like Defoe's picture of the dead-cart in the plague of London. Such is ever the end of departing from God—songs palsied into silence or turned into wailing when the judgment bursts; death stalking supreme, and silence brooding over all.

The crimes that ripened men for this terrible harvest are next set forth, in part, in verses 4 to 6. These verses partly coincide verbally with the previous indictment in Amos ii. 6, etc., which, however, is more comprehensive. Here only one form of sin is dealt with. And what was the sin that deserved the bad eminence of being thus selected as the chief sign that Israel was ripe and rotten? Precisely the one which gets most indulgence in the Christian Church; namely, eagerness to be rich, and sharp, unkindly dealing. These men, who were only fit to be swept out of the land, were most punctual in their religious duties. They would not on any account do business either on a festival or on Sabbath, but they were very impatient till—shall we say?

Monday morning came—that they might get to their
beloved work again.

Their lineal descendants are no strangers on the
exchanges, or in the churches of London or New York.
They were not only outwardly scrupulous and inwardly
weary of religious observances, but when they did get
to 'business,' they gave short measure and took a long
price, and knew how to turn the scales always in their
own favour. It was the expedient of rude beginners
in the sacred art of getting the best of a bargain, to
put a false bottom in the *ephah*, and to stick a piece of
lead below the shekel weight, which the purchaser had
to make go up in the scale with his silver. There are
much neater ways of doing the same thing now; and
no doubt some very estimable gentlemen in high repute
as Christians, who give respectability to any church or
denomination, could have taught these early practi-
tioners a lesson or two.

They were as cruel as they were greedy. They
bought their brethren as slaves, and if a poor man
had run into their debt for even a pair of shoes, they
would sell him up in a very literal sense. Avarice,
unbridled by the fear of God, leads by a short cut to
harshness and disregard of the claims of others. There
are more ways of buying the needy for a pair of shoes
than these people practised.

The last touch in the picture is meanness, which
turned everything into money. Even what fell through
the sieve when wheat was winnowed, which ought to
have been given to anybody, was carefully scraped up,
and, dirty as it was, sold. Is not 'nothing for nothing'
an approved maxim to-day? Are not people held up
as shining lights of commerce, who have the faculty of
turning everything into saleable articles? Some serious

reflections ought to be driven home to us who live in great commercial communities, and are in manifold ways tempted to 'learn their ways, and so get a snare unto our souls,' by this gibbeting of tempers and customs, very common among ourselves, as the very head and front of the sin of Israel, which determined its ripeness for destruction.

The catalogue of sins is left incomplete (compare with chapter ii.), as if holy indignation turned for relief to the thought of the certain judgment. That certainly is strongly affirmed by the representation of the oath of Jehovah. 'He can swear by no other,' therefore He 'swears by Himself'; and the 'excellency of Jacob' cannot with propriety mean anything else than Him who is, or ought to be, the sole ground of confidence and occasion of 'boasting' to the nation (Hos. v. 5). He gives His own being as the guarantee that judgment shall fall. As surely as God is God, injustice and avarice will ruin a nation. We talk now about necessary consequences and natural laws rendering penalties inevitable. The Bible suggests a deeper foundation for their certain incidence—even the very nature of God Himself. As long as He is what He is, covetousness and its child, harshness to the needy, will be sin against Him, and be avenged sooner or later. God has a long and a wide memory, and the sins which He 'remembers' are those which He has not forgiven, and will punish.

Amos heaps image on image to deepen the impression of terror and confusion. Everything is turned to its opposite. The solid land reels, rises, and falls, like the Nile in flood (see Revised Version). The sun sets at midday, and noon is darkness. Feasts change to mourning, songs to lamentations. Rich garments are put aside for sackcloth, and flowing locks drop off and leave bald heads. These are evidently all figures vividly piled together to express the same thought. The crash that destroyed their national prosperity and existence would shake the most solid things and darken the brightest. It would come suddenly, as if the sun plunged from the zenith to the west. It would make joy a stranger, and bring grief as bitter as when a father or a mother mourns the death of an only son. Besides all this, something darker beyond is dimly hinted in that awful, vague, final threat, 'The end thereof as a bitter day.'

Now all these threats were fulfilled in the fall of the kingdom of Israel; but that 'day of the Lord' was in principle a miniature foreshadowing of the great final judgment. Some of the very features of the description here are repeated with reference to it in the New Testament. We cannot treat such prophecies as this as if they were exhausted by their historical fulfilment. They disclose the eternal course of divine judgment, which is to culminate in a future day of judgment. The oath of God is not yet completely fulfilled. Assuredly as He lives and is God, so surely will modern sinners have to stand their trial; and, as of old, the chase after riches will bring down crashing ruin. We need that vision of judgment as much as Samaria did when Amos saw the basket of ripe fruit, craving, as it were, to be plucked. So do obstinate sinners invite destruction.

The last section specifies one feature of judgment, the deprivation of the despised word of the Lord (vs. 11-14). Like Saul, whose piteous wail in the witch's hovel was, 'God . . . answereth me no more,' they who paid no heed to the word of the Lord shall one day seek far and wearily for a prophet, and seek in vain. The

word rendered 'wander,' which is used in the other
description of people seeking for water in a literal
drought (iv. 8), means 'reel,' and gives the picture of
men faint and dizzy with thirst, yet staggering on in
vain quest for a spring. They seek everywhere, from
the Dead Sea on the east to the Mediterranean on the
west, and then up to the north, and so round again to
the starting-point. Is it because Judah was south that
that quarter is not visited? Perhaps, if they had gone
where the Temple was, they would have found the
stream from under its threshold, which a later prophet
saw going forth to heal the marshes and dry places.
Why was the search vain? Has not God promised to
be found of those that seek, however far they have
gone away? The last verse tells why. They still were
idolaters, swearing by the 'sin of Samaria,' which is
the calf of Beth-el, and by the other at Dan, and going
on idolatrous pilgrimages to Beer-sheba, far away in
the south, across the whole kingdom of Judah (Amos
v. 5). It was vain to seek for the word of the Lord
with such doings and worship.

The truth implied is universal in its application.
God's message neglected is withdrawn. Conscience
stops if continually unheeded. The Gospel may still
sound in a man's ears, but have long ceased to reach
farther. There comes a time when men shall wish
wasted opportunities back, and find that they can no
more return than last summer's heat. There may be
a wish for the prophet in time of distress, which means
no real desire for God's word, but only for relief from
calamity. There may be a sort of seeking for the word,
which seeks in the wrong places and in the wrong ways,
and without abandoning sins. Such quest is vain. But
if, driven by need and sorrow, a poor soul, feeling the

thirst after the living God, cries from ever so distant a land of bondage, the cry will be answered. But let us not forget that our Lord has told us to take heed how we hear, on the very ground that 'to him that hath shall be given; and from him that hath not, even that he hath shall be taken away.'

JONAH

GUILTY SILENCE AND ITS REWARD

'Now the word of the Lord came unto Jonah the son of Amittai, saying, 2. Arise, go to Nineveh, that great city, and cry against it; for their wickedness is come up before Me. 3. But Jonah rose up to flee unto Tarshish from the presence of the Lord, and went down to Joppa; and he found a ship going to Tarshish: so he paid the fare thereof, and went down into it, to go with them unto Tarshish from the presence of the Lord. 4. But the Lord sent out a great wind into the sea, and there was a mighty tempest in the sea, so that the ship was like to be broken. 5. Then the mariners were afraid, and cried every man unto his god, and cast forth the wares that were in the ship into the sea, to lighten it of them. But Jonah was gone down into the sides of the ship; and he lay, and was fast asleep. 6. So the shipmaster came to him, and said unto him, What meanest thou, O sleeper? arise, call upon thy God, if so be that God will think upon us, that we perish not. 7. And they said every one to his fellow, Come, and let us cast lots, that we may know for whose cause this evil is upon us. So they cast lots, and the lot fell upon Jonah. 8. Then said they unto him, Tell us, we pray thee, for whose cause this evil is upon us: What is thine occupation? and whence comest thou? what is thy country? and of what people art thou? 9. And he said unto them, I am an Hebrew; and I fear the Lord, the God of heaven, which hath made the sea and the dry land. 10. Then were the men exceedingly afraid, and said unto him, Why hast thou done this? For the men knew that he fled from the presence of the Lord, because he had told them. 11. Then said they unto him, What shall we do unto thee, that the sea may be calm unto us? for the sea wrought, and was tempestuous. 12. And he said unto them, Take me up, and cast me forth into the sea; so shall the sea be calm unto you: for I know that for my sake this great tempest is upon you. 13. Nevertheless the men rowed hard to bring it to the land; but they could not: for the sea wrought, and was tempestuous against them. 14. Wherefore they cried unto the Lord, and said, We beseech thee, O Lord, we beseech thee, let us not perish for this man's life, and lay not upon us innocent blood: for Thou, O Lord, hast done as it pleased Thee. 15. So they took up Jonah, and cast him forth into the sea; and the sea ceased from her raging. 16. Then the men feared the Lord exceedingly, and offered a sacrifice unto the Lord, and made vows. 17. Now the Lord had prepared a great fish to swallow up Jonah. And Jonah was in the belly of the fish three days and three nights.'—JONAH i. 1-17.

JONAH was apparently an older contemporary of Hosea and Amos. The Assyrian power was looming threateningly on the northern horizon, and a flash or two had already broken from that cloud. No doubt terror had wrought hate and intenser narrowness. To correct these by teaching, by an instance drawn from Assyria

itself, God's care for the Gentiles and their susceptibility to His voice, was the purpose of Jonah's mission.
He is a prophet of Israel, because the lesson of his
history was for them, though his message was for
Nineveh. He first taught by example the truth which
Jesus proclaimed in the synagogue of Nazareth, and
Peter learned on the housetop at Joppa, and Paul
took as his guiding star. A truth so unwelcome and
remote from popular belief needed emphasis when
first proclaimed; and this singular story, as it were,
underlines it for the generation which heard it first.
Its place would rather have been among the narratives
than the prophets, except for this aspect of it. So
regarded, Jonah becomes a kind of representative of
Israel; and his history sets forth large lessons as to its
function among the nations, its unwillingness to discharge it, the consequences of disobedience, and the
means of return to a better mind.

Note then, first, the Prophet's unwelcome charge.
There seems no sufficient reason for doubting the historical reality of Jonah's mission to Nineveh; for we
know that intercourse was not infrequent, and the
silence of other records is, in their fragmentary condition, nothing wonderful. But the fact that a prophet
of Israel was sent to a heathen city, and that not to
denounce destruction except as a means of winning to
repentance, declared emphatically God's care for the
world, and rebuked the exclusiveness which claimed
Him for Israel alone. The same spirit haunts the
Christian Church, and we have all need to ponder the
opposite truth, till our sympathies are widened to
the width of God's universal love, and we discern
that we are bound to care for all men, since He
does so.

Jonah sullenly resolved not to obey God's voice. What a glimpse into the prophetic office that gives us! The divine Spirit could be resisted, and the Prophet was no mere machine, but a living man who had to consent with his devoted will to bear the burden of the Lord. One refused, and his refusal teaches us how superb and self-sacrificing was the faithfulness of the rest. So we have each to do in regard to God's message intrusted to us. We must bow our wills, and sink our prejudices, and sacrifice our tastes, and say, 'Here am I; send me.'

Jonah represents the national feelings which he shared. Why did he refuse to go to Nineveh? Not because he was afraid of his life, or thought the task hopeless. He refused because he feared success. God's goodness was being stretched rather too far, if it was going to take in Nineveh. Jonah did not want it to escape. If he had been sent to destroy it, he would probably have gone gladly. He grudged that heathen should share Israel's privileges, and probably thought that gain to Nineveh would be loss to Israel. It was exactly the spirit of the prodigal's elder brother. There was also working in him the concern for his own reputation, which would be damaged if the threats he uttered turned out to be thunder without lightning, by reason of the repentance of Nineveh.

Israel was set among the nations, not as a dark lantern, but as the great lampstand in the Temple court proclaimed, to ray out light to all the world. Jonah's mission was but a concrete instance of Israel's charge. The nation was as reluctant to fulfil the reason of its existence as the Prophet was. Both begrudged sharing privileges with heathen dogs, both thought God's care wasted, and neither had such feelings

towards the rest of the world as to be willing to be
messengers of forgiveness to them. All sorts of
religious exclusiveness, contemptuous estimates of
other nations, and that bastard patriotism which
would keep national blessings for our own country
alone, are condemned by this story. In it dawns the
first faint light of that sun which shone at its full
when Jesus healed the Canaanite's daughter, or when
He said, 'Other sheep I have, which are not of this
fold.'

Note, next, the fatal consequences of refusal to obey
the God-given charge. We need not suppose that
Jonah thought that he could actually get away from
God's presence. Possibly he believed in a special
presence of God in the land of Israel, or, more probably, the phrase means to escape from service. At
any rate, he determined to do his flight thoroughly.
Tarshish was, to a Hebrew, at the other end of the
world from Nineveh. The Jews were no sailors, and
the choice of the sea as means of escape indicates the
obstinacy of determination in Jonah.

The storm is described with a profusion of unusual
words, all apparently technical terms, picked up on
board, just as Luke, in the only other account of a
storm in Scripture, has done. What a difference
between the two voyages! In the one, the unfaithful
prophet is the cause of disaster, and the only sluggard
in the ship. In the other, the Apostle, who has hazarded
his life to proclaim his Lord, is the source of hope,
courage, vigour, and safety. Such are the consequences
of silence and of brave speech for God. No wonder that
the fugitive Prophet slunk down into some dark corner,
and sat bitterly brooding there, self-accused and condemned, till weariness and the relief of the tension of

his journey lulled him to sleep. It was a stupid and heavy sleep. Alas for those whose only refuge from conscience is oblivion!

Over against this picture of the insensible Prophet, all unaware of the storm (which may suggest the parallel insensibility of Israel to the impending divine judgments), is set the behaviour of the heathen sailors, or 'salts,' as the story calls them. Their conduct is part of the lesson of the book; for, heathen as they are, they have yet a sense of dependence, and they pray; they are full of courage, battling with the storm, jettisoning the cargo, and doing everything possible to save the ship. Their treatment of Jonah is generous and chivalrous. Even when they hear his crime, and know that the storm is howling like a wild beast for him, they are unwilling to throw him overboard without one more effort; and when at last they do it, their prayer is for forgiveness, inasmuch as they are but carrying out the will of Jehovah. They are so much touched by the whole incident that they offer sacrifices to the God of the Hebrews, and are, in some sense, and possibly but for a time, worshippers of Him.

All this holds the mirror up to Israel, by showing how much of human kindness and generosity, and how much of susceptibility for the truth which Israel had to declare, lay in rude hearts beyond its pale. This crew of heathen of various nationalities and religions were yet men who could be kind to a renegade Prophet, peril their lives to save his, and worship Jehovah. 'I have not found so great faith, no, not in Israel,' is the same lesson in another form. We may find abundant opportunities for learning it; for the characters of godless men, and of some among the heathen, may well shame many a Christian.

Jonah's conduct in the storm is no less noble than his former conduct had been base. The burst of the tempest blew away all the fog from his mind, and he saw the stars again. His confession of faith; his calm conviction that he was the cause of the storm; his quiet, unhesitating command to throw him into the wild chaos foaming about the ship; his willing acceptance of death as the wages of his sin, all tell how true a saint he was in the depth of his soul. Sorrow and chastisement turn up the subsoil. If a man has any good in him, it generally comes to the top when he is afflicted and looks death in the face. If there is nothing but gravel beneath, it too will be brought up by the plough. There may be much selfish unfaithfulness overlying a real devoted heart.

Jonah represented Israel here too, both in that the consequence of the national unfaithfulness and greedy, exclusive grasp of their privileges would lead to their being cast into the roaring waves of the sea of nations, amid the tumult of the peoples, and in that, for them as for him, the calamity would bring about a better mind, the confession of their faith, and acknowledgment of their sin. The history of Israel was typified in this history, and the lessons it teaches are lessons for all churches, and for all God's children for all time. If we shirk our duty of witnessing for Him, or any other of His plain commands, unfaithfulness will be our ruin. The storm is sure to break where His Jonahs try to hide, and their only hope lies in bowing to the chastisement and consenting to be punished, and avowing whose they are and whom they serve. If we own Him while the storm whistles round us, the worst of it is past, and though we have to struggle amid its waves, He will take care of us, and

anything is possible rather than that we should be lost
in them.

The miracle of rescue is the last point. Jonah's
repentance saved his life. Tossed overboard impeni-
tent he would have been drowned. So Israel was
taught that the break-up of their national life would
not be their destruction if they turned to the Lord in
their calamity. The wider lesson of the means of
making chastisement into blessing, and securing a
way of escape—namely, by owning the justice of the
stroke, and returning to duty—is meant for us all.
He who sends the storm watches its effect on us, and
will not let His repentant servants be utterly over-
whelmed. That is a better use to make of the story
than to discuss whether any kind of known Mediterranean fish could swallow a man. If we believe in
miracles, the question need not trouble us. And
miracle there must be, not only in the coincidence of
the fish and the Prophet being in the same bit of sea at
the same moment, but in his living for so long in his
strange ' ark of safety.'

The ever-present providence of God, the possible
safety of the nation, even when in captivity, the preservation of every servant of God who turns to the
Lord in his chastisement, the exhibition of penitence as
the way of deliverance, are the purposes for which the
miracle was wrought and told. Flippant sarcasms are
cheap. A devout insight yields a worthy meaning.
Jesus Christ employed this incident as a symbol of His
Death and Resurrection. That use of it seems hard to
reconcile with any view but that the story is true.
But it does not seem necessary to suppose that our
Lord regarded it as an intended type, or to seek to find
in Jonah's history further typical prophecy of Him.

The salient point of comparison is simply the **three days'** entombment; and it is rather an illustrative analogy than an intentional prophecy. The subsequent action of the Prophet in Nineveh, and the effect of it, were true types of the preaching of the Gospel by the risen Lord, through His servants, to the Gentiles, and of their hearing the Word. But it requires considerable violence in manipulation to force the bestowing of Jonah, for safety and escape from death, in the fish's maw, into a proper prophecy of the transcendent fact of the Resurrection.

'LYING VANITIES'

'They that observe lying vanities forsake their own mercy.'—JONAH II. 8.

JONAH'S refusal to obey the divine command to go to Nineveh and cry against it is best taken, not as prosaic history, but as a poetical representation of Israel's failure to obey the divine call of witnessing for God. In like manner, his being cast into the sea and swallowed by the great fish, is a poetic reproduction, for homiletical purposes, of Israel's sufferings at the hands of the heathen whom it had failed to warn. The song which is put into Jonah's mouth when in the fish's belly, of which our text is a fragment, represents the result on the part of the nation of these hard experiences. 'Lying vanities' mean idols, and 'their own mercy' means God. The text is a brief, pregnant utterance of the great truth which had been forced home to Israel by sufferings and exile, that to turn from Jehovah to false gods was to turn from the sure source of tender care to lies and emptiness. That is but one case of the wider truth that an ungodly life is the acme of stupidity, a tragic mistake, as well as a great sin.

In confirmation and enforcement of our text we may consider:—

I. The illusory vanity of the objects pursued.

The Old Testament tone of reference to idols is one of bitter contempt. Its rigid monotheism was intensified and embittered by the universal prevalence of idolatry; and there is a certain hardness in its tone in reference to the gods of the nations round about, which has little room for pity, and finds expression in such names as those of our text—'vanities,' 'lies,' 'nothingness,' and the like. To the Jew, encompassed on all sides by idol-worshippers, the alternative was vehement indignation or entire surrender. The Mohammedan in British India exhibits much the same attitude to Vishnu and Sîva as the Jew did to Baal and Ashtoreth. It is easy to be tolerant of dead gods, but it becomes treason to Jehovah to parley with them when they are alive.

But the point which we desire to insist upon here is somewhat wider than the vanity of idols. It is the emptiness of all objects of human pursuit apart from God. These last three words need to be made very prominent; for in itself 'every creature of God is good,' and the emptiness does not inhere in themselves, but first appears when they are set in His place. He, and only He, can, and does, satisfy the whole nature—is authority for the will, peace for the conscience, love for the heart, light for the understanding, rest for all seeking. He, and He alone, can fill the past with the light in which is no regret, the present with a satisfaction rounded and complete, the future with a hope certain as experience, to which we shall ever approximate, and which we can never exhaust and outgrow. Any, or all, the other objects

of human endeavour may be won, and yet we may be
miserable. The inadequacy of all these ought to be
pressed home upon us more than it is, not only by
their limitations whilst they last, but by the transiency of them all. 'The fashion of this world passeth
away,' as the Apostle John puts it, in a forcible expression which likens all this frame of things to a
panorama being unwound from one roller and on to
another. The painted screen is but paint at the best,
and is in perpetual motion, which is not arrested by the
vain clutches of hands that would fain stop the irresistible and tragic gliding past.

These vanities are '*lying* vanities.' There is only one
aim of life which, being pursued and attained, fulfils
the promises by which it drew man after it. It is a
bald commonplace, reiterated not only by preachers
but by moralists of every kind, and confirmed by
universal experience, that a hope fulfilled is a hope
disappointed. There is only one thing more tragic
than a life which has failed in its aims, and it is a
life which has perfectly succeeded in them, and has
found that what promised to be bread turns to ashes.
The word of promise may be kept to the ear, but is
always broken to the hope. Many a millionaire loses
the power to enjoy his millions by the very process
by which he gains them. The old Jewish thinker
was wise not only in taking as the summing up of
all worldly pursuits the sad sentence, 'All is vanity,'
but in putting it into the lips of a king who had won
all he sought. The sorceress draws us within her
charmed circle by lying words and illusory charms,
and when she has so secured the captives, her
mask is thrown off and her native hideousness dis-
played.

II. The hard service which lying vanities require.

The phrase in our text is a quotation, slightly altered, from Psalm xxxi. 6: 'I hate them that regard lying vanities; but I trust in the Lord.' The alteration in the form of the verb as it occurs in Jonah expresses the intensity of regard, and gives the picture of watching with anxious solicitude, as the eyes of a servant turned to his master, or those of a dog to its owner. The world is a very hard master, and requires from its servants the concentration of thought, heart, and effort. We need only recall the thousand sermons devoted to the enforcement of 'the gospel of getting on,' which prosperous worldlings are continually preaching. A chorus of voices on every side of us is dinning into the ears of every young man and woman the necessity for success in life's struggle of taking for a motto, 'This one thing I do.' How many a man is there, who in the race after wealth or fame, has flung away aspirations, visions of noble, truthful love to life, and a hundred other precious things? Browning tells a hideous story of a mother flinging, one after another, her infants to the wolves as she urged her sledge over the snowy plain. No less hideous, and still more maiming, are the surrenders that men make when once their hearts have been filled with the foolish ambitions of worldly success. Let us fix it in our minds, that nothing that time and sense can give is worth the price that it exacts.

> 'It is only heaven that can be had for the asking;
> It is only God that is given away.'

All sin is slavery. Its yoke presses painfully on the neck, and its burden is heavy indeed, and the rest which it promises never comes.

III. The self-inflicted loss.

Our text suggests that there are two ways by which we may learn the folly of a godless life—One, the consideration of what it turns to, the other, the thought of what it departs from.

'They forsake their own Mercy,' that is God. The phrase is here almost equivalent to 'His name'; and it carries the blessed thought that He has entered into relations with every soul, so that each man of us—even if he have turned to 'lying vanities'—can still call Him, 'my own Mercy.' He is ours; more our own than is anything without us. He is ours, because we are made for Him, and He is all for us. He is ours by His love, and by His gift of Himself in the Son of His love. He is ours; if we take Him for ours by an inward communication of Himself to us in the innermost depths of our being. He becomes 'the Master-Light of all our seeing.' In the mysterious inwardness of mutual possession, the soul which has given itself to God and possesses Him, has not only communion, but may even venture to claim as its own the deeper and more mysterious *union* with God. Those multiform mercies, 'which endure for ever,' and speed on their manifold errands into every remotest region of His universe, gather themselves together, as the diffused lights of some nebulæ concentrate themselves into a sun. That sun, like the star that led the wise men from the East, and finally stood over one poor house in an obscure village, will shine lambent above, and will pass into, the humblest heart that opens for it. They who can say, as we all can if we will, 'My God,' can never want.

And if we turn to the alternative in our text, and consider who they are to whom we turn when we turn from God, there should be nothing more needed to drive home the wholesome conviction of the folly of the wisest, who deliberately prefers shadow to substance, lying vanities to the one true and only reality. I beseech you to take that which is your own, and which no man can take from you. Weigh in the scales of conscience, and in the light of the deepest necessities of your nature, the whole pile of those emptinesses that have been telling you lies ever since you listened to them; and place in the other scale the mercy of God, and the Christ who brings it to you, and decide which is the weightier, and which it becomes you to take for your pattern for ever.

THREEFOLD REPENTANCE

'And the word of the Lord came unto Jonah the second time, saying, 2. Arise, go unto Nineveh, that great city, and preach unto it the preaching that I bid thee. 3. So Jonah arose, and went unto Nineveh, according to the word of the Lord. Now Nineveh was an exceeding great city of three days' journey. 4. And Jonah began to enter into the city a day's journey, and he cried, and said, Yet forty days, and Nineveh shall be overthrown. 5. So the people of Nineveh believed God, and proclaimed a fast, and put on sackcloth, from the greatest of them even to the least of them. 6. For word came unto the king of Nineveh, and he arose from his throne, and he laid his robe from him, and covered him with sackcloth, and sat in ashes. 7. And he caused it to be proclaimed and published through Nineveh by the decree of the king and his nobles, saying, Let neither man nor beast, herd nor flock, taste anything; let them not feed, nor drink water: 8. But let man and beast be covered with sackcloth, and cry mightily unto God; yea, let them turn every one from his evil way, and from the violence that is in their hands. 9. Who can tell if God will turn and repent, and turn away from His fierce anger, that we perish not? 10. And God saw their works, that they turned from their evil way; and God repented of the evil, that He had said that He would do unto them; and He did it not.'—JONAH iii. 1-10.

THIS passage falls into three parts: Jonah's renewed commission and new obedience (vs. 1-4), the repentance of Nineveh (vs. 5-9), and the acceptance thereof by God (ver. 10). We might almost call these three the repentance of Jonah, of Nineveh, and of God. The evident intention of the narrative is to parallel the Ninevites turning from their sins, and God's turning from His anger and purpose of destruction; and if the word 'repentance' is not applied to Jonah, his conduct sufficiently shows the thing.

I. Note the renewed charge to the penitent Prophet, and his new eagerness to fulfil it. His deliverance and second commission are put as if all but simultaneous, and his obedience was swift and glad. Jonah did not venture to take for granted that the charge which he had shirked was still continued to him. If God commands to take the trumpet, and we refuse, we dare not assume that we shall still be honoured with the delivery of the message. The punishment of dumb lips is often dumbness. Opportunities of service, slothfully or faint-heartedly neglected, are often withdrawn. We can fancy how Jonah, brought back to the better mind which breathes in his psalm, longed to be honoured by the trust of preaching once more, and how rapturously his spirit would address itself to the task. Duties once unwelcome become sweet when we have passed through the experience of the misery that comes from neglecting them. It is God's mercy that gives us the opportunity of effacing past disobedience by new alacrity.

The second charge is possibly distinguishable from the first as being less precise. It may be that the exact nature of 'the preaching that I bid thee' was not told Jonah till he had to open his mouth in Nineveh; but, more probably, the second charge was identical with the first.

The word rendered 'preach' is instructive. It means 'to cry,' and suggests the manner befitting those who bear God's message. They should sound it out loudly, plainly, urgently, with earnestness and marks of emo-

tion in their voice. Languid whispers will not wake
sleepers. Unless the messenger is manifestly in earnest,
the message will fall flat. Not with bated breath, as if
ashamed of it; nor with hesitation, as if not quite sure
of it; nor with coldness, as if it were of little urgency,
—is God's Word to be pealed in men's ears. The
preacher is a crier. The substance of his message, too,
is set forth. 'The preaching which I bid thee'—not his
own imaginations, nor any fine things of his own
spinning. Suppose Jonah had entertained the Ninevites with dissertations on the evidences of his prophetic authority, or submitted for their consideration
a few thoughts tending to show the agreement of his
message with their current opinions in religion, or an
argument for the existence of a retributive Governor
of the world, he would not have shaken the city. The
less the Prophet shows himself, the stronger his influence. The more simply he repeats the stern, plain, short
message, the more likely it is to impress. God's Word,
faithfully set forth, will prove itself. The preacher or
teacher of this day has substantially the same charge
as Jonah had; and the more he suppresses himself,
and becomes but a voice through which God speaks,
the better for himself, his hearers, and his work.

Nineveh, that great aggregate of cities, was full, as
Eastern cities are, of open spaces, and might well be
a three days' journey in circumference. What a task
for that solitary stranger to thunder out his loud cry
among all these crowds! But he had learned to do
what he was bid; and without wasting a moment, he
'began to enter into the city a day's journey,' and, no
doubt, did not wait till the end of the day to proclaim
his message. Let us learn that there is an element of
threatening in God's most merciful message, and that

the appeal to terror and to the desire for self-preservation is part of the way to preach the Gospel. Plain
warnings of coming evil may be spoken tenderly, and
reveal love as truly as the most soothing words. The
warning comes in time. 'Forty days' of grace are
granted. The gospel warns us in time enough for
escape. It warns us because God loves; and they are
as untrue messengers of His love as of His justice who
slur over the declaration of His wrath.

II. Note the repentance of Nineveh (vs. 5-9). The
impression made by Jonah's terrible cry is perfectly
credible and natural in the excitable population of an
Eastern city, in which even now any appeal to terror,
especially if associated with religious and prophetic
claims, easily sets the whole in a frenzy. Think of the
grim figure of this foreign man, with his piercing voice
and half-intelligible speech, dropped from the clouds as
it were, and stalking through Nineveh, pealing out his
confident message, like that gaunt fanatic who walked
Jerusalem in its last agony, crying, 'Woe! woe unto
the bloody city!' or that other, who, with flaming fire
on his head and madness in his eyes, affrighted London
in the plague. No wonder that alarm was kindled, and,
being kindled, spread like wildfire. Apparently the
movement was first among the people, who began to
fast before the news penetrated to the seclusion of the
palace. But the contagion reached the king, and the
popular excitement was endorsed and fanned by a
royal decree. The specified tokens of repentance are
those of ordinary mourning, such as were common
all over the East, with only the strange addition, which
smacks of heathen ideas, that the animals were made
sharers in them.

There is great significance in that 'believed God'

(ver. 5). The foundation of all true repentance is crediting God's word of threatening, and therefore realising the danger, as well as the disobedience, of our sin. We shall be wise if we pass by the human instrument, and hear God speaking through the Prophet. Never mind about Jonah, believe God.

We learn from the Ninevites what is true repentance. They brought no sacrifices or offerings, but sorrow, self-abasement, and amendment. The characteristic sin of a great military power would be 'violence,' and that is the specific evil from which they vow to turn. The loftiest lesson which prophets found Israel so slow to learn, 'A broken and a contrite heart Thou wilt not despise,' was learned by these heathens. We need it no less. Nineveh repented on a peradventure that their repentance might avail. How pathetic that 'Who can tell?' (ver. 9) is! We *know* what they *hoped*. Their doubt might give fervour to their cries, but our certainty should give deeper earnestness and confidence to ours.

The deepest meaning of the whole narrative is set forth in our Lord's use of it, when He holds up the men of Nineveh as a condemnatory instance to the hardened consciences of His hearers. Probably the very purpose of the book was to show Israel that the despised and yet dreaded heathen were more susceptible to the voice of God than they were: 'I will provoke you to jealousy by them which are no people.' The story was a smiting blow to the proud exclusiveness and self-complacent contempt of prophetic warnings, which marked the entire history of God's people. As Ezekiel was told: 'Thou are not sent . . . to many peoples of a strange speech and of an hard language. . . . Surely, if I sent thee to them, they would hearken

N

unto thee. But the house of Israel will not hearken
unto thee.' It is ever true that long familiarity
with the solemn thoughts of God's judgment and
punishment of sin abates their impression on us. Our
Puritan forefathers used to talk about ' gospel-hardened
sinners,' and there are many such among us. The man
who lives by Niagara does not hear its roar as a stranger
does. The men of Nineveh will rise in the judgment
with other generations than that which was 'this
generation' in Christ's time; and that which is 'this
generation' to-day will, in many of its members, be
condemned by them.

But the wave of feeling soon retired, and there is no
reason to believe that more than a transient impression was made. It does not seem certain that the
Ninevites knew what 'God' they hoped to appease.
Probably their pantheon was undisturbed, and their
repentance lasted no longer than their fear. Transient
repentance leaves the heart harder than before, as half-
melted ice freezes again more dense. Let us beware
of frost on the back of a thaw. ' Repentance which is
repented of' is worse than none.

III. We note the repentance of God (ver. 10). Mark
the recurrence of the word 'turn,' employed in verses
8, 9, and 10 in reference to men and to God. Mark
the bold use of the word 'repent,' applied to God,
which, though it be not applied to the Ninevites in
the previous verses, is implied in every line of them.
The same expression is found in Exodus xxxii. 14,
which may be taken as the classical passage warrant-
ing its use. The great truth involved is one that is too
often lost sight of in dealing with prophecy; namely,
that all God's promises and threatenings are conditional. Jeremiah learned that lesson in the house of

the potter, and we need to keep it well in mind. God threatens, precisely in order that He may not have to perform His threatenings. Jonah was sent to Nineveh to cry, 'Yet forty days, and Nineveh shall be overthrown,' in order that it might not be overthrown. What would have been the use of proclaiming the decree, if it had been irreversible? There is an implied 'if' in all God's words. 'Except ye repent' underlies the most absolute threatenings of evil. 'If we hold fast the beginning of our confidence firm unto the end,' is presupposed in the brightest and broadest promises of good.

The word 'repent' is denied and affirmed to have application to God. He is not 'a son of man, that He should repent,' inasmuch as His immutability and steadfast purpose know no variableness. But just because they cannot change, and He must ever be against them that do evil, and ever bless them that turn to Him with trust, therefore He changes His dealings with us according to our relation to Him, and because He cannot repent, or be other than He was and is, 're-pents of the evil that He had said that He would do' unto sinners when they repent of the evil that they have done against Him, inasmuch as He leaves His threatening unfulfilled, and 'does it not.'

So we might almost say that the purpose of this book of Jonah is to teach the possibility and efficacy of repentance, and to show how the penitent man, heathen or Jew, ever finds in God changed dealings corresponding to his changed heart. The widest charity, the humbling lesson for people brought up in the blaze of revelation, that dwellers in the twilight or in the darkness are dear to God and may be more susceptible of divine impressions than ourselves, the rebuke of all pluming ourselves on our privileges, the boundlessness of God's mercy, are among the other lessons of this strange book; but none of them is more precious than its truly evangelic teaching of the blessedness of true penitence, whether exemplified in the renegade Prophet returning to his high mission, or the fierce Ninevites humbled and repentant, and finding mercy from the God of the whole earth.

MICAH

IS THE SPIRIT OF THE LORD STRAITENED?

'O thou that art named the house of Jacob, is the Spirit of the Lord straitened? Are these His doings?'—MICAH ii. 7.

THE greater part of so-called Christendom is to-day[1] celebrating the gift of a Divine Spirit to the Church; but it may well be asked whether the religious condition of so-called Christendom is not a sad satire upon Pentecost. There seems a woful contrast, very perplexing to faith, between the bright promise at the beginning and the history of the development in the future. How few of those who share in to-day's services have any personal experience of such a gift! How many seem to think that that old story is only the record of a past event, a transient miracle which has no kind of relation to the experience of the Christians of this day! There were a handful of believers in one of the towns of Asia Minor, to whom an Apostle came, and was so startled at their condition that he put to them in wonder the question that might well be put to multitudes of so-called Christians amongst us: 'Did you receive the Holy Ghost when you believed?' And their answer is only too true a transcript of the experience of large masses of people who call themselves Christians: 'We have not so much as heard whether there be any Holy Ghost.'

I desire, then, dear brethren, to avail myself of this

[1] Whitsunday.

197

day's associations in order to press upon your consciences and upon my own some considerations naturally suggested by them, and which find voice in these
two indignant questions of the old Prophet:—' Is the
Spirit of the Lord straitened?' 'Are these'—the phenomena of existing popular Christianity—'are these His
doings?' And if we are brought sharp up against the
consciousness of a dreadful contrast, it may do us good
to ask what is the explanation of so cloudy a day
following a morning so bright.

I. First, then, I have to ask you to think with me of
the promise of the Pentecost.

What did it declare and hold forth for the faith of
the Church? I need not dwell at any length upon
this point. The facts are familiar to you, and the inferences drawn from them are commonplace and
known to us all. But let me just enumerate them
as briefly as may be.

'Suddenly there came a sound, as of the rushing of
a mighty wind, and it filled all the house where they
were sitting. And there appeared cloven tongues as of
fire, and it sat upon each of them; and they were all
filled with the Holy Ghost.'

What lay in that? First, the promise of a Divine
Spirit by symbols which express some, at all events, of
the characteristics and wonderfulness of His work.
The 'rushing of a mighty wind' spoke of a power
which varies in its manifestations from the gentlest
breath that scarce moves the leaves on the summer
trees to the wildest blast that casts down all which
stands in its way.

The natural symbolism of the wind, to popular apprehension the least material of all material forces, and
of which the connection with the immaterial part of a

man's personality has been expressed in all languages, points to a divine, to an immaterial, to a mighty, to a life-giving power which is free to blow whither it listeth, and of which men can mark the effects, though they are all ignorant of the force itself.

The other symbol of the fiery tongues which parted and sat upon each of them speaks in like manner of the divine influence, not as destructive, but full of quick, rejoicing energy and life, the power to transform and to purify. Whithersoever the fire comes, it changes all things into its own substance. Whithersoever the fire comes, there the ruddy spires shoot upwards towards the heavens. Whithersoever the fire comes, there all bonds and fetters are melted and consumed. And so this fire transforms, purifies, ennobles, quickens, sets free ; and where the fiery Spirit is, there are energy, swift life, rejoicing activity, transforming and transmuting power which changes the recipient of the flame into flame himself.

Then, still further, in the fact of Pentecost there is the promise of a Divine Spirit which is to influence all the moral side of humanity. This is the great and glorious distinction between the Christian doctrine of inspiration and all others which have, in heathen lands, partially reached similar conceptions—that the Gospel of Jesus Christ has laid emphasis upon the *Holy* Spirit, and has declared that holiness of heart is the touchstone and test of all claims of divine inspiration. Gifts are much, graces are more. An inspiration which makes wise is to be coveted, an inspiration which makes holy is transcendently better. There we find the safeguard against all the fanaticisms which have sometimes invaded the Christian Church, namely, in the thought that the Spirit which dwells in men, and makes them free from the obligations of outward law and cold morality, is a Spirit that works a deeper holiness than law dreamed, and a more spontaneous and glad conformity to all things that are fair and good, than any legislation and outward commandment could ever enforce. The Spirit that came at Pentecost is not merely a Spirit of rushing might and of swift-flaming energy, but it is a Spirit of holiness, whose most blessed and intimate work is the production in us of all homely virtues and sweet, unpretending goodnesses which can adorn and gladden humanity.

Still further, the Pentecost carried in it the promise and prophecy of a Spirit granted to all the Church. 'They were all filled with the Holy Ghost.' This is the true democracy of Christianity, that its very basis is laid in the thought that every member of the body is equally close to the Head, and equally recipient of the life. There is none now who has a Spirit which others do not possess. The ancient aspiration of the Jewish law-giver: 'Would God that all the Lord's people were prophets, and that the Lord would put His Spirit upon them,' is fulfilled in the experience of Pentecost; and the handmaiden and the children, as well as the old men and the servants, receive of that universal gift. Therefore sacerdotal claims, special functions, privileged classes, are alien to the spirit of Christianity, and blasphemies against the inspiring God. If 'one is your Master, all ye are brethren,' and if we have all been made to drink into one Spirit, then no longer hath any man dominion over our faith nor power to intervene and to intercede with God for us.

And still further, the promise of this early history

was that of a Spirit which should fill the whole
nature of the men to whom He was granted; filling—
in the measure, of course, of their receptivity—them
as the great sea does all the creeks and indentations
along the shore. The deeper the creek, the deeper the
water in it; the further inland it runs, the further
will the refreshing tide penetrate the bosom of the
continent. And so each man, according to his character, stature, circumstances, and all the varying conditions which determine his power of receptivity, will
receive a varying measure of that gift. Yet it is
meant that all shall be full. The little vessel, the tiny
cup, as well as the great cistern and the enormous vat,
each contains according to its capacity. And if all are
filled, then this quick Spirit must have the power to
influence all the provinces of human nature, must
touch the moral, must touch the spiritual. The tem-
porary manifestations and extraordinary signs of His
power may well drop away as the flower drops when
the fruit has set. The operations of the Divine Spirit
are to be felt thrilling through all the nature, and
every part of the man's being is to be recipient of the
power. Just as when you take a candle and plunge it
into a jar of oxygen it blazes up, so my poor human
nature immersed in that Divine Spirit, baptized in
the Holy Ghost, shall flame in all its parts into un-
suspected and hitherto inexperienced brightness. Such
are the elements of the promise of Pentecost.

II. And now, in the next place, look at the apparent
failure of the promise.

'Is the Spirit of the Lord straitened?' Look at
Christendom. Look at all the churches. Look at
yourselves. Will any one say that the religious condition of any body of professed believers at this

moment corresponds to Pentecost? Is not the gap so
wide that to fill it up seems almost impossible? Is
not the stained and imperfect fulfilment a miserable
satire upon the promise? 'If the Lord be with us,'
said one of the heroes of ancient Israel, 'wherefore
is all this come upon us?' I am sure that we may
say the same. If the Lord be with us, what is the
meaning of the state of things which we see around
us, and must recognise in ourselves? Do any existing churches present the final perfect form of Christianity as embodied in a society? Would not the best
thing that could happen, and the thing that will have
to happen some day, be the disintegration of the
existing organisations in order to build up a more
perfect habitation of God through the Spirit? I do
not wish to exaggerate. God knows there is no need
for exaggerating. The plain, unvarnished story, without any pessimistic picking out of the black bits and
forgetting all the light ones, is bad enough.

Take three points on which I do not dwell and apply
them to yourselves, dear brethren, and estimate by
them the condition of things around us. First, say
whether the ordinary tenor of our own religious life
looks as if we had that Divine Spirit in us which
transforms everything into its own beauty, and
makes men, through all the regions of their nature,
holy and pure. Then ask yourselves the question
whether the standard of devotion and consecration in
any church witnesses of the presence of a Divine
Spirit. A little handful of people, the best of them
very partially touched with the life of God, and very
imperfectly consecrated to His service, surrounded by
a great mass about whom we can scarcely, in the
judgment of charity, say even so much, that is the

description of most of our congregations. 'Are these His doings?' Surely somebody else's than His.

Take another question. Do the relations of modern Christians and their churches to one another attest the presence of a unifying Spirit? 'We have all been made to drink into one Spirit,' said Paul. Alas, alas! does it seem as if *we* had? Look round professing Christendom, look at the rivalries and the jealousies between two chapels in adjoining streets. Look at the gulfs between Christian men who differ only on some comparative trifle of organisation and polity, and say if such things correspond to the Pentecostal promise of one Spirit which is to make all the members into one body? 'Is the Spirit of the Lord straitened? Are these *His* doings?'

Take another branch of evidence. Look at the comparative impotence of the Church in its conflict with the growing worldliness of the world. I do not forget how much is being done all about us to-day, and how still Christ's Gospel is winning triumphs, but I do not suppose that any man can look thoughtfully and dispassionately on the condition, say, for instance, of Manchester, or of any of our great towns, and mark how the populace knows nothing and cares nothing about us and our Christianity, and never comes into our places of worship, and has no share in our hopes any more than if they lived in Central Africa, and that after eighteen hundred years of nominal Christianity, without feeling that some malign influence has arrested the leaping growth of the early Church, and that somehow or other that lava stream, if I might so call it, which poured hot from the heart of God in the old days has had its flow checked, and over its burning bed there has spread a black and wrinkled crust, whatso-

ever lingering heat there may still be at the centre.
'If God be with us, why has all this come upon us?'

III. And now, lastly, let us think for a moment of
the solution of the contradiction.

The indignant questions of my text may be taken,
with a little possibly permissible violence, as expressing and dismissing some untrue explanations. One
explanation that sometimes is urged is, the Spirit of
the Lord *is* straitened. That explanation takes two
forms. Sometimes you hear people saying, 'Christianity is effete. We have to go now to fresh fountains
of inspiration, and turn away from these broken
cisterns that can hold no water.' I am not going to
argue that question. I do not think for my part that
Christianity will be effete until the world has got up
to it and beyond it in its practice, and it will be a good
while before that happens. Christianity will not be
worn out until men have copied and reduced to practice
the example of Jesus Christ, and they have not quite
got that length yet. No shadow of a fear that the
gospel has lost its power, or that God's Spirit has
become weak, should be permitted to creep over our
hearts. The promise is, 'I will send another Com-
forter, and He shall abide with you *for ever.*' It is a
permanent gift that was given to the Church on that
day. We have to distinguish in the story between the
symbols, the gift, and the consequences of the gift.
The first and the last are transient, the second is permanent. The symbols were transient. The people
who came running together saw no tongues of fire.
The consequences were transient. The tongues and
the miraculous utterances were but for a time. The
results vary according to the circumstances; but the
central thing, the gift itself, is an irrevocable gift,

and once bestowed is ever with the Church to all
generations.

Another form of the explanation is the theory that
God in His sovereignty is pleased to withhold His Spirit
for reasons which we cannot trace. But it is not true
that the gift once given varies in the degree in which
it is continued. There is always the same flow from
God. There are ebbs and flows in the spiritual power
of the Church. Yes! and the tide runs out of your
harbours. Is there any less water in the sea because
it does? So the gift may ebb away from a man, from
a community, from an epoch, not because God's manifestation and bestowment fluctuate, but because our
receptivity changes. So we dismiss, and are bound to
dismiss, if we are Christians, the unbelieving explanation, 'The Spirit of the Lord *is* straitened,' and not to
sit with our hands folded, as if an inscrutable sovereignty, with which we have nothing to do, sometimes
sent more and sometimes less of His spiritual gifts
upon a waiting Church. It is not so. 'With Him is
no variableness.' The gifts of God are without repentance; and the Spirit that was given once, according to
the Master's own word already quoted, is given that
He may abide with us for ever.

Therefore we have to come back to this, which is
the point to which I seek to bring you and myself, in
lowly penitence and contrite acknowledgment—that it
is all our own fault and the result of evils in ourselves
that may be remedied, that we have so little of that
divine gift; and that if the churches of this country
and of this day seem to be cursed and blasted in so
much of their fruitless operations and formal worship,
it is the fault of the churches, and not of the Lord of
the churches. The stream that poured forth from the

throne of God has not lost itself in the sands, nor is it
shrunken in its volume. The fire that was kindled on
Pentecost has not died down into grey ashes. The
rushing of the mighty wind that woke on that morning has not calmed and stilled itself into the stagnancy
and suffocating breathlessness of midday heat. The
same fulness of the Spirit which filled the believers on
that day is available for us all. If, like that waiting
Church of old, we abide in prayer and supplication,
the gift will be given to us too, and we may repeat and
reproduce, if not the miracles which we do not need,
yet the necessary inspiration of the highest and the
noblest days and saints in the history of the Church.
'If ye, being evil, know how to give good gifts to your
children, how much more will your Heavenly Father
give the Holy Spirit to them that ask Him?' 'Ask
and ye shall receive,' and be filled 'with the Holy Ghost
and with power.'

CHRIST THE BREAKER

'The Breaker is come up before them: they have broken up, and have passed
through the gate, and are gone out by it: and their king shall pass before them,
and the Lord on the head of them.'—MICAH ii. 13.

MICAH was contemporary with Isaiah. The two
prophets stand, to a large extent, on the same level
of prophetic knowledge. Characteristic of both of
them is the increasing clearness of the figure of the
personal Messiah, and the increasing fulness of detail
with which His functions are described. Characteristic
of both of them is the presentation which we find in
this text of that Messiah's work as being the gathering
together of the scattered captive people and the leading
them back in triumph into the blessed land.

Such is the image which underlies my text. Of course I have nothing to do now with questions as to any narrower and nearer historical fulfilment, because I believe that all these Messianic prophecies which were susceptible of, and many of which obtained, a historical and approximate fulfilment in the restoration of the Jews from the Babylonish captivity, have a higher and broader and more real accomplishment in that great deliverance wrought by Jesus Christ, of which all these earlier and partial and outward manifestations were themselves prophecies and shadows.

So I make no apology for taking the words before us as having their only real accomplishment in the office and working of Jesus Christ. He is 'the Breaker which is come up before us.' He it is that has broken out the path on which we may travel, and in whom, in a manner which the Prophet dreamed not of, 'the Lord is at the head' of us, and our King goes before us. So that my object is simply to take that great name, the Breaker, and to see the manifold ways in which in Scripture it is applied to the various work of Jesus Christ in our redemption.

I. I follow entirely the lead of corresponding passages in other portions of Scripture, and to begin with, I ask you to think of that great work of our Divine Redeemer by which He has broken for the captives the prison-house of their bondage.

The image that is here before us is either that of some foreign land in which the scattered exiles were bound in iron captivity, or more probably some dark and gloomy prison, with high walls, massive gates, and barred windows, wherein they were held; and to them sitting hopeless in the shadow of death, and bound in affliction and iron, there comes one mysterious figure whom the Prophet could not describe more particularly, and at His coming the gates flew apart, and the chains dropped from their hands; and the captives had heart put into them, and gathering themselves together into a triumphant band, they went out with songs and ever-lasting joy upon their heads; freemen, and on the march to the home of their fathers. 'The Breaker is gone up before them; they have broken, and passed through the gate, and are gone out by it.'

And is not that our condition? Many of us know not the bondage in which we are held. We are held in it all the more really and sadly because we conceit ourselves to be free. Those poor, light-hearted people in the dreadful days of the French Revolution, used to keep up some ghastly mockery of society and cheerful-ness in their prisons; and festooned the bars with flowers, and made believe to be carrying on their life freely as they used to do; but for all that, day after day the tumbrils came to the gates, and morning after morning the jailer stood at the door of the dungeons with the fatal list in his hand, and one after another of the triflers was dragged away to death. And so men and women are living a life which they fancy is free, and all the while they are in bondage, held in a prison-house. You, my brother! are chained by guilt; you are chained by sin, you are chained by the habit of evil with a strength of which you never know till you try to shake it off.

And there comes to each of us a mighty Deliverer, who breaks the gates of brass, and who cuts the bars of iron in sunder. Christ comes to us. By His death He has borne away the guilt; by His living Spirit He will bear away the dominion of sin from our hearts; and if the Son will make us free we shall be free indeed.

Oh! ponder that deep truth, I pray you, which the Lord Christ has spoken in words that carry conviction in their very simplicity to every conscience: 'He that committeth sin is the slave of sin.' And as you feel sometimes—and you all feel sometimes—the catch of the fetter on your wrists when you would fain stretch out your hands to good, listen as to a true gospel to this old word which, in its picturesque imagery, carries a truth that should be life. To us all 'the Breaker is gone up before us,' the prison gates are open. Follow His steps, and take the freedom which He gives; and be sure that you 'stand fast in the liberty wherewith Christ hath made you free, and be not entangled again with any yoke of bondage.'

Men and women! Some of you are the slaves of your own lusts. Some of you are the slaves of the world's maxims. Some of you are held in bondage by some habit that you abominate, but cannot get away from. Here is freedom for you. The dark walls of the prison are round us all. 'The Scripture hath shut up all in sin, that He might have mercy upon all.' Blessed be His name! As the angel came to the sleeping Apostle, and to his light touch the iron gates swung obedient on their hinges, and Roman soldiers who ought to have watched their prey were lulled to sleep, and fetters that held the limbs dropped as if melted; so, silently, in His meek and merciful strength, the Christ comes to us all, and the iron gate which leadeth out into freedom opens of its own accord at His touch, and the fetters fall from our limbs, and we go forth free men. 'The Breaker is gone up before us.'

II. Again, take another application of this same figure found in Scripture, which sets forth Jesus Christ as being the Opener of the path to God.

o

'I am the Way and the Truth and the Life, no man cometh to the Father but by Me,' said He. And again, 'By a new and living way which He hath opened for us through the veil' (that is to say, His flesh), we can have free access 'with confidence by the faith of Him.' That is to say, if we rightly understand our natural condition, it is not only one of bondage to evil, but it is one of separation from God. Parts of the divine character are always beautiful and sweet to every human heart when it thinks about them. Parts of the divine character stand frowning before a man who knows himself for what he is; and conscience tells us that between God and us there is a mountain of impediment piled up by our own evil. To us Christ comes, the Path-finder and the Path; the Pioneer who breaks the way for us through all the hindrances, and leads us up to the presence of God.

For we do not know God as He is except by Jesus Christ. We see fragments, and often distorted fragments, of the divine nature and character apart from Jesus, but the real divine nature as it is, and as it is in its relation to me, a sinner, is only made known to me in the face of Jesus Christ. When we see Him we see God; Christ's tears are God's pity, Christ's gentleness is God's meekness, Christ's tender, drawing love is not only a revelation of a most pure and sweet Brother's heart, but a manifestation through that Brother's heart of the deepest depths of the divine nature. Christ is the heart of God. Apart from Him, we come to the God of our own consciences and we tremble; we come to the God of our own fancies and we presume; we come to the God dimly guessed at and pieced together from out of the hints and indications of His works, and He is little more than a dead name to us. Apart from

Christ we come to a peradventure which we call a God; a shadow through which you can see the stars shining. But we know the Father when we believe in Christ. And so all the clouds rising from our own hearts and consciences and fancies and misconceptions, which we have piled together between God and ourselves, Christ clears away; and thus He opens the path to God.

And He opens it in another way too, on which I cannot dwell. It is only the God manifest in Jesus Christ that draws men's hearts to Him. The attractive power of the divine nature is all in Him who has said, 'I, if I be lifted up, will draw all men unto Me.' The God whom men know, or think they know, outside of the revelation of divinity in Jesus Christ, is a God before whom they sometimes tremble, who is far more often their terror than their love, who is their 'ghastliest doubt' still more frequently than He is their 'dearest faith.' But the God that is in Christ woos and wins men to Him, and from His great sweetness there streams out, as it were, a magnetic influence that draws hearts to Him. The God that is in Christ is the only God that humanity ever loved. Other gods they may have worshipped with cowering terror and with far-off lip reverence, but this God has a heart, and wins hearts because He has. So Christ opens the way to Him.

And still further, in a yet higher fashion, that Saviour is the Path-breaker to the Divine Presence, in that He not only makes God known to us, and not only makes Him so known to us as to draw us to Him, but in that likewise He, by the fact of His Cross and passion, has borne and borne away the impediments of our own sin and transgression which rise for ever between us and Him, unless He shall sweep them out

of the way. He has made 'the rough places plain and
the crooked things straight'; levelled the mountains
and raised the valleys, and cast up across all the
wilderness of the world a highway along which 'the
wayfaring man though a fool' may travel. Narrow
understandings may know, and selfish hearts may love,
and low-pitched confessions may reach the ear of the
God who comes near to us in Christ, that we in Christ
may come near to Him. The Breaker is gone up before
us ; 'having therefore, brethren, boldness to enter into
the holiest of all . . . by a new and living way, which
He hath consecrated for us . . . let us draw near with
true hearts.'

III. Then still further, another modification of this
figure is found in the frequent representations of
Scripture, by which our Lord is the Breaker, going up
before us in the sense that He is the Captain of our
life's march.

We have, in the words of my text, the image of the
gladly-gathered people flocking after the Leader. 'They
have broken up, and have passed through the gate, and
are gone out by it; and their King shall pass before
them, and the Lord on the head of them.' The Prophet
knew not that the Lord their King, of whom it is
enigmatically said that He too, as well as 'the Breaker,'
is to go before them, was in mysterious fashion to
dwell in that Breaker ; and that those two, whom He
sees separately, are yet in a deep and mysterious sense
one. The host of the captives, returning in triumphant
march through the wilderness and to the promised
land, is, in the Prophet's words, headed both by the
Breaker and by the Lord. We know that the Breaker
is the Lord, the Angel of the Covenant in whom is the
name of Jehovah.

And so we connect with all these words of my text such words as designate our Saviour as the Captain of our salvation; such words as His own in which He says, 'When He putteth forth His sheep He goeth before them'—such words as His Apostle used when he said, 'Leaving us an ensample that we should follow in His steps.' And by all there is suggested this—that Christ, who breaks the prison of our sins, and leads us forth on the path to God, marches at the head of our life's journey, and is our Example and Commander; and Himself present with us through all life's changes and its sorrows.

Here is the great blessing and peculiarity of Christian morals that they are all brought down to that sweet obligation: 'Do as I did.' Here is the great blessing and strength for the Christian life in all its difficulties —you can never go where you cannot see in the desert the footprints, haply spotted with blood, that your Master left there before you, and planting your trembling feet in the prints, as a child might imitate his father's strides, may learn to recognise that all duty comes to this: 'Follow Me'; and that all sorrow is calmed, ennobled, made tolerable, and glorified, by the thought that He has borne it.

The Roman matron of the legend struck the knife into her bosom, and handed it to her husband with the words, 'It is not painful!' Christ has gone before us in all the dreary solitude, and in all the agony and pains of life. He has hallowed them all, and has taken the bitterness and the pain out of each of them for them that love Him. If we feel that the Breaker is before us, and that we are marching behind Him, then whithersoever He leads us we may follow, and whatsoever He has passed through we may pass through

We carry in His life the all-sufficing pattern of duty.
We have in His companionship the all-strengthening
consolation. Let us leave the direction of our road in
His hands, who never says 'Go!' but always 'Come!'
This General marches in the midst of His battalions
and sets His soldiers on no enterprises or forlorn hopes
which He has not Himself dared and overcome.

So Christ goes as our Companion before us, the true
pillar of fire and cloud in which the present Deity abode,
and He is with us in real companionship. Our joyful
march through the wilderness is directed, patterned,
protected, companioned by Him, and when He 'putteth
forth His own sheep,' blessed be His name, 'He goeth
before them.'

IV. And now, lastly, there is a final application of
this figure which sets forth our Lord as the Breaker for
us of the bands of death, and the Forerunner 'entered
for us into the heavens.'

Christ's resurrection is the only solid proof of a future
life. Christ's present resurrection life is the power by
partaking in which, 'though we were dead, yet shall
we live.'

He has trodden that path, too, before us. He has
entered into the great prison-house into which the
generations of men have been hounded and hurried;
and where they lie in their graves, as in their narrow
cells. He has entered there; with one blow He has
struck the gates from their hinges, and has passed out,
and no soul can any longer be shut in as for ever into
that ruined and opened prison. Like Samson, He has
taken the gates which from of old barred its entrance,
and borne them on His strong shoulders to the city
on the hill, and now Death's darts are blunted, his
fetters are broken, and his gaol has its doors wide

open, and there is nothing for him to do now but to fall upon his sword and to kill himself, for his prisoners are free. 'Oh, death! I will be thy plague; oh, grave! I will be thy destruction.' 'The Breaker has gone up before us'; therefore it is not possible that we should be holden of the impotent chains that He has broken.

The Forerunner is for us entered and passed through the heavens, and entered into the holiest of all. We are too closely knit to Him, if we love Him and trust Him, to make it possible that we shall be where He is not, or that He shall be where we are not. Where He has gone we shall go. In heaven, blessed be His name! He will still be the leader of our progress and the captain at the head of our march. For He crowns all His other work by this, that having broken the prison-house of our sins, and opened for us the way to God, and been the leader and the captain of our march through all the pilgrimage of life, and the opener of the gate of the grave for our joyful resurrection, and the opener of the gate of heaven for our triumphal entrance, He will still as the Lamb that is in the midst of the Throne, go before us, and lead us into green pastures and by the still waters, and this shall be the description of the growing blessedness and power of the saints' life above, 'These are they which follow the Lamb whithersoever He goeth.'

AS GOD, SO WORSHIPPER

'. . . All the peoples will walk every one in the name of his god, and we will walk in the name of the Lord our God for ever and ever.'—MICAH iv. 5 (R.V.).

THIS is a statement of a general truth which holds good of all sorts of religion. 'To walk' is equivalent to carrying on a course of practical activity. 'The name'

of a god is his manifested character. So the expression
'Walk in the name' means, to live and act according to,
and with reference to, and in reliance on, the character
of the worshipper's god. In the Lord's prayer the
petition 'Hallowed be Thy name' precedes the petition
'Thy will be done.' From reverent thoughts about the
name must flow life in reverent conformity to the will.

I. A man's god is what rules his practical life.

Religion is dependence upon a Being recognised to be
perfect and sovereign, whose will guides, and whose
character moulds, the whole life. That general statement may be broken up into parts; and we may dwell
upon the attitude of dependence, or of that of submission, or upon that of admiration and recognition of
ideal perfection, or upon that of aspiration; but we
come at last to the one thought—that the goal of
religion is likeness and the truest worship is imitation.
Such a view of the essence of religion gives point to the
question, What is our god? and makes it a very
easily applied, and very searching test, of our lives.
Whatever we profess, that which we feel ourselves
dependent on, that which we invest, erroneously or
rightly, with supreme attributes of excellence, that
which we aspire after as our highest good, that which
shapes and orders the current of our lives, is our god.
We call ourselves Christians. I am afraid that if we
tried ourselves by such a test, many of us would fail to
pass it. It would thin the ranks of all churches as
effectually as did Gideon's ordeal by water, which
brought down a mob of ten thousand to a little steadfast band of three hundred. No matter to what church
we belong, or how flaming our professions, our practical
religion is determined by our answer to the question,
What do we most desire? What do we most eagerly

pursue? England has as much need as ever the house
of Jacob had of the scathing words that poured like
molten lead from the lips of Isaiah the son of Amoz,
'Their land is full of silver and gold, neither is there
any end of their treasures. Their land is also full of
idols: they worship the work of their own hands.'
Money, knowledge, the good opinion of our fellows,
success in a political career—these, and the like, are
our gods. There is a worse idolatry than that which
bows down before stocks and stones. The aims
that absorb us; our highest ideal of excellence; that
which possessed, we think would secure our blessedness; that lacking which everything else is insipid and
vain—these are our gods: and the solemn prohibition
may well be thundered in the ears of the unconscious
idolaters not only in the English world, but also in the
English churches. 'Thou shalt not give My glory to
another, nor My praise to graven images.'

II. The worshipper will resemble his god in character.

As we have already said, the goal of religion is likeness, and the truest worship is imitation. It is proved
by the universal experience of humanity that the level
of morality will never rise above the type enshrined in
their gods; or if it does, in consequence of contact with
a higher type in a higher religion, the old gods will be
flung to the moles and the bats. 'They that make them
are like unto them; so is every one that trusteth in
them.' That is a universal truth. The worshippers
were in the Prophet's thought as dumb and dead as the
idols. They who 'worship vanity' inevitably 'become
vain.' A Venus or a Jupiter, a Baal or an Ashtoreth,
sets the tone of morals.

This truth is abundantly enforced by observation of
the characters of the men amongst us who are practical

idolaters. They are narrowed and lowered to correspond with their gods. Low ideals can never lead to lofty lives. The worship of money makes the complexion yellow, like jaundice. A man who concentrates his life's effort upon some earthly good, the attainment of which seems to be, so long as it is unattained, his passport to bliss, thereby blunts many a finer aspiration, and makes himself blind to many a nobler vision. Men who are always hunting after some paltry and perishable earthly good, become like dogs who follow scent with their noses at the ground, and are unconscious of everything a yard above their heads. We who live amidst the rush of a great commercial community see many instances of lives stiffened, narrowed, impoverished, and hardened by the fierce effort to become rich. And wherever we look with adequate knowledge over the many idolatries of English life, we see similar processes at work on character. Everywhere around us 'the peoples are walking every one in the name of his god.' That character constitutes the worshipper's ideal; it is a pattern to which he aims to be assimilated; it is a good the possession of which he thinks will make him blessed; it is that for which he willingly sacrifices much which a clearer vision would teach him is far more precious than that for which he is content to barter it.

The idolaters walking in the name of their god is a rebuke to the Christian men who with faltering steps and many an aberration are seeking to walk in the name of the Lord their God. If He is in any real and deep sense 'our God,' we shall see in Him the realised ideal of all excellence, the fountain of all our blessedness, the supreme good for our seeking hearts, the sovereign authority to sway our wills; the measure of our conscious possession of Him will be the measure of our glad imitation of Him, and our joyful spirits, enfranchised by the assurance of our loving possession of Him who is love, will hear Him ever whisper to us, 'Be ye perfect as your Father which is in heaven is perfect.' The desire to reproduce in the narrow bounds of our human spirits the infinite beauties of the Lord our God will give elevation to our lives, and dignity to our actions attainable from no other source. If we hallow His name, we shall do His will, and earth will become a foretaste of heaven.

III. The worshipper will resemble his god in fate.

We may observe that it is only of God's people that Micah in our text applies the words 'for ever and ever.' 'The peoples'' worship perishes. They walk for a time in the name of their god, but what comes of it at last is veiled in silence. It is Jehovah's worshippers who walk in His name for ever and ever, and of whom the great words are true, 'Because I live ye shall live also.' We may be sure of this that all the divine attributes are pledged for our immortality; we may be sure, too, that a soul which here follows in the footsteps of Jesus, which in its earthly life walked in the name of the Lord its God, will continue across the narrow bridge, and go onward 'for ever and ever' in direct progress in the same direction in which it began on earth. The imitation, which is the practical religion of every Christian, has for its only possible result the climax of likeness. The partial likeness is attained on earth by contemplation, by aspiration, and by effort; but it is perfected in the heavens by the perfect vision of His perfect face. 'We shall be like Him, for we shall see Him as He is.' Not till it has reached its goal can the Christian life begun here be conceived as ended. It shall never be said of any one who tried by God's help to walk 'in the name of the Lord' that he was lost in the desert, and never reached his journey's end. The peoples who walked in the name of any false god will find their path ending as on the edge of a precipice, or in an unfathomable bog; loss, and woe, and shame will be their portion. But 'the name of the Lord is a strong tower,' into which whoever will may run and be safe, and to walk in the name of the Lord is to walk on a way 'that shall be called the Way of Holiness, whereon no ravenous beast shall go up, but the redeemed shall walk there,' and all that are on it 'shall come with singing to Zion, and everlasting joy shall be upon their heads.'

'A DEW FROM THE LORD'

'The remnant of Jacob shall be in the midst of many people as a dew from the Lord, that tarrieth not for man, nor waiteth for the sons of men.'—MICAH v. 7.

THE simple natural science of the Hebrews saw a mystery in the production of the dew on a clear night, and their poetic imagination found in it a fit symbol for all silent and gentle influences from heaven that refreshed and quickened parched and dusty souls. Created by an inscrutable process in silence and darkness, the dewdrops lay innumerable on the dry plains and hung from every leaf and thorn, each little globule a perfect sphere that reflected the sun, and twinkled back the beams in its own little rainbow. Where they fell the scorched vegetation lifted its drooping head. That is what Israel is to be in the world, says Micah. He saw very deep into God's mind and into the function of the nation.

It may be a question as to whether the text refers

more especially to the place and office of Israel when planted in its own land, or when dispersed among the nations. For, as you see, he speaks of 'the remnant of Jacob' as if he was thinking of the survivors of some great calamity which had swept away the greater portion of the nation. Both things are true. When settled in its own land, Israel's office was to teach the nations God; when dispersed among the Gentiles, its office ought to have been the same. But be that as it may, the conception here set forth is as true to-day as ever it was. For the prophetic teachings, rooted though they may be in the transitory circumstances of a tiny nation, are 'not for an age, but for all time,' and we get a great deal nearer the heart of them when we grasp the permanent truths that underlie them, than when we learnedly exhume the dead history which was their occasion.

Micah's message comes to all Christians, and very eminently to English Christians. The subject of Christian missions is before us to-day, and some thoughts in the line of this great text may not be inappropriate.

We have here, then,

I. The function of each Christian in his place.

'The remnant of Jacob shall be as a dew from the Lord in the midst of many nations.' What made Israel 'as a dew'? One thing only; its religion, its knowledge of God, and its consequent purer morality. It could teach Greece no philosophy, no art, no refinement, no sensitiveness to the beautiful. It could teach Rome no lessons of policy or government. It could bring no wisdom to Egypt, no power or wealth to Assyria. But God lit His candle and set it on a candlestick, that it 'might give light to all that were in the house.' The

same thing is true about Christian people. We cannot
teach the world science, we cannot teach it philosophy
or art, but we can teach it God. Now the possibility
brings with it the obligation. The personal experience
of Jesus Christ in our hearts, as the dew that brings to
us life and fertility, carries with it a commission as
distinct and imperative as if it had been pealed into
each single ear by a voice from heaven. That which
made Israel the 'dew amidst many nations,' parched for
want of it, makes Christian men and women fit to fill
the analogous office, and calls upon them to discharge
the same functions. For—in regard to all our possessions, and therefore most eminently and imperatively
in regard to the best—that which we have, we have as
stewards, and the Gospel, as the Apostle found, was
not only given to him for his own individual enjoy-
ment, elevation, ennobling, emancipation, salvation,
but was 'committed to his charge,' and he was
'entrusted' with it, as he says, as a sacred deposit.

Remember, too, that, strange as it may seem, the
only way by which that knowledge of God which was
bestowed upon Israel could become the possession of
the world was by its first of all being made the possession of a few. People talk about the unfairness, the
harshness, of the providential arrangement by which
the whole world was not made participant of the
revelation which was granted to Israel. The fire is
gathered on to a hearth. Does that mean that the
corners of the room are left uncared for? No! the
brazier is in the middle—as Palestine was, even geo-
graphically in the centre of the then civilised world—
that from the centre the beneficent warmth might
radiate and give heat as well as light to 'all them that
are in the house.'

So it is in regard to all the great possessions of the race. Art, literature, science, political wisdom, they are all intrusted to a few who are made their apostles; and the purpose is their universal diffusion from these human centres. It is in the line of the analogy of all the other gifts of God to humanity, that chosen men should be raised up in whom the life is lodged, that it may be diffused.

So to us the message comes: 'The Lord hath need of thee.' Christ has died; the Cross is the world's redemption. Christ lives that He may apply the power and the benefits of His death and of His risen life to all humanity. But the missing link between the all-sufficient redemption that is in Christ Jesus, and the actual redemption of the world, is 'the remnant of Jacob,' the Christian Church which is to be 'in the midst of many people, as a dew from the Lord.'

Now, that diffusion from individual centres of the life that is in Jesus Christ is the chiefest reason—or at all events, is one chief reason—for the strange and inextricable intertwining in modern society, of saint and sinner, of Christian and non-Christian. The seed is sown among the thorns; the wheat springs up amongst the tares. Their roots are so matted together that no hand can separate them. In families, in professions, in business relations, in civil life, in national life, both grow together. God sows His seed thin that all the field may smile in harvest. The salt is broken up into many minute particles and rubbed into that which it is to preserve from corruption. The remnant of Jacob is in the *midst* of many peoples; and you and I are encompassed by those who need our Christ, and who do not know Him or love Him; and one great reason for the close intertwining is that, scattered, we may diffuse,

and that at all points the world may be in contact with
those who ought to be working to preserve it from
putrefaction and decay.

Now there are two ways by which this function may
be discharged, and in which it is incumbent upon every
Christian man to make his contribution, be it greater
or smaller, to the discharge of it. The one is by direct
efforts to impart to others the knowledge of God in
Jesus Christ which we have, and which we profess to
be the very root of our lives. We can all do that if we
will, and we are here to do it. Every one of us has
somebody or other close to us, bound to us, perhaps,
by the tie of kindred and love, who will listen to us
more readily than to anybody else. Christian men and
women, have you utilised these channels which God
Himself, by the arrangements of society, has dug for
you, that through them you may pour upon some
thirsty ground the water of life? We could also help,
and help far more than any of us do, in associated
efforts for the same purpose. The direct obligation to
direct efforts to impart the Gospel cannot be shirked,
though, alas! it is far too often ignored by us professing Christians.

But there is another way by which 'the remnant of
Jacob' is to be 'a dew from the Lord,' and that is by
trying to bring to bear Christian thoughts and Christian
principles upon all the relations of life in which we stand,
and upon all the societies, be they greater or smaller—
the family, the city, or the nation—of which we form
parts. We have heard a great deal lately about what
people that know very little about it, are pleased to call
'the Nonconformist conscience.' I take the compliment,
which is not intended, but is conveyed by the word.
But I venture to say that what is meant, is not

the 'Nonconformist' conscience, it is the *Christian* conscience. We Nonconformists have no monopoly, thank God, of that. Nay, rather, in some respects, our friends in the Anglican churches are teaching some of us a lesson as to the application of Christian principles to civic duty and to national life. I beseech you, although I do not mean to dwell upon that point at all at this time, to ask yourselves whether, as citizens, the vices, the godlessness, the miseries—the removable miseries—of our great town populations, lie upon your hearts. Have you ever lifted a finger to abate drunkenness? Have you ever done anything to help to make it possible that the masses of our town communities should live in places better than the pigsties in which many of them have to wallow? Have you any care for the dignity, the purity, the Christianity of our civic rulers; and do you, to the extent of your ability, try to ensure that Christ's teaching shall govern the life of our cities? And the same question may be put yet more emphatically with regard to wider subjects, namely, the national life and the national action, whether in regard to war or in regard to other pressing subjects for national consideration. I do not touch upon these; I only ask you to remember the grand ideal of my text, which applies to the narrowest circle—the family; and to the wider circles —the city and the nation, as well as to the world. Time was when a bastard piety shrank back from intermeddling with these affairs and gathered up its skirts about it in an ecstasy of unwholesome unworldliness. There is not much danger of that now, when Christian men are in the full swim of the currents of civic, professional, literary, national life. But I will tell you of what there is a danger—Christian men and women

P

moving in their families, going into town councils, going into Parliament, going to the polling-booths, and leaving their Christianity behind them. 'The remnant of Jacob shall be as a dew from the Lord.'

Now let me turn for a moment to a second point, and that is

II. The function of English Christians in the world.

I have suggested in an earlier part of this sermon that possibly the application of this text originally was to the scattered remnant. Be that as it may, wherever you go, you find the Jew and the Englishman. I need not dwell upon the ubiquity of our race. I need not point you to the fact that, in all probability, our language is destined to be the world's language some day. I need do nothing more than recall the fact that a man may go on board ship, in Liverpool or London, and go round the world; everywhere he sees the Union Jack, and everywhere he lands upon British soil. The ubiquity of the scattered Englishman needs no illustration.

But I do wish to remind you that that ubiquity has its obligation. We hear a great deal to-day about Imperialism, about 'the Greater Britain,' about 'the expansion of England.' And on one side all that new atmosphere of feeling is good, for it speaks of a vivid consciousness which is all to the good in the pulsations of the national life. But there is another side to it that is not so good. What is the expansion sought for? Trade? Yes! necessarily; and no man who lives in Lancashire will speak lightly of that necessity. Vulgar greed, and earth-hunger? *that* is evil. Glory? that is cruel, blood-stained, empty. My text tells us why expansion should be sought, and what are the obliga-tions it brings with it. 'The remnant of Jacob shall be

in the midst of many people as a dew from the Lord.'
There are two kinds of Imperialism : one which regards
the Empire as a thing for the advantage of us here, in
this little land, and another which regards it as a
burden that God has laid on the shoulders of the men
whom John Milton, two centuries ago, was not afraid
to call 'His Englishmen.'

Let me remind you of two contrasted pictures which
will give far more forcibly than anything I can say, the
two points of view from which our world-wide dominion
may be regarded. Here is one of them : ' By the strength
of my hand I have done it, and by my wisdom, for I am
prudent. And I have removed the bounds of the people,
and have robbed their treasures, and my hand hath
found as a nest the riches of the people ; and as one
gathereth eggs that are left, have I gathered all the
earth ; and there was none that moved a wing, or
opened a mouth, or peeped.' That is the voice of the
lust for Empire for selfish advantages.   And here is
the other one : 'The kings of Tarshish and of the isles
shall bring presents ; yea, all kings shall fall down
before Him ; all nations shall serve Him, for He shall
deliver the needy when he crieth, the poor also, and
him that hath no helper. He shall redeem their soul
from deceit and violence, and precious shall their blood
be in His sight.' That is the voice that has learned :
'He that is greatest among you, let him be your
servant'; and that the dominion founded on unselfish
surrender for others is the only dominion that will last.
Brethren! that is the spirit in which alone England will
keep its Empire over the world.

I need not remind you that the gift which we have
to carry to the heathen nations, the subject peoples
who are under the ægis of our laws, is not merely our

literature, our science, our Western civilisation, still less
the products of our commerce, for all of which some of
them are asking; but it is *the* gift that they do *not* ask
for. The dew 'waiteth not for man, nor tarrieth for
the sons of men.' We have to create the demand by
bringing the supply. We have to carry Christ's Gospel
as the greatest gift that we have in our hands.

And now, I was going to have said a word, lastly, but
I see it can only be a word, about—

III. The failure to fulfil the function.

Israel failed. Pharisaism was the end of it—a hugging itself in the possession of the gift which it did not
appreciate, and a bitter contempt of the nations, and
so destruction came, and the fire on the hearth was
scattered and died out, and the vineyard was taken
from them and 'given to a nation bringing forth the
fruits thereof.' Change the name, as the Latin poet
says, and the story is told about us. England largely
fails in this function; as witness in India godless
civilians; as witness on every palm-shaded coral beach
in the South Seas, profligate beach-combers, drunken
sailors, unscrupulous traders; as witness the dying out
of races by diseases imported with profligacy and gin
from this land. 'A dew from the Lord!'; say rather a
malaria from the devil! 'By you,' said the Prophet,
'is the name of God blasphemed among the Gentiles.'
By Englishmen the missionary's efforts are, in a hundred
cases, neutralised, or hampered if not neutralised.

We have failed because, as Christian people, we have
not been adequately in earnest. No man can say with
truth that the churches of England are awake to the
imperative obligation of this missionary enterprise. 'If
God spared not the natural branches, take heed lest He
spare not thee.' Israel's religion was **not** diffusive,

therefore it corrupted; Israel's religion did not reach out a hand to the nations, therefore its heart was paralysed and stricken. They who bring the Gospel to others increase their own hold upon it. There is a joy of activity, there is a firmer faith, as new evidences of its power are presented before them. There is the blessing that comes down upon all faithful discharge of duty; 'If the house be not worthy, your peace shall return to you.' After all, our Empire rests on moral foundations, and if it is administered by us—and we each have part of the responsibility for all that is done—on the selfish ground of only seeking the advantage of 'the predominant partner,' then our hold will be loosened. There is no such cement of empire as a common religion. If we desire to make these subject peoples loyal fellow-subjects, we must make them true fellow-worshippers. The missionary holds India for England far more strongly than the soldier does. If we apply Christian principles to our administration of our Empire, then instead of its being knit together by iron bands, it will be laced together by the intertwining tendrils of the hearts of those who are possessors of 'like precious faith.' Brethren, there is another saying in the Old Testament, about the dew. 'I will be as the dew unto Israel,' says God through the Prophet. We must have Him as the dew for our own souls first. Then only shall we be able to discharge the office laid upon us, to be in the midst of many peoples as 'dew from the Lord.' If our fleece is wet and we leave the ground dry, our fleece will soon be dry, though the ground may be bedewed.

GOD'S REQUIREMENTS AND GOD'S GIFT

'What doth the Lord require of thee, but to do justly, and to love mercy, and to walk humbly with thy God?'—MICAH vi. 8.

THIS is the Prophet's answer to a question which he puts into the mouth of his hearers. They had the superstitious estimate of the worth of sacrifice, which conceives that the external offering is pleasing to God, and can satisfy for sin. Micah, like his great contemporary Isaiah, and the most of the prophets, wages war against that misconception of sacrifice, but does not thereby protest against its use. To suppose that he does so is to misunderstand his whole argument. Another misuse of the words of my text is by no means uncommon to-day. One has heard people say, 'We are plain men; we do not understand your theological subtleties; we do not quite see what you mean by "Repentance toward God, and faith in Jesus Christ." "To do justly, and to love mercy, and to walk humbly with my God," that is my religion, and I leave all the rest to you.' That is our religion too, but notice that word 'require.' It is a harsh word, and if it is the last word to be said about God's relation to men, then a great shadow has fallen upon life.

But there is another word which Micah but dimly caught uttered amidst the thunders of Sinai, and which you and I have heard far more clearly. The Prophet read off rightly God's *requirements*, but he had not anything to say about God's *gifts*. So his word is a half-truth, and the more clearly it is seen, and the more earnestly a man tries to live up to the standard of the requirements laid down here, the more will he feel that there

is something else needed, and the more will he see that
the great central peculiarity and glory of Christianity
is not that it reiterates or alters God's requirements,
but that it brings into view God's gifts. 'To do justly,
to love mercy, to walk humbly with our God,' is
possible only through repentance towards God, and
faith in our Lord Jesus Christ. And if you suppose
that these words of my text disclose the whole truth
about God's relation to men, and men's to God, you
have failed to apprehend the flaming centre of the
Light that shines from heaven.

I. So, then, the first thing that I wish to suggest is
God's requirements.

Now, I do not need to say more than just a word or
two about the summing-up in my text of the plain,
elementary duties of morality and religion. It covers
substantially the same ground, in a condensed form, as
does the Decalogue, only that Moses began with the
deepest thing and worked outwards, as it were; laying
the foundation in a true relation to God, which is the
most important, and from which will follow the true
relation to men. Micah begins at the other end, and
starting with the lesser, the more external, the purely
human, works his way inwards to that which is the
centre and the source of all.

'To do justly,' that is elementary morality in two
words. Whatever a man has a right to claim from
you, give him; that is the sum of duty. And yet not
altogether so, for we all know the difference between a
righteous man and a good man, and how, if there is
only rigidly righteous action, there is something wanting to the very righteousness of the action and to the
completeness of the character. 'To do' is not enough;
we must get to the heart, and so '*love* mercy.' Justice

is not all. If each man gets his deserts, as Shakespeare says, 'who of us shall scape whipping?' There must be the mercy as well as the justice. In a very deep sense no man renders to his fellows all that his fellows have a right to expect of him, who does not render to them mercy. And so in a very deep sense, mercy is part of justice, and you have not given any poor creature all that that poor creature has a right to look for from you, unless you have given him all the gracious and gentle charities of heart and hand. Justice and mercy do, in the deepest view, run into one.

Then Micah goes deeper. 'And to walk humbly with thy God.' Some people would say that this summary of the divine requirements is defective, because there is nothing in it about a man's duty to himself, which is as much a duty as his duty to his fellows, or his duty to God. But there is a good deal of my duty to myself crowded into that one word, 'humbly.' For I suppose we might almost say that the basis of all our obligations to our own selves lies in this, that we shall take the right view—that is, the lowly view—of ourselves. But I pass that.

'To walk humbly with thy God.' 'Can two walk together unless they be agreed?' For walking with God there must be communion, based in love, and resulting in imitation. And that communion must be constant, and run through all the life, like a golden thread through some web. So, then, here is the minimum of the divine requirements, to give everybody what he has a right to, including the mercy to which he has a right, to have a lowly estimate of myself, and to live continually grasping the hand of God, and conscious of His overshadowing wing at all moments, and of conformity to His will at every step of the road. That

is the minimum; and the people who so glibly say,
'That is my religion,' have little consciousness of how
far-reaching and how deep-down-going the requirements of this text are. The requirements result from
the very nature of God, and our relation to Him, and
they are endorsed by our own consciences, for we all
know that these, and nothing less than these are the
duties that we owe to God. So much for God's requirements.

II. Our failure.

There is not one of us that has come up to the
standard. Man after man may be conceived of as
bringing in his hands the actions of his life, and laying
them in the awful scales which God's hand holds. In
the one are God's requirements, in the other my life;
and in every case down goes the weight, and 'weighed
in the balances we are altogether lighter than vanity.'
We stand before the great Master in the school, and
one by one we take up our copybooks; and there is not
one of them that is not black with blots and erasures
and swarming with errors. The great cliff stands in
front of us with the victor's prize on its topmost ledge,
and man after man tries to climb, and falls bruised and
broken at the base. 'There is none righteous, no, not
one.' Micah's requirements come to every man that
will honestly take stock of his life and his character
as the statement of an unreached and unreachable
ideal to which he never has climbed nor ever can climb.

Oh, brethren! if these words are all the words that
are to be said about God and me, then I know not
what lies before the enlightened conscience except
shuddering despair, and a paralysing consciousness of
inevitable failure. I beseech you, take these words,
and go apart with them, and test your daily life by

them. God requires me to do justly. Does there not
rise before my memory many an act in which, in
regard to persons and in regard to circumstances, I
have fallen beneath that requirement? He requires
me 'to love mercy.' He requires me 'to walk humbly,'
and I have often been inflated and self-conceited and
presumptuous. He requires me to walk with Himself,
and I have shaken away His hand from me, and passed
whole days without ever thinking of Him, and 'the
God in whose hands' my 'breath is, and whose are all'
my 'ways,' I have 'not glorified.' I cannot hammer
this truth into your consciences. You have to do it for
yourselves. But I beseech you, recognise the fact that
you are implicated in the universal failure, and that
God's requirement is God's condemnation of each of us.

If, then, that is true, that all have come short of the
requirement, then there should follow a universal sense
of guilt, for there is the universal fact of guilt, whether
there be the sense of it or not. There must follow, too,
consequences resulting from the failure of each of us to
comply with these divine requirements, consequences
very alarming, very fatal; and there must follow a
darkening of the thought of God. 'I knew thee that
thou wert an austere man, reaping where thou didst
not sow, and gathering where thou didst not straw.'
That is the God of all the people who take my text as
the last word of their religion—God 'requires of me.
The blessed sun in the heavens becomes a lurid ball of
fire when it is seen through the mist of such a conception of the divine character, and its relation to men.
There is nothing that so drapes the sky in darkness,
and hides out the great light of God, as the thought
of His requirements as the last thought we cherish
concerning Him.

There follows, too, upon this conception, and the failure that results to fulfil the requirements, a hopelessness as to ever accomplishing that which is demanded of us. Who amongst us is there that, looking back upon his past in so far as it has been shaped by his own effort and his own unaided strength, can look forward to a future with any hope that it will mend the past? Brethren! experience teaches us that we have not fulfilled, and cannot fulfil, what remains our plain duty, notwithstanding our inability to discharge it—viz., 'To do justly, and to love mercy, and to walk humbly with our God.' To think of God's requirements, and of my own failure, is the sure way to paralyse all activity; just as that man in the parable who said, 'Thou art an austere man,' went away and hid his talent in the earth. To think of God's requirements and my own failures, if heaven has nothing more to say to me than this stern 'Thou shalt,' is the short way to despair. And that is why most of us prefer to be immersed in the trivialities of daily life rather than to think of God, and of what He asks from us. For the only way by which some of us can keep our equanimity and our cheerfulness is by ignoring Him and forgetting what He demands, and never taking stock of our own lives.

III. Lastly, my text leads us to think of God's gift.

I said it is a half-truth, for it only tells us of what He desires us to be, and does not tell us of how we may be it. It is meant, like the law of which it is a condensation, to be the *pedagogue*, to lead the child to Jesus Christ, the true Master, and the true Gift of God.

God 'requires.' Yes, and He requires, in order that we should say to Him, 'Lord, Thou hast a right to ask this, and it is my blessedness to give it, but I cannot.

Do Thou give me what Thou dost require, and then I
can.'

The gift of God is Jesus Christ, and that gift meets
all our failures. I have spoken of the sense of guilt
that rises from the consciousness of failure to keep the
requirements of the divine law; and the gift of God
deals with that. It comes to us as we lie wounded,
bruised, conscious of failure, alarmed for results, sen-
sible of guilt, and dreading the penalties, and it says to
us, 'Thine iniquity is taken away, and thy sin purged.'
'God requires of thee what thou hast not done. Trust
yourselves to Me, and all iniquity is passed from your
souls.'

I spoke of the hopelessness of future performance,
which results from experience of past failures; and the
gift of God deals with that. You cannot meet the
requirements. Christ will put His Spirit into your
spirits, if you will trust yourselves to Him, and then
you will meet them, for the things which are impossible with men are possible with God. So, if led by
Micah, we pass from God's requirements to His gifts,
look at the change in the aspect which God bears to
us. He is no longer standing strict to mark, and stern
to judge and condemn: but bending down graciously
to help. His last word to us is not 'Thou shalt do' but
'I will give.' His utterance in the Gospel is not 'do,'
but it is 'take'; and the vision of God, which shines
out upon us from the life and from the Cross of Jesus
Christ, is not that of a great Taskmaster, but that of
Him who helps all our weakness, and makes it strength.
A God who 'requires' paralyses men, shuts men out
from hope and joy and fellowship; a God who gives
draws men to His heart, and makes them diligent in
fulfilling all His blessed requirements.

Think of the difference which the conception of God as giving makes to the spirit in which we work. No longer, like the Israelites in Egypt, do we try to make bricks without straw, and break our hearts over our failures, or desperately abandon the attempt, and live in neglect of God and His will; but joyfully, with the clear confidence that 'our labour is not in vain in the Lord,' we seek to keep the commandments which we have learned to be the expressions of His love. One of the Fathers puts all in one lovely sentence: 'Give what Thou commandest, and command what Thou wilt.'

Think, too, of the difference which this conception of the giving rather than of the requiring God brings into what we have to do. We have not to begin with effort, we have to begin with faith. The fountain must be filled from the spring before it can send up its crystal pillar flashing in the sunlight; and we must receive by our trust the power to will and to do. First fill the lamp with oil, and let the Master light it, and then let its blaze beam forth. First, we have to go to the giving God, with thanks 'unto Him for His unspeakable gift'; and then we have to say to Him, 'Thou hast given me Thy Son. What dost Thou desire that I shall give to Thee?' We have first to accept the gift, and then, moved by the mercy of God, to ask, 'Lord! what wilt Thou have me to do?'

HABAKKUK

THE IDEAL DEVOUT LIFE

'The Lord God is my Strength, and He will make my feet like hinds' feet, and He will make me to walk upon mine high places.'—HABAKKUK iii. 19.

So ends one of the most magnificent pieces of imaginative poetry in Scripture or anywhere else. The singer has been describing a great delivering manifestation of the Most High God, which, though he knew it was for the deliverance of God's people, shed awe and terror over his soul. Then he gathers himself together to vow that in this God, thus manifested as the God of his salvation, he 'will rejoice,' whatever penury or privation may attach to his outward life. Lastly, he rises, in these final words, to the apprehension of what this God, thus rejoiced in, will become to those who so put their trust and their gladness upon Himself.

The expressions are of a highly metaphorical and imaginative character, but they admit of being brought down to very plain facts, and they tell us the results in heart and mind of true faith and communion with God.

It is to be noticed that a parallel saying, almost verbatim the same as that of my text, occurs in the 18th psalm, and that there, too, it is the last and joyous result of a tremendous manifestation of the delivering energy of God.

Without any attempt to do more than bring out the

deep meaning of the words, I note that the three clauses
of our text present three aspects of what our lives and
ourselves may steadfastly be if we, too, will rejoice in
the God of our salvation.

I. First, such communion with God brings God to a
man for his strength.

The 18th psalm, which is closely parallel, as I have
remarked, with this one, gives a somewhat different
and inferior version of that thought when it says, 'It
is the Lord that girdeth me with strength.' But
Habakkuk, though perhaps he could not have put into
dogmatic shape all that he meant, had come farther
than that with this: 'The Lord *is* my strength.' He
not only *gives*, as one might put a coin into the hand
of a beggar, while standing separate from him all the
while, but 'He *is* my strength.'

And what does that mean? It is an anticipation of
that most wonderful and highest of all the New Testament truths which the Apostle declared when he said:
'I can do all things in Christ which strengtheneth me
within.' It is the anticipation in experience—which
always comes before dogmatic formulas that reduce
experiences into articulate utterances, of what the
Apostle recorded when he said that he had heard the
voice that declared, 'My grace is sufficient for thee,
and My strength is made perfect in weakness.'

Ah, brother! do not let us deprive ourselves of the
lofty consolations and the mysterious influx of power
which may be ours, if we will open our eyes to see, and
our hearts to receive, what is really the central blessing of the Gospel, the communication through the same
faith as Habakkuk exercised when he said, 'I will
rejoice in the God of my salvation,' of an actual divine
strength to dwell in and manifest itself majestically

and triumphantly through, our weakness. 'The Lord is my strength,' and if we will rejoice in the Lord we shall find that Habakkuk's experience was lower than ours, inasmuch as he knew less of God than we do; and we shall be able to surpass his saying with the other one of the Prophet: 'The Lord is my strength and song; He also is become my salvation.' That is the first blessing that this ancient believer, out of the twilight of early revelation, felt as certain to come through communion with God.

II. The second is like unto it. Such rejoicing communion with God will give light-footedness in the path of life.

'He makes my feet like hinds' feet.' The stag is, in all languages spoken by people that have ever seen it, the very type and emblem of elastic, springing ease, of light and bounding gracefulness, that clears every obstacle, and sweeps swiftly over the moor. And when this singer, or his brother psalmist in the other psalm that we have referred to, says, 'Thou makest my feet like hinds' feet,' what he is thinking about is that light and easy, springing, elastic gait, that swiftness of advance. What a contrast that is to the way in which most of us get through our day's work! Plod, plod, plod, in a heavy-footed, spiritless grind, like that with which the ploughman toils down the sticky furrows of a field, with a pound of clay at each heel; or like that with which a man goes wearied home from his work at night. The monotony of trivial, constantly recurring doings, the fluctuations in the thermometer of our own spirits; the stiff bits of road that we have all to encounter sooner or later; and as days go on, our diminishing buoyancy of nature, and the love of walking a little slower than we used to do; we all know these things, and our gait is affected by them. But then my text brings a bright assurance, that swift and easy and springing as the course of a stag on a free hill-side may be the gait with which we run the race set before us.

It is the same thought, under a somewhat different garb, which the Apostle has when he tells us that the Christian soldier ought to have his 'feet shod with the alacrity that comes from the gospel of peace.' We are to be always ready to run, and to run with light hearts when we do. That is a possible result of Christian communion, and ought, far more than it is, to be an achieved reality with each of us. Of course physical conditions vary. Of course our spirits go up and down. Of course the work that we have to do one day seems easier than the same work does another. All these fluctuations and variations, and causes of heavy-footed-ness—and sometimes more sinful ones, causes of slug-gishness—will survive; but in spite of them all, and beneath them all, it is possible that we may have ourselves thus equipped for the road, and may rejoice in our work 'as a strong man to run a race,' and may cheerily welcome every duty, and cast ourselves into all our tasks. It is possible, because communion with God manifest in Christ does, as we have been seeing, actually breathe into men a vigour, and consequently a freshness and a buoyancy that do not belong to themselves, and do not come from nature or from surrounding things. Unless that is true, that Chris-tianity gives to a man the divine gladness which makes him ready for work, I do not know what is the good of his Christianity to him.

But not only is that so, but this same communion with God, which is the opening of the heart for the

Q

influx of the divine power, brings to bear upon all
our work new motives which redeem it from being
oppressive, tedious, monotonous, trivial, too great for
our endurance, or too little for our effort. All work
that is not done in fellowship with Jesus Christ tends
to become either too heavy to be tackled successfully,
or too trivial to demand our best energies, and in
either case will be done perfunctorily, and as the days
go on, mechanically and wearisomely, as a grind and a
plod. 'Thou makest my feet like hinds' feet'—if I get
the new motive of love to God in Christ well into my
heart so that it comes out and influences all my actions,
there will be no more tasks too formidable to under-
take, or too small to be worth an effort. There will be
nothing unwelcome. The rough places will be made
plain, and the crooked things straight, and our feet
will be shod with the preparedness of the gospel of
peace.

If we live in daily communion with God, another
thought, too, will come in, which will, in like manner,
make us ready 'to run with' cheerfulness 'the race
that is set before us.' We shall connect everything
that befalls us, and everything that we have to do, with
the final issue, and life will become solemn, grave, and
blessed, because it is the outer court and vestibule of
the eternal life with God in Christ. They that hold
communion with Him, and only they, will, as another
prophet says, 'run and not be weary,' when there come
the moments that require a special effort; and 'will
walk and not faint' through the else tediously long
hours of commonplace duty and dusty road.

III. The last of the thoughts here is—Communion
with God brings elevation.

'He will make me to walk upon my high places.

One sees the herd on the skyline of the mountain ridge,
and at home up there, far above dangers and attack;
able to keep their footing on cliff and precipice, and
tossing their antlers in the pure air. One wave of the
hand, and they are miles away. 'He sets me upon my
high places'; if we will keep ourselves in simple,
loving fellowship with God in Christ; and day by day,
even when 'the fig-tree does not blossom, and there is
no fruit in the vine,' will still 'rejoice in the God of our
salvation,' He will lift us up, and Isaiah's other clause
in the verse which I have quoted will be fulfilled:
'They shall mount up with wings as eagles.' Communion with God does not only help us to plod and to
travel, but it helps us to soar. If we keep ourselves in
touch with Him, we shall be like a weight that is hung
on to a balloon. The buoyancy of the one will lift the
leadenness of the other. If we hold fast by Christ's
hand that will lift us up to the high places, the heights
of God, in so far as we may reach them in this world;
and we shall be at home up there. They will be '*my
high places,*' that I never could have got at by my own
scrambling, but to which Thou hast lifted me up, and
which, by Thy grace, have become my natural abode.
I am at home there, and walk at liberty in the loftiness,
and fear no fall amongst the cliffs.

Are you and I familiar with these upper ranges of
thought and experience and life? Do we feel at home
there more than down in the bottoms, amongst the
swamps, and the miasma, and the mists? Where is
your home, brother? The Mass begins with *Sursum
corda*: 'Up with your hearts,' and that is the word for
us. But the way to get up is to keep ourselves in touch
with Jesus Christ, and then He will, even whilst our
feet are travelling along this road of earth, set us at

His own right hand in the heavenly places, and make them ' *our* high places.' It is safe up there. The air is pure; the poison mists are down lower; the hunters do not come there; their arrows or their rifles will not carry so far. It is only when the herd ventures a little down the hill that it is in danger from shots.

But the elevation will not be such as to make us despise the low paths on which duty—the sufficient and loftiest thing of all—lies for us. Our souls may be like stars, and dwell apart, and yet may lay the humblest duties upon themselves, and whilst we live in the high places, we ' may travel on life's common way in cheerful godliness.' Communion with Him will make us light-footed, and lift us high, and yet it will keep us at desk, and mill, and study, and kitchen, and nursery, and shop, and we shall find that the high places are reachable in every life, and in every task. So we may go on until at last we shall hear the Voice that says, ' Come up higher,' and shall be lifted to the mountain of God, where the living waters are, and shall fear no snares or hunters any more for ever.

ZEPHANIAH

ZION'S JOY AND GOD'S

'Sing, O daughter of Zion; shout, O Israel; be glad and rejoice with all the heart, O daughter of Jerusalem. . . . 17. He will rejoice over thee with joy; He will rest in His love, He will joy over thee with singing.'—ZEPHANIAH iii. 14, 17.

WHAT a wonderful rush of exuberant gladness there is in these words! The swift, short clauses, the triple invocation in the former verse, the triple promise in the latter, the heaped together synonyms, all help the impression. The very words seem to dance with joy. But more remarkable than this is the parallelism between the two verses. Zion is called to rejoice in God because God rejoices in her. She is to shout for joy and sing because God's joy too has a voice, and breaks out into singing. For every throb of joy in man's heart, there is a wave of gladness in God's. The notes of our praise are at once the echoes and the occasions of His. We are to be glad because He is glad: He is glad because we are so. We sing for joy, and He joys over us with singing because we do.

I. God's joy over Zion.

It is to be noticed that the former verse of our text is followed by the assurance: 'The Lord is in the midst of thee'; and that the latter verse is preceded by the same assurance. So, then, intimate fellowship and communion between God and Israel lies at the root both of God's joy in man and man's joy in God.

We are solemnly warned by 'profound thinkers' of

letting the shadow of our emotions fall upon God. No
doubt there is a real danger there; but there is a worse
danger, that of conceiving of a God who has no life
and heart; and it is better to hold fast by this—that
in Him is that which corresponds to what in us is
gladness. We are often told, too, that the Jehovah of
the Old Testament is a stern and repellent God, and
the religion of the Old Testament is gloomy and
servile. But such a misconception is hard to maintain
in the face of such words as these. Zephaniah, of
whom we know little, and whose words are mainly
forecasts of judgments and woes pronounced against
Zion that was rebellious and polluted, ends his prophecy
with these companion pictures, like a gleam of sunshine which often streams out at the close of a dark
winter's day. To him the judgments which he prophesied
were no contradiction of the love and gladness of God.
The thought of a glad God might be a very awful
thought; such an insight as this prophet had gives a
blessed meaning to it. We may think of the joy that
belongs to the divine nature as coming from the completeness of His being, which is raised far above all that
makes of sorrow. But it is not in Himself alone that
He is glad; but it is because He loves. The exercise of
love is ever blessedness. His joy is in self-impartation;
His delights are in the sons of men: 'As the bride-
groom rejoiceth over the bride, so shall thy God rejoice
over thee.' His gladness is in His children when they let
Him love them, and do not throw back His love on
itself. As in man's physical frame it is pain to have
secretions dammed up, so when God's love is forced
back upon itself and prevented from flowing out in
blessing, some shadow of suffering cannot but pass
across that calm sky. He is glad when His face is

mirrored in ours, and the rays from Him are reflected from us.

But there is another wonderfully bold and beautiful thought in this representation of the gladness of God. Note the double form which it assumes : 'He will rest' —literally, be silent—'in His love ; He will joy over thee with singing.' As to the former, loving hearts on earth know that the deepest love knows no utterance, and can find none. A heart full of love rests as having attained its desire and accomplished its purpose. It keeps a perpetual Sabbath, and is content to be silent.

But side by side with this picture of the repose of God's joy is set with great poetic insight the precisely opposite image of a love which delights in expression, and rejoices over its object with singing. The combination of the two helps to express the depth and intensity of the one love, which like a song-bird rises with quivering delight and pours out as it rises an ever louder and more joyous note, and then drops, composed and still, to its nest upon the dewy ground.

II. Zion's joy in God.

To the Prophet, the fact that 'the Lord is in the midst of thee' was the guarantee for the confident assurance 'Thou shalt not fear any more'; and this assurance was to be the occasion of exuberant gladness, which ripples over in the very words of our first text. That great thought of 'God dwelling in the midst' is rightly a pain and a terror to rebellious wills and alienated hearts. It needs some preparation of mind and spirit to be glad because God is near; and they who find their satisfaction in earthly sources, and those who seek for it in these, see no word of good news, but rather a 'fearful looking for of judgment' in the thought that God is in their midst. The word rendered 'rejoices' in the first verse of our text is not the same as that so translated in the second. The latter means literally, to move in a circle; while the former literally means, to leap for joy. Thus the gladness of God is thought of as expressing itself in dignified, calm movements, whilst Zion's joy is likened in its expression to the more violent movements of the dance. True human joy is like God's, in that He delights in us and we in Him, and in that both He and we delight in the exercise of love. But we are never to forget that the differences are real as the resemblances, and that it is reserved for the higher form of our experiences in a future life to 'enter into the joy of the Lord.'

It becomes us to see to it that our religion is a religion of joy. Our text is an authoritative command as well as a joyful exhortation, and we do not fairly represent the facts of Christian faith if we do not 'rejoice in the Lord always.' In all the sadness and troubles which necessarily accompany us, as they do all men, we ought by the effort of faith to set the Lord always before us that we be not moved. The secret of stable and perpetual joy still lies where Zephaniah found it—in the assurance that the Lord is with us, and in the vision of His love resting upon us, and rejoicing over us with singing. If thus our love clasps His, and His joy finds its way into our hearts, it will remain with us that our 'joy may be full'; and being guarded by Him whilst still there is fear of stumbling, He will set us at last 'before the presence of His glory without blemish in exceeding joy.'

HAGGAI

VAIN TOIL

' Ye have sown much, and bring in little; ye eat, but ye have not enough; ye drink, but ye are not filled with drink; ye clothe you, but there is none warm; and he that earneth wages earneth wages to put it into a bag with holes.'—HAGGAI i. 6

A LARGE emigration had taken place from the land of captivity to Jerusalem. The great purpose which the returning exiles had in view was the rebuilding of the Temple, as the centre-point of the restored nation. With true heroism, and much noble and unselfish enthusiasm, they began the work, postponing to it all considerations of personal convenience. But the usual fate of all great national enthusiasms attended this. Political difficulties, hard practical realities, came in the way, and the task was suspended for a time. A handful remained true to the original ideas; the rest fell away. Personal comfort, love of ease, the claims of domestic life, the greed of gain, all the ignoble motives which, like gravitation and friction, check such movements after the first impulse is exhausted, came into play. Like every great cause, this one was launched amidst high hopes and honest zeal: but by degrees the hopes faded and became nothing better than 'godly imaginations.' The exiles took to building their own ceiled houses, and let the House of God lie waste. They began to think more of settling on the land than of building the Temple. No doubt they said all the things with which men are wont to hide their selfishness under the mask of duty:

—'Men must live; we must take care of ourselves; it is mad enthusiasm to build a temple when we have not homes; we mean to build it some time, but we are practical men and must provide for our wants first.'

This wisdom of theirs turned out folly, as it generally does. There came, as we learn from this prophet, a season of distress, in which the harvest, for which they had sacrificed their duties and their calling, failed: and in spite of their prudent diligence, or rather, just because of their misplaced and selfish attention to their worldly wellbeing, they were poor and hungry. 'The heaven over them was stayed from dew, and the earth from her fruit.' Haggai was sent by God to interpret the calamity, and to urge to the fulfilment of their earlier purposes.

His words apply to a supernatural condition of things with which he is dealing, but they contain truths illustrated by it and true for ever. For us all, as truly as for those Jews, the first thing, the primary, all-embracing duty, is to serve God, to obey, love, and live with Him. The same selfish and worldly excuses have force with us: 'We have business to look after; men must live; we have no time to think about religion; I have built a new mill that occupies my thoughts; I have found a new plaything, and I must try it; I have married a wife, and therefore I cannot come.' So God and His claims, Christ and His love, are hustled into a corner to be attended to when opportunity serves, but to be neglected in the meantime. And the same result follows, not by miracle, but by natural necessity. Haggai puts these results in our text with bitter, indignant amplification. His words are all the working out of one idea—the unprofitableness, on the whole and in the long-run, of a godless life. He illustrates this in the clauses of our text in various forms, and my purpose now is simply to apply each of these to the realities of a godless life.

I. It is a life of fruitless toil.

The Prophet pictures the sowing, the abundant seed thrown broadcast, the long waiting, and then, finally, a wretched harvest—a few prematurely yellow ears and short stalks. I remember a friend telling me that when he was a boy he went out reaping with his father in one of our years of great drought; and after a day's work threshed out all that he had cut, and carried it home with him in his handkerchief. That is what Haggai saw realised in fact, because the sowing had been without God. It is what we may see in others and feel in ourselves. It is the very law and curse of godless toil with its unproductive harvest. The builders set out to build a tower whose top shall reach to heaven, and they never get higher than a story or two. There is nothing more tragic than the contrast between what a man actually accomplishes in his life and what he planned when he began it. Many and many of our lives are like the half-built houses in Pompeii, where the stones are lying that had been all squared and polished, and have never been lifted to their place in the unfinished walls. Much of the seed never comes up at all; and what we gather is always less than what we expected. The prize gleams before us; when we get it, is it as good as it looked when it hung tempting at the unreached goal? A fox-brush is scarcely sufficient payment for riding over half a county. Ah! but you say, there is the enthusiasm and stir of the pursuit. Well, yes; it is something if it is *training* you for something, and if you can say that faculties worth the cultivating are developed in that way: and whether that is

so depends on what you think a man is made for, and
on whether these are faculties which will last and find
their scope as long as you last.   Consider what you are,
what you seek; and then say whether the most fruitful
harvest from which God and His love are left out is
not little.

This fruitlessness of toil is inevitable unless it springs
from a motive which in itself is sufficient, pursues a
purpose which will surely be accomplished, and is done
in hope of the world where 'our works do follow us.'
If we are allied to Christ, then whether our work be
great or small, apparently successful or frustrated, it
will be all right.   Though we do not see our fruit, we
know that He will bless the springing thereof, and that
no least deed done for Him but shall in the harvest-day
be found waving a nodding head of multiplied results.
'God giveth it a body as it hath pleased Him'; and 'he
that goeth forth weeping shall doubtless return, bringing his sheaves with him.'   'Your labour is not in vain
in the Lord.'

II. A godless life is one of unsatisfied hunger and
thirst.

The poor results of the exiles' toil did not avail to
stay gnawing hunger nor slake burning thirst, and the
same result applies only too sadly to lives lived apart
from God.   There are a multitude of desires proper to
the human soul besides those which belong to the
bodily frame, and these have their proper objects.   Is
it true that the objects are sufficient to satisfy the
desires?   Does any one of the things for which we toil
feed us full when we have it?   Do we not always want
just a little more?   And is not that want accompanied
with a real and sharp sense of hunger?   Is it not true
the appetite grows with what it feeds on?   And even

if a man schools himself to something like content, it comes not because the desire is satisfied, but because it is somehow bridled. Cerberus often breaks his chain, in spite of honied cakes that have been tossed into the wide mouths of his tripled heads. What do wealth and ambition do for their votaries? And even he who thirsts for nobler occupations and lives for higher aims is often obliged to admit, in weariness, that 'this also is vanity.'

But even when the desire is satisfied, the man desiring is not. To feed their bodies men starve their souls. How many longings are crushed or neglected by him who pushes eagerly after any one longing! We have either to race from one course to another, splitting life into intolerable distractions, or we have to circumscribe and limit ourselves in order to devote all our power to securing one; and if we secure it, then a hundred others will bark like a kennel of hounds.

And if you say, 'I know nothing about all this; I have my aims, and on the whole I secure a tolerable satisfaction for them,' do you not know a nameless unrest? If you do not, then you are so much the poorer and the lower, and you have murdered part of yourself. Some one single tyrannous desire sits solitary in your heart. He has slain all his brethren that he may rule, as sultans used to do in Constantinople. One big fish in the aquarium has eaten up all the others.

God only satisfies the soul. It is only the 'bread which came down from Heaven,' of which if we eat our souls shall live, and be filled as with marrow and fatness. That One is all-sufficient in His Oneness. Possessing Him, we know no satiety; possessing Him, we do not need to maim any part of our nature; possessing Him, we shall not covet divers multifarious objects. The loftiest powers of the soul find in Him their adequate, inexhaustible, eternal object. The lowest desires may, like the beasts of the forest, seek their meat from God. If we take Him for our own and live on Him by faith, our blessed experience will be, 'I am full: I have all and abound.'

III. The godless life is one of futile defences.

'Ye clothe you, but there is none warm.' The clothing was to guard against the nipping air that blew shrewdly on their hills, and it failed to keep them from the weather. We may be indulging in fancy in this application of our text, but still raiment is as needful as food, and its failure to answer its purpose points to a real sorrow and insufficiency of a life lived without God. In it there is no real defence against the manifold evils which storm upon all of us. When the bitter, biting weather comes, what have you to shelter you from the cold blast? Some rags of stoical resignation or proverbial commonplaces? 'What is done cannot be helped'; 'What cannot be cured must be endured'; 'It is a long lane that has no turning,' and the like. But what are these? You may have other occupations to interest you, but these will not heal, though they may divert your attention from, your gaping wounds. You have friends, and the like, but though you have all these and much beside, these will not avail. 'The covering is shorter than that a man can wrap himself in it.' Naked and shivering, exposed to the pelting and the pitiless storm, with rags soaked through, and chilled to the bone, what is there but death before the man in the wild weather on some trackless moor? And what is there for us if we have to bear the storms and cold of life without God? No doubt most of us struggle through somehow. Time heals much; work does a great deal:

to live is so much, that no living being can be wholly
miserable. Other cares and other occupations blossom
and grow, and the brown mounds get covered with
sweet springing grass. But how many lie down and
die? How many for the rest of their lives go crushed
and broken-spirited? How many carry about with
them, deep in their hearts, a sleepless sorrow? How
many have to bear passionate paroxysms of agony
and bursts of angry grief, all of which might have been
softened and soothed and made to gleam with the
mellow light of hope as from a hidden sun, if only,
instead of defiantly and weakly fronting the world
alone, they had found in the man Christ the refuge
from the storm and the covert from the tempest. How
can a man face all the awful possibilities and the solemn
certainties of life without God and not go mad? It is
impossible to work without Him; it is impossible to
rejoice without Him ; but more impossible still, if that
could be, is it to endure without Him. It is in union
with Jesus Christ, and with Him alone, that we shall
receive 'the pure linen, clean and white,' which is a
surer defence than the warrior's mail, and 'being
clothed we shall not be found naked.'

IV. A godless life is one of fleeting riches.

In Haggai's strong metaphor, the poor day-labourer
earns his small wage and puts it into a ragged bag, or
as we should say, a pocket with a hole in it; and when
he comes to look for it, it is gone, and all his toil is for
nothing. What a picture this is of the very experience that befalls all men who work for less wages than
God's 'Well done.' Take an instance or two: here is a
man who works hard for a long time, and puts his
money into some bank, and one morning he gets a
letter to tell him the bank's doors are closed, and his

savings gone—a bag with holes. Here is a man who
climbs by slow degrees to the head of his profession and
lives in popular admiration, and some day he sees a
younger competitor shooting ahead of him, and all is
lost—a bag with holes. Here is a man who has, by
some great discovery, established his fame or his
fortune, and a new man, standing on his shoulders,
makes a greater, and his fame dwarfs and his trade
runs into other channels—a bag with holes. Here is a
man who has conquered a world, and dies on the rock
of St. Helena, with his pompous titles stripped off him,
and instead of kingdoms a rood or two of garden, and
instead of his legions, half a dozen soldiers, a doctor,
and a jailer—a bag with holes. Here is a man who,
having amassed his riches and kept them without loss
all his life, is dying. They cannot go with him. That
would not matter; but unfortunately he has to live
yonder, and he will have 'nothing of all his labour that
he can carry away in his hands'—a bag with holes.

Such loss and final separation befall us all; but he
who loves God loses none of his real treasure when he
parts from earthly treasures. Fortune may turn her
wheel as she pleases, his wealth cannot be taken from
him. His riches are laid up in a sure storehouse,
'where neither moth nor rust doth corrupt.' We each
live for ever. Should we not have for our object in life
that which is eternal as ourselves? Why should we
fix our hopes on that which is not abiding—on things
that can perish, on things that we must lose? Let us
not run this awful risk. Do not impoverish or darken
life here; do not condemn yourselves to unfruitful toil,
to unsatisfied desires, to unguarded calamities, to un-
stable possessions; but come, as sinful men ought to
come, to Jesus Christ for pardon and for life. Then, in

due season, you will reap if you faint not; and the harvest will not be little, but 'some sixty-fold and some an hundred-fold'; then you will 'hunger no more, neither thirst any more,' but 'He that hath mercy on you will lead you to living fountains of water'; then you will not have to draw your poor rags round you for warmth, but shall be clothed with the robe of righteousness and the garment of praise; then you will never need to fear the loss of your riches, but bear with you whilst you live your treasures beyond the reach of change, and will find them multiplied a thousand-fold when you die and go to God, your portion and your joy for ever.

BRAVE ENCOURAGEMENTS

'In the seventh month, in the one and twentieth day of the month, came the word of the Lord by the prophet Haggai, saying, 2. Speak now to Zerubbabel the son of Shealtiel, governor of Judah, and to Joshua the son of Josedech, the high priest, and to the residue of the people, saying, 3. Who is left among you that saw this house in her first glory? and how do ye see it now? is it not in your eyes in comparison of it as nothing? 4. Yet now be strong, O Zerubbabel, saith the Lord; and be strong, O Joshua, son of Josedech, the high priest; and be strong, all ye people of the land, saith the Lord, and work: for I am with you, saith the Lord of Hosts: 5. According to the word that I covenanted with you when ye came out of Egypt, so My Spirit remaineth among you: fear ye not. 6. For thus saith the Lord of Hosts; Yet once, it is a little while, and I will shake the heavens, and the earth, and the sea, and the dry land; 7. And I will shake all nations, and the desire of all nations shall come: and I will fill this house with glory, saith the Lord of Hosts. 8. The silver is Mine, and the gold is Mine, saith the Lord of Hosts. 9. The glory of this latter house shall be greater than of the former, saith the Lord of hosts: and in this place will I give peace, saith the Lord of Hosts.'—HAGGAI ii. 1-9.

THE second year of Darius, in which Haggai prophesied, was 520 B.C. Political intrigues had stopped the rebuilding of the Temple, and the enthusiasm of the first return had died away in the face of prolonged difficulties. The two brave leaders, Zerubbabel and Joshua, still survived, and kept alive their own zeal; but the mass of

R

the people were more concerned about their comforts
than about the restoration of the house of Jehovah.
They had built for themselves 'ceiled houses,' and
were engrossed with their farms.

The Book of Ezra dwells on the external hindrances
to the rebuilding. Haggai goes straight at the selfishness and worldliness of the people as the great hindrance.
We know nothing about him beyond the fact that he
was a prophet working in conjunction with Zechariah.
He has been thought to have been one of the original
company who came back with Zerubbabel, and it has
been suggested, though without any certainty, that he
may have been one of the old men who remembered
the former house. But these conjectures are profitless,
and all that we know is that God sent him to rouse the
slackened earnestness of the people, and that his words
exercised a powerful influence in setting forward the
work of rebuilding. This passage is the second of his
four short prophecies. We may call it a vision of the
glory of the future house of Jehovah.

The prophecy begins with fully admitting the depress-
ing facts which were chilling the popular enthusiasm.
Compared with the former Temple, this which they had
begun to build could not but be 'as nothing.' So the
murmurers said, and Haggai allows that they are quite
right. Note the turn of his words: 'Who is left . . .
that saw this house in its former glory?' There had
been many eighteen years ago; but the old eyes that
had filled with tears then had been mostly closed by
death in the interval, and now but few survived. Perhaps if the eyes had not been so dim with age, the
rising house would not have looked so contemptible.
The pessimism of the aged is not always clear-sighted,
nor their comparisons of what was, and what is begin-

ning to be, just. But it is always wise to be frank in
admitting the full strength of the opinions that we
oppose; and encouragements to work will never tell
if they blink difficulties or seek to deny plain facts.
Haggai was wise when he began with echoing the old
men's disparagements, and in full view of them, pealed
out his brave incitements to the work.

The repetition of the one exhortation, 'Be strong,
be strong, be strong,' is very impressive. The very
monotony has power. In the face of the difficulties
which beset every good work the cardinal virtue is
strength. 'To be weak is to be miserable,' and is the
parent of failures. One hears in the exhortation an
echo of that to Joshua, to whom and to his people the
command 'Be strong and of good courage' was given
with like repetition (Joshua i.).

But there is nothing more futile than telling feeble
men to be strong, and trembling ones to be very
courageous. Unless the exhorter can give some means
of strength and some reason for courage, his word is
idle wind. So Haggai bases his exhortation upon its
sufficient ground, 'For I am with you, saith Jehovah of
hosts.' Strength is a duty, but only if we have a source
of strength available. The one basis of it is the
presence of God. His name reveals the immensity of
His power, who commands all the armies of heaven,
angels, or stars, and to whom the forces of the universe
are as the ordered ranks of His disciplined army; and
who is, moreover, the Captain of earthly hosts, ever
giving victory to those who are His 'willing soldiers in
the day of His power.' It is not vain to bid a man be
strong, if you can assure him that God is with him.
Unless you can, you may save your breath.

Here is the temper for all Christian workers. Let

them realise the duty of strength; let them have recourse to the Fountain of strength; let them mark the purpose of strength, which is 'work,' as Haggai puts it so emphatically. We have nothing to do with the magnitude of what we may be able to build. It may be very poor beside the great houses that greater ages or men have been able to rear. But whether it be a temple brave with gold and cedar, or a log-hut, it is our business to put all our strength into the task, and to draw that strength from the assurance that God is with us.

The difficulties connected with the translation of verse 5 need not concern us here. For my purpose, the general sense resulting from any translation is clear enough. The covenant made of old, when Israel came from an earlier captivity, is fresh as ever, and God's Spirit is with the people; therefore they need not fear. 'Fear ye not' is another of the well-meant exhortations which often produce the opposite effect from the intended one. One can fancy some of the people saying, ' It is all very well to talk about not being afraid; but look at our feebleness, our defence-lessness, our enemies; we cannot but fear, if we open our eyes.' Quite true; and there is only one antidote to fear, and that is the assurance that God's covenant binds Him to take care of me. Unless one believes that, he must be strangely blind to the facts of life if he has not a cold dread coiled round his heart and ever ready to sting.

The Prophet rises into grand predictions of the glory of the poor house which the weak hands were raising. Verses 6-9 set things invisible over against the visible. In general terms the Prophet announces a speedy con-vulsion, partly symbolical and partly real, in which 'all nations' shall be revolutionised, and as a consequence, shall become Jehovah's worshippers, bringing their treasures to the Temple, and so filling the house with glory. This shall be because Jehovah is the true Possessor of all their wealth. But the scope of verse 9 seems to transcend these promises, and to point to an undescribed 'glory,' still greater than that of the universal flocking of the nations with their gifts, and to reach a climax in the wide promise of peace given in the Temple, and thence, as is implied, flowing out 'like a river' through a tranquillised world.

'Yet once, it is a little while.' How long did the little while last? There were, possibly, some feeble incipient fulfilments of the prophecy in the immediate future; for, after the exile, there were convulsions in the political world which resulted in security to the Jews, and the religion of Israel began to draw some scattered proselytes. But the prophecy is not completely fulfilled even now, and it covers the entire development of the 'kingdom that cannot be moved' until the end of time. The writer of the Epistle to the Hebrews thus understands the prophecy (Hebrews xii. 26, 27), and there are echoes of it in Revelation xxi., which describes the final form of the Holy City, the New Jerusalem. So the chronology of prophecy is not altogether that of history; and while the events stand clear, their perspective is foreshortened. All the ages are but 'a little while' in the calendar of heaven. In regard to the whole of the prophetic utterances, we have often to say with the disciples, 'What is this that he saith, a little while?' Eighteen centuries have rolled away since the seer heard, 'Behold, I come quickly,' and the vision still tarries.

The old interpretation of 'the desire of all nations'

as meaning Jesus Christ gave a literal fulfilment of
the prophecy by His presence in the Temple; but that
meaning of the phrase is untenable, both because the
verb is in the plural, which would be impossible if a
person were meant, and because the only interpretation which gives relevancy to verse 8 is that the
expression means the silver and gold, there declared
to be Jehovah's.   That venerable explanation, then,
cannot stand.   There were offerings from heathen
kings, such as those from Darius recorded in Ezra vi.
6-10, and the gifts of Artaxerxes (Ezra vii. 15), which
may be regarded as incipient accomplishments; but
such facts as these cannot exhaust the prophecy.

It must be admitted that nothing happened during
the history of that Temple to answer to the full meaning of this prophecy.   But was it therefore a delusion
that God spoke by Haggai?   We must distinguish
between form and substance.   The Temple was the
centre point of the kingdom of God on earth, the place
of meeting between God and men, the place of sacrifice.
The fulfilment of the prophecy is not to be found in any
house made with hands, but in the true Temple which
Jesus Christ has builded.   He in His own humanity
was all that the Temple shadowed and foretold.   It is in
Him, and in the spiritual Temple which He has reared,
that Haggai's vision will find its full realisation, which is
yet future.   The powers that issue from Him shattered
the Roman empire, have ever since been casting earth's
kingdoms into new moulds, and have still destructive
work to do.   The ' once more ' began when Jesus came,
but the final ' shaking' lies in front still.   Every smaller
revolution in thought or sweeping away of institutions
is a prelude to that great 'shaking' when everything
will go except the kingdom that cannot be moved.   Its

result shall be that the treasures of the nations shall be poured at His feet who is ' worthy to receive riches,' even as other prophecies have foretold that 'men shall bring unto Thee the wealth of the nations' (Isaiah lx. 11 ; Revelation xxi. 24, 26).

In that true Temple the glory of the Shechinah, which was wanting in the second, for ever abides, ' the glory as of the only-begotten of the Father'; and in it dwells for ever the dove of peace, ready to glide into every heart that enters to worship at the shrine. Jesus Christ is not the ' desire of all nations' which shall come to the Temple, but is the Temple to which the wealth of all nations shall be brought, in whom the true glory of a manifested God abides, and from whom the peace of God which passeth all understanding, and is His own peace too, shall enter reconciled souls, and calm turbulent passions, and reconcile contending peoples, and diffuse its calm through all the nations of the saved who there ' walk in the light of the Lord.'

ZECHARIAH

DYING MEN AND THE UNDYING WORD

' Your fathers, where are they ? and the prophets, do they live for ever ? 6. But My words and My statutes, which I commanded My servants the prophets, did they not take hold of your fathers?'—ZECHARIAH 1. 5, 6.

ZECHARIAH was the Prophet of the Restoration. Some sixteen years before this date a feeble band of exiles had returned from Babylon, with high hopes of re-building the ruined Temple. But their designs had been thwarted, and for long years the foundations stood unbuilded upon. The delay had shattered their hopes and flattened their enthusiasm; and when, with the advent of a new Persian king, a brighter day dawned, the little band was almost too dispirited to avail itself of it. At that crisis, two prophets 'blew soul-animating strains,' and as the narrative says else-where, ' the work prospered through the prophesying of Haggai and Zechariah.'

My text comes from the first of Zechariah's pro-phecies. In it he lays the foundation for all that he has subsequently to say. He points to the past, and summons up the august figures of the great pre-Exilic prophets, and reminds his contemporaries that the words which they spoke had been verified in the experience of past generations. He puts himself in line with these, his mighty predecessors, and declares that, though the hearers and the speakers of that prophetic word had glided away into the vast un-

known, the word remained, lived still, and on his
lips demanded the same obedience as it had vainly
demanded from the generation that was past.

It has sometimes been supposed that of the two
questions in my text the first is the Prophet's—' Your
fathers, where are they?' and that the second is the
retort of the people—'The prophets, do *they* live for
ever?' 'It is true that our fathers are gone, but
what about the prophets that you are talking of? Are
they any better off? Are they not dead, too?' But
though the separation of the words into dialogue gives
vivacity, it is wholly unnecessary. And it seems to
me that Zechariah's appeal is all the more impressive
if we suppose that he here gathers the mortal hearers
and speakers of the immortal word into one class, and
sets over against them the Eternal Word, which lives
to-day as it did then, and has new lessons for a new
generation. So it is from that point of view that I
wish to look at these words now, and try to gather
from them some of the solemn, and, as it seems to me,
striking lessons which they inculcate. I follow with
absolute simplicity the Prophet's thoughts.

I. The mortal hearers and speakers of the abiding
Word.

'Your fathers, where are they? and the prophets, do
they live for ever?' It is all but impossible to invest
that well-known thought with any fresh force; but,
perhaps, if we look at it from the special angle from
which the Prophet here regards it, we may get some
new impression of the old truth. That special angle
is to bring into connection the Eternal Word and the
transient vehicles and hearers of it.

Did you ever stand in some roofless, ruined cathedral
or abbey church, and try to gather round you the

generations that had bowed and worshipped there?
Did you ever step across the threshold of some ancient
sanctuary, where the feet of vanished generations had
worn down the sand-stone steps at the entrance? It
is solemn to think of the fleeting series of men; it is
still more striking to bring them into connection with
that everlasting Word which once they heard, and
accepted or rejected.

But let me bring the thought a little closer. There
is not a sitting in our churches that has not been sat
in by dead people. As I stand here and look round
I can re-people almost every pew with faces that we
shall see no more. Many of you, the older *habitués*
of this place, can do the same, and can look and think,
'Ah! *he* used to sit there; *she* used to be in that
corner.' And I can remember many mouldering lips
that have stood in this place where I stand, of friends
and brethren that are gone. 'Your fathers, where
are they?' 'Graves under us, silent,' is the only
answer. 'And the prophets, do they live for ever?'
No memories are shorter-lived than the memories of
the preachers of God's Word.

Take another thought, that all these past hearers and
speakers of the Word had that Word verified in their
lives. 'Took it not hold of your fathers?' Some of
them neglected it, and its burdens were upon them, little
as they felt them sometimes. Some of them clave to it,
and accepted it, and its blessed promises were all fulfilled to them. Not one of those who, for the brief
period of their earthly lives, came in contact with that
divine message but realised, more or less consciously,
some blessedly and some in darkened lives and ruined
careers, the solemn truth of its promises and of its
threatenings. The Word may have been received, or it

may have been neglected, by the past generations; but whether the members thereof put out a hand to accept, or withheld their grasp, whether they took hold of it or it took hold of them—wherever they are now, their earthly relation to that word is a determining factor in their condition. The syllables died away into empty air, the messages were forgotten, but the men that ministered them are eternally influenced by the faithfulness of their ministrations, and the men that heard them are eternally affected by the reception or rejection of that word. So, when we summon around us the congregation of the dead, which is more numerous than the audience of the living to whom I now speak, the lesson that their silent presence teaches us is, ' Wherefore we should give the more earnest heed to the things that we have heard.'

II. Let us note the abiding Word, which these transient generations of hearers and speakers have had to do with.

It is maddening to think of the sure decay and dissolution of all human strength, beauty, wisdom, unless that thought brings with it immediately, like a pair of coupled stars, of which the one is bright and the other dark, the corresponding thought of that which does not pass, and is unaffected by time and change. Just as reason requires some unalterable substratum, below all the fleeting phenomena of the changeful creation— a God who is the Rock-basis of all, the staple to which all the links hang—so we are driven back and back and back, by the very fact of the transiency of the transient, to grasp, for a refuge and a stay, the permanency of the permanent. ' In the year that King Uzziah died I saw the Lord sitting upon a throne'—the passing away of the mortal shadow of sovereignty revealed the undying and true King. It is blessed for us when the lesson which the fleeting of all that *can* flee away reads to us is that, beneath it all, there is the Unchanging. When the leaves drop from the boughs of the trees that veil the face of the cliff, then the steadfast rock is visible; and when the generations, like leaves, drop and rot, then the rock background should stand out the more clearly.

Zechariah meant by the 'word of God' simply the prophetic utterances about the destiny and the punishment of his nation. We ought to mean by the 'word of God, which liveth and abideth for ever,' not merely the written embodiment of it in the Old or New Testament, but the Personal Word, the Incarnate Word, the everlasting Son of the Father, who came upon earth to be God's mouthpiece and utterance, and who is for us all *the* Word, the Eternal Word of the living God. It is His perpetual existence rather than the continuous duration of the written word, declaration of Himself though it is, that is mighty for our strength and consolation when we think of the transient generations.

Christ lives. That is the deepest meaning of the ancient saying, 'All flesh is grass. . . . The Word of the Lord endureth for ever.' He lives; therefore we can front change and decay in all around calmly and triumphantly. It matters not though the prophets and their hearers pass away. Men depart; Christ abides. Luther was once surprised by some friends sitting at a table from which a meal had been removed, and thoughtfully tracing with his fingers upon its surface with some drop of water or wine the one word 'Vivit'; He lives. He fell back upon that when all around was dark. Yes, men may go; what of that? Aaron

may have to ascend to the summit of Hor, and put off
his priestly garments and die there. Moses may have
to climb Pisgah, and with one look at the land which
he must never tread, die there alone by the kiss of God,
as the Rabbis say. Is the host below leaderless? The
Pillar of Cloud lies still over the Tabernacle, and burns
steadfast and guiding in front of the files of Israel.
'Your fathers, where are they? The prophets, do they
live for ever?' 'Jesus Christ is the same yesterday
and to-day and for ever.'

Another consideration to be drawn from this contrast
is, since we have this abiding Word, let us not dread
changes, however startling and revolutionary. Jesus
Christ does not change. But there is a human element
in the Church's conceptions of Jesus Christ, and still
more in its working out of the principles of the Gospel
in institutions and forms, which partakes of the transiency of the men from whom it has come. In such a
time as this, when everything is going into the melting-
pot, and a great many timid people are trembling for
the Ark of God, quite unnecessarily as it seems to me,
it is of prime importance for the calmness and the
wisdom and the courage of Christian people, that they
should grasp firmly the distinction between the divine
treasure which is committed to the churches, and the
earthen vessels in which it has been enshrined. Jesus
Christ, the man Jesus, the divine person, His incarnation, His sacrifice, His resurrection, His ascension, the
gift of His Spirit to abide for ever with His Church
—these are the permanent 'things which cannot be
shaken.' And creeds and churches and formulas and
forms—these are the human elements which are capable of variation, and which need variation from time
to time. No more is the substance of that eternal

Gospel affected by the changes, which are possible on
its vesture, than is the stateliness of some cathedral
touched, when the reformers go in and sweep out the
rubbish and the trumpery which have masked the fair
outlines of its architecture, and vulgarised the majesty
of its stately sweep. Brethren! let us fix this in our
hearts, that nothing which is of Christ can perish, and
nothing which is of man can or should endure. The
more firmly we grasp the distinction between the permanent and the transient in existing embodiments of
Christian truth, the more calm shall we be amidst the
surges of contending opinions. 'He that believeth shall
not make haste.'

III. Lastly, the present generation and its relation to
the abiding Word.

Zechariah did not hesitate to put himself in line with
the mighty forms of Isaiah, and Jeremiah, and Ezekiel,
and Hosea. He, too, was a prophet. We claim, of
course, no such authority for present utterers of that
eternal message, but we do claim for our message a
higher authority than the authority of this ancient
Prophet. He felt that the word of God that was put
into his lips was a new word, addressed to a new
generation, and with new lessons for new circumstances, fitting as close to the wants of the little
band of exiles as the former messages, which it succeeded, had fitted to the wants of their generation.
We have no such change in the message, for Jesus
Christ speaks to us all, speaks to all times and to all
circumstances, and to every generation. And so, just
as Zechariah based upon the history of the past his
appeal for obedience and acceptance, the considerations
which I have been trying to dwell upon bring with
them stringent obligations to us who stand, however

unworthy, in the place of the generations that are gone, as the hearers and ministers of the Word of God.

Let me put two or three very simple and homely exhortations. First, see to it, brother, that you accept that Word. By acceptance I do not mean a mere negative attitude, which is very often the result of lack of interest, the negative attitude of simply not reject-ing; but I mean the opening not only of your minds but of your hearts to it. For if what I have been say-ing is true, and the Word of God has for its highest manifestation Jesus Christ Himself, then you cannot accept a person by pure head-work. You must open your hearts and all your natures, and let Him come in with His love, with His pity, with His inspiration of strength and virtue and holiness, and you must yield yourselves wholly to Him. Think of the generations that are gone. Think of their brief moment when the great salvation was offered to them. Think of how, whether they received or rejected it, that Word took hold upon them. Think of how they regard it now, wherever they are in the dimness; and be you wise in time and be not as those of your fathers who rejected the Word.

Hold it fast. In this time of unrest make sure of your grasp of the eternal, central core of Christianity, Jesus Christ Himself, the divine-human Saviour of the world. There are too many of us whose faith oozes out at their finger ends, simply because they have so many around them that question and doubt and deny. Do not let the floating icebergs bring down *your* temperature; and have a better reason for not believing, if you do not believe, than that so many and such influential and authoritative men have ceased to believe. When Jesus asks, 'Will ye also go away?' our answer should be,

'Lord, to whom shall we go? Thou hast the words of eternal life.'

Accept Him, hold Him fast, trust to His guidance in present day questions. Zechariah felt that his message belonged to the generation to whom he spoke. It was a new message. We have no new message, but there are new truths to be evolved from the old message. The questionings and problems, social, economical, intellectual, moral—shall I say political?—of this day, will find their solution in that ancient word, 'God so loved the world, that He gave His only begotten Son, that whosoever believeth in Him should not perish.' There is the key to all problems. 'In Him are hid all the treasures and wisdom of knowledge.'

Zechariah pointed to the experiences of a past generation as the basis of his appeal. We can point back to eighteen centuries, and say that the experiences of these centuries confirm the truth that Jesus Christ is the Saviour of the world. The blessedness, the purity, the power, the peace, the hope which He has breathed into humanity, the subsidiary and accompanying material and intellectual prosperity and blessings that attend His message, its independence of human instruments, its adaptation to all varieties of class, character, condition, geographical position, its power of recuperating itself from corruptions and distortions, its undiminished adaptedness to the needs of this generation and of each of us—enforce the stringency of the exhortation, and confirm the truth of the assertion: 'This is My beloved Son; hear ye Him!' 'The voice said, Cry. And I said, What shall I cry? All flesh is grass, and all the goodliness thereof as the flower of the field: the grass withereth, and the flower thereof falleth away: but the Word of our God shall stand for ever.' Three hundred years after Isaiah a triumphant Apostle added, 'This is the word which by the Gospel is preached unto you.' Eighteen hundred years after Peter we can echo his confident declaration, and, with the history of these centuries to support our faith, can affirm that the Christ of the Gospel and the Gospel of the Christ are in deed and in truth the Living Word of the Living God.

THE CITY WITHOUT WALLS

'Jerusalem shall be inhabited as towns without walls. . . . 5. For I, saith the Lord, will be unto her a wall of fire round about, and will be the glory in the midst of her.'—ZECHARIAH ii. 4, 5.

ZECHARIAH was the Prophet of the returning exiles, and his great work was to hearten them for their difficult task, with their small resources and their many foes, and to insist that the prime condition to success, on the part of that portion of the nation that had returned, was holiness. So his visions, of which there is a whole series, are very largely concerned with the building of the Temple and of the city. In this one, he sees a man with a measuring-rod in his hand coming forth to take the dimensions of the still un-existing city of God. The words that I have read are the centre portion of that vision. You notice that there are three clauses, and that the first in order is the conse-quence of the other two. 'Jerusalem shall be builded as a city without walls . . . for I will be a wall of fire round about her, and the glory in the midst of her.'

And that exuberant promise was spoken about the Jerusalem over which Christ wept when he foresaw its inevitable destruction. When the Romans had cast a torch into the Temple, and the streets of the city were

8

running with blood, what had become of Zechariah's
dream of a wall of fire round about her? Then can the
divine fire be quenched? Yes. And who quenched it?
Not the Romans, but the people that lived within that
flaming rampart. The apparent failure of the promise
carries the lesson for churches and individuals to-day,
that in spite of such glowing predictions, there may
again sound the voice that the legend says was heard
within the Temple, on the night before Jerusalem fell.
'Let us depart,' and there was a rustling of unseen
wings, and on the morrow the legionaries were in the
shrine. 'If God spared not the natural branches, take
heed lest He also spare not thee.'

Now let us look, in the simplest possible way, at these
three clauses, and the promises that are in them; keeping in mind that, like all the divine promises, they are
conditional.

The first is this :—

I. 'I will be a wall of fire round about her.'

I need not dwell on the vividness and beauty of that
metaphor. These encircling flames will consume all
antagonism, and defy all approach. But let me remind
you that the conditional promise was intended for
Judæa and Jerusalem, and was fulfilled in literal fact.
So long as the city obeyed and trusted God it was impregnable, though all the nations stood round about it,
like dogs round a sheep. The fulfilment of the promise
has passed over, with all the rest that characterised
Israel's position, to the Christian Church, and to-day,
in the midst of all the agitations of opinion, and all the
vauntings of men about an effete Christianity, and
dead churches, it is as true as ever it was that the living
Church of God is eternal. If it had not been that there
was a God as a wall of fire round about the Church, it

would have been wiped off the face of the earth long
ago. If nothing else had killed it the faults of its
members would have done so. The continuance of the
Church is a perpetual miracle, when you take into
account the weakness, and the errors, and the follies,
and the stupidities, and the narrownesses, and the sins,
of the people who in any given day represent it. That
it should stand at all, and that it should conquer,
seems to me to be as plain a demonstration of the
present working of God, as is the existence still, as a
separate individuality amongst the peoples of the earth,
of His ancient people, the Jews. Who was it who said,
when somebody asked him for the best proof of the
truth of Christianity, 'The Jews'? and so we may say,
if you want a demonstration that God is working in
the world, 'Look at the continuance of the Christian
Church.'

In spite of all the vauntings of people that have
already discounted its fall, and are talking as if it
needed no more to be reckoned with, that calm confidence is the spirit in which we are to look around and
forward. It does not become any Christian ever to
have the smallest scintillation of a fear that the ship
that bears Jesus Christ can fail to come to land, or can
sink in the midst of the waters. There was once a
timid would-be helper who put out his hand to hold up
the Ark of God. He need not have been afraid. The
oxen might stumble, and the cart roll about, but the
Ark was safe and stable. A great deal may go, but the
wall of fire will be around the Church. In regard to its
existence, as in regard to the immortal being of each
of its members, the great word remains for ever true:
'Because I live ye shall live also.'

But do not let us forget that this great promise does

not belong only to the Church as a whole, but that we have each to bring it down to our own individual lives, and to be quite sure of this, that in spite of all that sense says, in spite of all that quivering hearts and weeping eyes may seem to prove, there *is* a wall of fire round each of us, if we are keeping near Jesus Christ, through which it is as impossible that any real evil should pass and get at us, as it would be impossible that any living thing should pass through the flaming battlements that the Prophet saw round his ideal city. Only we have to interpret that promise by faith and not by sense, and we have to make it possible that it shall be fulfilled by keeping inside the wall, and trusting to it. As faith dwindles, the fiery wall burns dim, and evil can get across its embers, and can get at us. Keep within the battlements, and they will flame up bright and impassable, with a fire that on the outer side consumes, but to those within is a fire that cherishes and warms.

II. The next point of the promise passes into a more intimate region. It is well to have a defence from that which is without us; but it is more needful to have, if a comparison can be made between the two, a glory 'in the midst' of us.

The one is external defence; the other inward illumination, with all which light symbolises—knowledge, joy, purity.

There is even more than that meant by this great promise. For notice that emphatic little word *the—the* glory, not *a* glory—in the midst of her. Now you all know what 'the glory' was. It was that symbolic Light that spoke of the special presence of God, and went with the Children of Israel in their wanderings, and sat between the Cherubim. There was no 'Shechinah,' as it is technically called, in that second Temple. But yet the Prophet says, 'The glory'—the actual presence of God—'shall be in the midst of her,' and the meaning of that great promise is taught us by the very last vision in the New Testament, in which the Seer of the Apocalypse says, 'The glory of the Lord did lighten it' (evidently quoting Zechariah), 'and the Lamb is the light thereof.' So the city is lit as by one central glow of radiance that flashes its beams into every corner, and therefore 'there shall be no night there.'

Now this promise, too, bears on churches and on individuals. On the Church as a whole it bears in this way: the only means by which a Christian community can fulfil its function, and be the light of the world, is by having the presence of God, in no metaphor, the actual presence of the illuminating Spirit in its midst. If it has not that, it may have anything and everything else—wealth, culture, learning, eloquence, influence in the world—but all is of no use; it will be darkness. We are light only in proportion as we are 'light in the Lord.' As long as we, as communities, keep our hearts in touch with Him, so long do we shine. Break the contact, and the light fades and flickers out.

The same thing is true, dear brethren, about individuals. For each of us the secret of joy, of purity, of knowledge, is that we be holding close communion with God. If we have Him in the depths of our hearts, then, and only then, shall we be 'light in the Lord.'

And now look at the last point which follows, as I have said, as the result of the other two.

III. 'Jerusalem shall be without walls.'

It is to be like the defenceless villages scattered up and down over Israel. There is no need for bulwarks of stone. The wall of fire is round about. The Prophet

has a vision of a great city, of a type unknown in those
old times, though familiar to us in our more peaceful
days, where there was no hindrance to expansion by
encircling ramparts, no crowding together of the people
because they needed to hide behind the city walls; and
where the growing community could spread out into
the outer suburbs, and have fresh air and ample space.
That is the vision of the manner of city that Jerusalem
was to be. It did not come true, but the ideal was this.
It has not yet come true sufficiently in regard to the
churches of to-day, but it ought to be the goal to which
they are tending. The more a Christian community is
independent of external material supports and defences
the better.

I am not going to talk about the policy or impolicy
of Established Churches, as they are called. But it
seems to me that the principle that is enshrined in this
vision is their condemnation. Never mind about stone
and lime walls, trust in God and you will not need them,
and you will be strong and 'established' just in the
proportion in which you are cut loose from all dependence upon, and consequent subordination to, the civil
power.

But there is another thought that I might suggest,
though I do not know that it is directly in the line of
the Prophet's vision; and that is—a Christian Church
should neither depend on, nor be cribbed and cramped
by, men-made defences of any kind. Luther tells us
somewhere, in his parabolic way, of people that wept
because there were no visible pillars to hold up the
heavens, and were afraid that the sky would fall upon
their heads. No, no, there is no fear of that happening,
for an unseen hand holds them up. A church that
hides behind the fortifications of its grandfathers'

erection has no room for expansion; and if it has no room for expansion it will not long continue as large as it is. It must either grow greater, or grow, and deserve to grow, less.

The same thing is true, dear brethren, about ourselves individually. Zechariah's prophecy was never meant to prevent what he himself helped to further, the building of the actual walls of the actual city. And our dependence upon God is not to be so construed as that we are to waive our own common-sense and our own effort. That is not faith; it is fanaticism.

We have to build ourselves round, in this world, with other things than the 'wall of fire,' but in all our building we have to say, 'Except the Lord build the house, they labour in vain that build it. Except the Lord keep the city, the watchers watch in vain.' But yet neither Jerusalem nor the Church, nor the earthly state of that believer who lives most fully the life of faith, exhausts this promise. It waits for the day when the city shall descend, 'like a bride adorned for her husband, having no need of the sun nor of the moon, for the glory . . . lightens it.' Having walls, indeed, but for splendour, not for defence; and having gates, which have only one of the functions of a gate—to stand wide open, to the east and the west, and the north and the south, for the nations to enter in; and never needing to be barred against enemies by day, 'for there shall be no night there.'

A VISION OF JUDGMENT AND CLEANSING

'And he shewed me Joshua the high priest standing before the Angel of the Lord, and Satan standing at his right hand to resist him. 2. And the Lord said unto Satan, The Lord rebuke thee, O Satan; even the Lord that hath chosen Jerusalem rebuke thee: is not this a brand plucked out of the fire? 3. Now Joshua was clothed with filthy garments, and stood before the Angel. 4. And He answered and spake unto those that stood before Him, saying, Take away the filthy garments from him. And unto him He said, Behold, I have caused thine iniquity to pass from thee, and I will clothe thee with change of raiment. 5. And I said, Let them set a fair mitre upon his head. So they set a fair mitre upon his head, and clothed him with garments. And the Angel of the Lord stood by. 6. And the Angel of the Lord protested unto Joshua, saying, 7. Thus saith the Lord of Hosts, If thou wilt walk in My ways, and if thou wilt keep My charge, then thou shalt also judge My house, and shalt also keep My courts, and I will give thee places to walk among these that stand by. 8. Hear now, O Joshua the high priest, thou, and thy fellows that sit before thee: for they are men wondered at: for, behold, I will bring forth My servant The BRANCH. 9. For behold the stone that I have laid before Joshua; upon one stone shall be seven eyes: behold, I will engrave the graving thereof, saith the Lord of Hosts, and I will remove the iniquity of that land in one day. 10. In that day, saith the Lord of Hosts, shall ye call every man his neighbour under the vine and under the fig-tree.'—ZECHARIAH iii. 1-10.

ZECHARIAH worked side by side with Haggai to quicken the religious life of the people, and thus to remove the gravest hindrances to the work of rebuilding the Temple. Inward indifference, not outward opposition, is the real reason for slow progress in God's work, and prophets who see visions and preach repentance are the true practical men.

This vision followed Haggai's prophecy at the interval of a month. It falls into two parts—a symbolical vision and a series of promises founded on it.

I. The Symbolical Vision (vs. 1-5).—The scene of the vision is left undetermined, and the absence of any designation of locality gives the picture the sublimity of indefiniteness. Three figures, seen he knows not where, stand clear before the Prophet's inward eye. They were shown him by an unnamed person, who is evidently Jehovah Himself. The real and the ideal are marvellously mingled in the conception of Joshua the high priest—the man whom the people saw every day

going about Jerusalem—standing at the bar of God, with
Satan as his accuser. The trial is in process when the
Prophet is permitted to see. We do not hear the plead-
ings on either side, but the sentence is solemnly recorded.
The accusations are dismissed, their bringer rebuked,
and in token of acquittal, the filthy garments which
the accused had worn are changed for the full festal
attire of the high priest.

What, then, is the meaning of this grand symbolism?
The first point to keep well in view is the representative character of the high priest. He appears as laden
not with individual but national sins. In him Israel is,
as it were, concentrated, and what befalls him is the
image of what befalls the nation. His dirty dress is
the familiar symbol of sin; and he wears it, just as he
wore his sacerdotal dress, in his official capacity, as the
embodied nation. He stands before the judgment seat,
bearing not his own but the people's sins.

Two great truths are thereby taught, which are as
true to-day as ever. The first is that representation is
essential to priesthood. It was so in shadowy and
external fashion in Israel; it is so in deepest and most
blessed reality in Christ's priesthood. He stands before
God as our representative—'And the Lord hath made
to meet on Him the iniquity of us all.' If by faith we
unite ourselves with Him, there ensues a wondrous
transference of characteristics, so that our sin becomes
His, and His righteousness becomes ours; and that in
no mere artificial or forensic sense, but in inmost reality.
Theologians talk of a *communicatio idiomatum* as between the human and the divine elements in Christ.
There is an analogous passage of the attributes of
either to the other, in the relation of the believer to his
Saviour.

The second thought in this symbolic appearance of Joshua before the angel of the Lord is that the sins of God's people are even now present before His perfect judgment, as reasons for withdrawing from them His favour. That is a solemn truth, which should never be forgotten. A Christian man's sins do accuse him at the bar of God. They are all visible there; and so far as their tendency goes, they are like wedges driven in to rend him from God.

But the second figure in the vision is 'the Satan,' standing in the plaintiff's place at the Judge's right hand, to accuse Joshua. The Old Testament teaching as to the evil spirit who 'accuses' good men is not so developed as that of the New, which is quite natural, inasmuch as the shadow of bright light is deeper than that of faint rays. It is most full in the latest books, as here and in Job; but doctrinal inferences drawn from such highly imaginative symbolism as this are precarious. No one who accepts the authority of our Lord can well deny the existence and activity of a malignant spirit, who would fain make the most of men's sins, and use them as a means of separating their doers from God. That is the conception here.

But the main stress of the vision lies, not on the accuser or his accusation, but on the Judge's sentence, which alone is recorded. 'The Angel of the Lord' is named in verse 1 as the Judge, while the sentence in verse 2 is spoken by 'the Lord.' It would lead us far away from our purpose to inquire whether that Angel of the Lord is an earlier manifestation of the eternal Son, who afterwards became flesh—a kind of preluding or rehearsing of the Incarnation. But in any case, God so dwells in Him as that what the Angel says God says and the speaker varies as in our text. The accuser is rebuked, and God's rebuke is not a mere word, but brings with it punishment. The malicious accusations have failed, and their aim is to be gathered from the language which announces their miscarriage. Obviously Satan sought to procure the withdrawal of divine favour from Joshua, because of his sin; that is, to depose the nation from its place as the covenant people, because of its transgressions of the covenant. Satan here represents what might otherwise have been called, in theological language, 'the demands of justice.' The answer given him is deeply instructive as to the grounds of the divine forbearance.

Note that Joshua's guilt as the representative of the people is not denied, but tacitly admitted and actually spoken of in verse 4. Why, then, does not the accuser have his way? For two reasons. God has chosen Jerusalem. His great purpose, the fruit of His undeserved mercy, is not to be turned aside by man's sins. The thought is the same as that of Jeremiah: 'If heaven above can be measured . . . then I will also cast off all the seed of Israel for all that they have done' (Jer. xxxi. 37). Again, the fact that Joshua was 'a brand plucked from the burning'—that is, that the people whom he represented had been brought unconsumed from the furnace of captivity—is a reason with God for continuing to extend His favour, though they have sinned. God's past mercies are a motive with him. Creatural love is limited, and too often says, 'I have forgiven so often, that I am wearied, and can do it no more.' He *has*, therefore he *will*. We often come to the end of our longsuffering a good many times short of the four hundred and ninety a day which Christ prescribes. But God never does. True, Joshua and his people have sinned, and that since their restoration, and Satan had a good argument in pointing to these transgressions; but God does not say, 'I will put back the half-burned brand in the fire again, since the evil is not burned out of it,' but forgives again, because He has forgiven before.

The sentence is followed by the exchange of the filthy garments symbolical of sin, for the full array of the high priest. Ministering angels are dimly seen in the background, and are summoned to unclothe and clothe Joshua. The Prophet ventures to ask that the sacerdotal attire should be completed by the turban or mitre, probably that headdress which bore the significant writing 'Holiness to the Lord,' expressive of the destination of Israel and of its ceremonial cleanness. The meaning of this change of clothing is given in verse 4: 'I have caused thine iniquity to pass from thee.' Thus the complete restoration of the pardoned and cleansed nation to its place as a nation of priests to Jehovah is symbolised. To us the gospel of forgiveness fills up the outline in the vision; and we know how, when sin testifies against us, we have an Advocate with the Father, and how the infinite love flows out to us notwithstanding all sin, and how the stained garment of our souls can be stripped off, and the 'fine linen clean and white,' the priestly dress on the day of atonement, be put on us, and we be made priests unto God.

II. The remainder of the vision is the address of the Angel of the Lord to Joshua, developing the blessings now made sure to him and his people by this renewed consecration and cleansing. First (verse 7) is the promise of continuance in office and access to God's presence, which, however, are contingent on obedience. The forgiven man must keep God's charge, if he is to retain his standing. On that condition, he has 'a place of

access among those that stand by'; that is, the privilege of approach to God, like the attendant angels.
This promise may be taken as surpassing the prerogatives hitherto accorded to the high priest, who had
only the right of entrance into the holiest place once a
year, but now is promised the *entrée* to the heavenly
court, as if he were one of the bright spirits who stand
there. They who have access with confidence within
the veil because Christ is there, have more than the
ancient promise of this vision.

The main point of verse 8 is the promise of the
Messiah, but the former part of the verse is remarkable. Joshua and his fellows are summoned to listen,
'for they are men which are a sign.' The meaning
seems to be that he and his brethren who sat as his
assessors in official functions, are collectively a sign or
embodied prophecy of what is to come. Their restoration to their offices was a shadowy prophecy of a greater
act of forgiving grace, which was to be effected by the
coming of the Messiah.

The name 'Branch' is used here as a proper name.
Jeremiah (Jer. xxiii. 5 ; xxxiii. 15) had already employed
it as a designation of Messiah, which he had apparently
learned from Isaiah iv. 2. The idea of the word is that
of the similar names used by Isaiah, 'a shoot out of the
stock of Jesse, and a Branch out of his roots' (Isaiah
xi. 1), and 'a tender plant, and as a root out of a dry
ground' (Isaiah liii. 2) ; namely, that of his origin from
the fallen house of David, and the lowliness of his
appearance.

The Messiah is again meant by the 'stone' in verse 9.
Probably there was some great stone taken from the
ruins, to which the symbol attaches itself. The foundation of the second Temple had been laid years before

the prophecy, but the stone may still have been visible.
The Rabbis have much to say about a great stone which
had been in the first Temple, and there used for the support of the ark, but in the second was set in the empty
place where the ark should have been. Isaiah had
prophesied of the 'tried cornerstone' laid in Zion, and
Psalm cxviii. 22 had sung of the stone rejected and
made the head of the corner. We go in the track, then,
of established usage, when we see in this stone the
emblem of Messiah, and associate with it all thoughts
of firmness, preciousness, support, foundation of the
true Temple, basis of hope, ground of certitude, and
whatever other substratum of fixity and immovable-
ness men's hearts or lives need. In all possible aspects
of the metaphor, Jesus is the Foundation.

And what are the 'seven eyes on the stone'? That
may simply be a vivid way of saying that the fulness
of divine Providence would watch over the Messiah,
bringing Him when the time was ripe, and fitting Him
for His work. But if we remember the subsequent
explanation (iv. 10) of the 'seven,' as 'the eyes of the
Lord which run to and fro through the whole earth,'
and connect this with Revelation v. 6, we can scarcely
rest content with that meaning, but find here the
deeper thought that the fulness of the divine Spirit
was given to Messiah, even as Isaiah (xi. 2) prophesies
of the sevenfold Spirit.

'I will engrave the graving thereof' is somewhat
obscure. It seems to mean that the seven eyes will be
cut on the stone, like masons' marks. If the seven eyes
are the full energies of the Holy Spirit, God's cutting of
them on the stone is equivalent to His giving them to
His Son; and the fulfilment of the promise was when
He gave the Holy Spirit not 'by measure unto Him.'

The blessed purpose of Messiah's coming and endowment with the Spirit is gloriously stated in the last clause of verse 9: 'I will remove the iniquity of that land in one day.' Jesus Christ has 'once for all' made atonement, as the Epistle to the Hebrews so often says. The better Joshua by one offering has taken away sin. 'The breadth of Thy land, O Immanuel,' stretched far beyond the narrow bounds which Zechariah knew for Israel's territory. It includes the whole world. As has been beautifully said, 'That one day is the day of Golgotha.'

The vision closes with a picture of the felicity of Messianic times, which recalls the description of the golden age of Solomon, when 'Judah and Israel dwelt safely, every man under his vine and under his fig-tree' (1 Kings iv. 25). In like manner the nation, cleansed, restored to its priestly privilege of free access to God by the Messiah who comes with the fulness of the Spirit, shall dwell in safety, and shall be knit together by friendship, and unenvyingly shall each share his good with all others, recognising in every man a neighbour, and gladly welcoming him to partake of all the blessings which the true Solomon has brought to his house and heart.

THE RIGHT OF ENTRY

'I will give thee places to walk among these that stand by.'—ZECHARIAH iii. 7.

A WORD or two of explanation will probably be necessary in order to see the full meaning of this great promise. The Prophet has just been describing a vision of judgment which he saw, in which the high priest, as representative of the nation, stood

before the Angel of the Lord as an unclean person.
He is cleansed and clothed, his foul raiment stripped
off him, and a fair priestly garment, with 'Holiness to
the Lord' written on the front of it, put upon him.
And then follow a series of promises, of which the
climax is the one that I have read. 'I will give thee
a place of access,' says the Revised Version, instead of
'places to walk'; 'I will give thee a place of access
among those that stand by'; the attendant angels are
dimly seen surrounding their Lord. And so the
promise of my text, in highly figurative fashion, is
that of free and unrestrained approach to God, of a
life that is like that of the angels that stand before
His Face.

So, then, the words suggest to us, first, what a
Christian life may be.

There are two images blended together in the great
words of my text; the one is that of a king's court,
the other is that of a temple. With regard to the
former it is a privilege given to the highest nobles of a
kingdom—or it was so in old days—to have the right of
entrée, at all moments and in all circumstances, to the
monarch. With regard to the latter, the prerogative of
the high priest, who was the recipient of this promise,
as to access to the Temple, was a very restricted one.
Once a year, with the blood that prevented his annihilation by the brightness of the Presence into which he
ventured, he passed within the veil, and stood before
that mysterious Light that coruscated in the darkness
of the Holy of Holies. But this High Priest is promised
an access on all days and at all times; and that He
may stand there, beside and like the seraphim, who
with one pair of wings veiled their faces in token of
the incapacity of the creature to behold the Creator;

'with twain veiled their feet' in token of the unworthiness of creatural activities to be set before Him, 'and with twain did fly' in token of their willingness to serve Him with all their energies. This Priest passes within the veil when He will. Or, to put away the two metaphors, and to come to the reality far greater than either of them, we can, whensoever we please, pass into the presence before which the splendours of an earthly monarch's court shrink into vulgarity, and attain to a real reception of the light that irradiates the true Holy Place, before which that which shone in the earthly shrine dwindles and darkens into a shadow. We may live with God, and in Him, and wrap a veil and 'privacy of glorious light' about us, whilst we pilgrim upon earth, and may have hidden lives which, notwithstanding all their surface occupation with the distractions and duties and enjoyments of the present, deep down in their centres are knit to God. Our lives may on the outside thus be largely amongst the things seen and temporal, and yet all the while may penetrate through these, and lay hold with their true roots on the eternal. If we have any religious life at all, the measure in which we possess it is the measure in which we may ever more dwell in the house of the Lord, and have our hearts in the secret place of the Most High, amid the stillnesses and the sanctities of His immediate dwelling.

Our Master is the great Example of this, of whom it is said, not only in reference to His mysterious and unique union of nature with the Father in His divinity, but in reference to the humanity which He had in common with us all, yet without sin, that the Son of Man came down from heaven, and even in the act of coming, and when He had come, was yet the Son of

T

Man 'which *is in heaven.*' Thus we, too, may have 'a
place of access among them that stand by,' and not
need to envy the angels and the spirits of the just
made perfect, the closeness of their communion, and
the vividness of their vision, for the same, in its degree,
may be ours. We, too, can turn all our desires into
petitions, and of every wish make a prayer. We, too,
can refer all our needs to His infinite supply. We, too,
may consciously connect all our doings with His will
and His glory; and for us it is possible that there shall
be, as if borne on those electric wires that go striding
across pathless deserts, and carry their messages
through unpeopled solitudes, between Him and us a
communication unbroken and continuous, which, by a
greater wonder than even that of the telegraph, shall
carry two messages, going opposite ways simultane-
ously, bearing to Him the swift aspirations and
supplications of our spirits, and bringing to us the
abundant answer of His grace. Such a conversation in
heaven, and such association with the bands of the
blessed is possible even for a life upon earth.

Secondly, let us consider this promise as a pattern
for us of what Christian life should be, and, alas! so
seldom is.

All privilege is duty, and everything that is possible
for any Christian man to become, it is imperative on
him to aim at. There is no greater sin than living
beneath the possibilities of our lives, in any region,
whether religious or other it matters not. Sin is not
only going contrary to the known law of God, but also
a falling beneath a divine ideal which is capable of
realisation. And in regard to our Christian life, if God
has flung open His temple-gates and said to us, 'Come
in, My child, and dwell in the secret place of the Most

High, and abide there under the shadow of the Almighty, finding protection and communion and companionship in My worship,' there can be nothing more insulting to Him, and nothing more fatally indicative of the alienation of our hearts from Him, than that we should refuse to obey the merciful invitation.

What should we say of a subject who never presented himself in the court to which he had the right of free *entrée*? His absence would be a mark of disloyalty, and would be taken as a warning-bell in preparation for his rebellion. What should we say of a son or a daughter, living in the same city with their parents, who never crossed the threshold of the father's house, but that they had lost the spirit of a child, and that if there was no desire to be near there could be no love?

So, if we will ask ourselves, 'How often do I use this possibility of communion with God, which might irradiate all my daily life?' I think we shall need little else, in the nature of evidence, that our piety and our religious experience are terribly stunted and dwarfed, in comparison with what they ought to be.

There is an old saying, 'He that can tell how often he has thought of God in a day has thought of Him too seldom.' I dare say many of us would have little difficulty in counting on the fingers of one hand, and perhaps not needing them all, the number of times in which, to-day, our thoughts have gone heavenwards. What we may be is what we ought to be, and not to use the prerogatives of our position is the worst of sins.

Again, my text suggests to us what every Christian life will hereafter perfectly be.

Some commentators take the words of my text to

refer only to the communion of saints from the earth, with the glorified angels, in and after the Resurrection. That is a poor interpretation, for heaven is here to-day. But still there is a truth in the interpretation which we need not neglect. Only let us remember that nothing— so far as Scripture teaches us—begins yonder except the full reaping of the fruits of what has been sown here, and that if a man's feet have not learned the path into the Temple when he was here upon earth, death will not be the guide for him into the Father's presence. All that here has been imperfect, fragmentary, occasional, interrupted, and marred in our communion with God, shall one day be complete. And then, oh! then, who can tell what undreamed-of depths and sweetnesses of renewed communion and of intercourses begun, for the first time then, between 'those that stand by,' and have stood there for ages, will then be realised?

'Ye are come'—even here on earth—'to an innumerable company of angels, to the general assembly and Church of the first-born,' but for us all there may be the quiet hope that hereafter we shall 'dwell in the house of the Lord for ever'; and 'in solemn troops and sweet societies' shall learn what fellowship, and brotherhood, and human love may be.

Lastly, notice, not from my text but from its context, how any life may become thus privileged.

The promise is preceded by a condition: 'If thou wilt walk in My ways, and if thou wilt keep My charge, then . . . I will give thee access among those that stand by.' That is to say, you cannot keep the consciousness of God's presence, nor have any blessedness of communion with Him, if you are living in disobedience of His commandments or in neglect of manifest duty. A thin film of vapour in our sky to-night will hide the moon. Though the vapour itself may be invisible, it will be efficacious as a veil. And any sin, great or small, fleecy and thin, will suffice to shut me out from God. If we are keeping His commandments, then, and only then, shall we have access with free hearts into His presence.

But to lay down that condition seems the same thing as slamming the door in every man's face. But let us remember what went before my text, the experience of the priest to whom it was spoken in the vision. His filthy garments were stripped off him, and the pure white robes worn on the great Day of Atonement, the sacerdotal dress, were put upon him. It is the *cleansed* man that has access among 'those that stand by.' And if you ask how the cleansing is to be effected, take the great words of the Epistle to the Hebrews as an all-sufficient answer, coinciding with, but transcending, what this vision taught Zechariah: 'Having, therefore, brethren, boldness to enter into the holiest of all, by the blood of Jesus, . . . and having a High Priest over the house of God; let us draw near with a true heart, in full assurance of faith, having our hearts sprinkled from an evil conscience.' Cleansed by Christ, and with Him for our Forerunner, we have boldness and 'access with confidence by the faith of Him,' who proclaims to the whole world, 'No man cometh to the Father but by Me.'

THE SOURCE OF POWER

'And the Angel that talked with me came again, and waked me, as a man that is wakened out of his sleep, 2. And said unto me, What seest thou? And I said, I have looked, and behold, a candlestick all of gold, with a bowl upon the top of it, and his seven lamps thereon, and seven pipes to the seven lamps which are upon the top thereof : 3. And two olive-trees by it, one upon the right side of the bowl, and the other upon the left side thereof. 4. So I answered and spake to the Angel that talked with me, saying, What are these, my Lord? 5. Then the Angel that talked with me answered and said unto me, Knowest thou not what these be? And I said, No, my Lord. 6. Then He answered and spake unto me, saying, This is the word of the Lord unto Zerubbabel, saying, Not by might, nor by power, but by My Spirit, saith the Lord of Hosts. 7. Who art thou, O great mountain? before Zerubbabel thou shalt become a plain : and he shall bring forth the head-stone thereof with shoutings, crying, Grace, grace unto it. 8. Moreover, the word of the Lord came unto me, saying, 9. The hands of Zerubbabel have laid the foundation of this house; his hands shall also finish it ; and thou shalt know that the Lord of Hosts hath sent me unto you. 10. For who hath despised the day of small things? for they shall rejoice, and shall see the plummet in the hand of Zerubbabel with those seven ; they are the eyes of the Lord, which run to and fro through the whole earth.'—ZECHARIAH iv. 1-10.

THE preceding vision had reference to Joshua the priest, and showed him restored to his prerogative of entrance into the sanctuary. This one concerns his colleague Zerubbabel, the representative of civil power, as he of ecclesiastical, and promises that he shall succeed in rebuilding the Temple. The supposition is natural that the actual work of reconstruction was mainly in the hands of the secular ruler.

Flesh is weak, and the Prophet had fallen into deep sleep, after the tension of the previous vision. That had been shown him by Jehovah, but in this vision we have the same angel interpreter who had spoken with Zechariah before. He does not bring the vision, but simply wakes the Prophet that he may see it, and directs his attention to it by the question, 'What seest thou?' The best way to teach is to make the learner put his conceptions into definite words. We see things more clearly, and they make a deeper impression, when we tell what we see. How many lazy looks we give at things temporal as well as at things eternal, after which we should be unable to answer the Angel's question! It is not every one who sees what he looks at.

The passage has two parts—the vision and its interpretation, with related promises.

The vision may be briefly disposed of. Its original is the great lamp which stood in the tabernacle, and was replaced in the Solomonic Temple by ten smaller ones. These had been carried away at the Captivity, and we do not read of their restoration. But the main thing to note is the differences between this lamp and the one in the tabernacle. The description here confines itself to these: They are three—the 'bowl' or reservoir above the lamp, the pipes from it to the seven lights, and the two olive-trees which stood on either side of the lamp and replenished from their branches the supply in the reservoir. The tabernacle lamp had no reservoir, and consequently no pipes, but was fed with oil by the priests. The meaning of the variations, then, is plain. They were intended to express the fuller and more immediately divine supply of oil. If the Revised Version's rendering of the somewhat doubtful numerals in verse 2 be accepted, each several light had seven pipes, thus expressing the perfection of its supplies.

Now, there can be no doubt about the symbolism of the tabernacle lamp. It represented the true office of Israel, as it rayed out its beams into the darkness of the desert. It meant the same thing as Christ's words, 'Ye are the light of the world,' and as the vision of the seven golden candlesticks, in Revelation i. 12, 13, 20. The substitution of separate lamps for one with seven lights may teach the difference between the mere formal unity of the people of God in the Old Testament and the true oneness, conjoined with diversity, in the New Testament Church, which is one because Christ walks in the midst. Zechariah's lamp, then, called to the minds of the little band of restored exiles their high vocation, and the changed arrangements for the supply of that oil, which is the standing emblem for divine communications fitting for service, or, to keep to the metaphor, fitting to shine, signified the abundance of these.

The explanation of the vision is introduced, as at Zechariah i. 9, 19, by the Prophet's question of its meaning. His angelic teacher is astonished at his dullness, as indeed heavenly eyes must often be at ours, and asks if he does not know so familiar an object. The Prophet's 'No, my Lord,' brings full explanation. Ingenuously acknowledged ignorance never asks Heaven for enlightenment in vain.

First, the true source of strength and success, as shown by the vision, is declared in plain terms. What fed the lamp? Oil, which symbolises the gift of a divine Spirit, if not in the full personal sense as in the New Testament, yet certainly as a God-breathed influence, preparing prophets, priests, kings, and even artificers, for their several forms of service. Whence came the oil? From the two olive-trees, which though, as verse 14 shows, they represented the two leaders, yet set forth the truth that their power for their work was from God; for the Bible knows nothing of 'nature' as a substitute for or antithesis to God, and the growth of the olive and its yield of oil is His doing.

This, then, was the message for Zerubbabel and his people, that God would give such gifts as they needed, in order that the light which He Himself had kindled should not be quenched. If the lamp was fed with oil, it would burn, and there would be a Temple for it to stand in. If we try to imagine the feebleness of the handful of discouraged men, and the ring of enemies round them, we may feel the sweetness of the promise which bade them not despond because they had little of what the word calls might.

We all need the lesson; for the blustering world is apt to make us forget the true source of all real strength for holy service or for noble living. The world's power at its mightiest is weak, and the Church's true power, at her feeblest, is omnipotent, if only she grasps the strength which is hers, and takes the Spirit which is given. The eternal antithesis of man's weakness at his haughtiest, and God's strength even in its feeblest possessors, is taught by that lamp flaming, whatever envious hands or howling storms might seek to quench it, because fed by oil from on high. Let us keep to God's strength, and not corrupt His oil with mixtures of foul-smelling stuff of our own compounding.

Next, in the strength of that revelation of the source of might a defiant challenge is blown to the foe. The 'great mountain' is primarily the frowning difficulties which lifted themselves against Zerubbabel's enterprise, and more widely the whole mass of worldly opposition encountered by God's servants in every age. It seems to bar all advance; but an unseen Hand crushes it down, and flattens it out into a level, on which progress is easy. The Hebrew gives the suddenness and completeness of the transformation with great force; for the whole clause, 'Thou shalt become a plain,' is one word in the original.

Such triumphant rising above difficulties is not presumption when it has been preceded by believing gaze on the source of strength. If we have taken to heart the former words of the Prophet, we shall not be in danger of rash overconfidence when we calmly front obstacles in the path of duty, assured that every mountain shall be made low. A brave scorn of the world, both in its sweetnesses and its terrors, befits God's men, and is apt to fulfil its own confidences; for most of these terrors are like ghosts, who will not wait to be spoken to, but melt away if fairly faced. Nor should we forget the other side of this thought; namely, that it is the constant drift of Providence to abase the lofty in mind, and to raise the lowly. What is high is sure to get many knocks which pass over lower heads. To men of faith every mountain shall either become a plain or be cast into the sea.

Then follows, on the double revelation of the source of strength and the futility of opposition, the assurance of the successful completion of the work. The stone which is to crown the structure shall be brought forth and set in its place amid jubilant prayers not offered in vain, that 'grace'—that is, the protecting favour of God—may rest on it.

The same thought is reiterated and enlarged in the next 'word,' which is somewhat separated from the former, as if the flow of prophetic communication had paused for a moment, and then been resumed. In verse 9 we have the assurance, so seldom granted to God's workers, that Zerubbabel shall be permitted to complete the task which he had begun. It is the fate of most of us to inherit unfinished work from our predecessors, and to bequeath the like to our successors. And in one aspect, all human work is unfinished, as being but a fragment of the fulfilment of the mighty purpose which runs through all the ages. Yet some

are more happy than others, in that they see an approximate completion of their work. But whether it be
so or not, our task is to 'do the little we can do, and
leave the rest with God,' sure that He will work all the
fragments into a perfect whole, and content to do the
smallest bit of service for Him. Few of us are strong
enough to do separate building. We are like coral
insects, whose reef is one, though its makers are
millions.

Zerubbabel finished his task, but its end was but a
new beginning of an order of things of which he did
not see the end. There are no beginnings or endings,
properly speaking, in human affairs, but all is one
unbroken flow. One man only has made a real new
beginning, and that is Jesus Christ; and He only will
really carry His work to its very last issues. He is
Alpha and Omega, the beginning and the ending. He
is the Foundation of the true Temple, and He is also
the Headstone of the corner, the foundation on which
all rests, the apex to which all runs up. 'When He
begins, He will also make an end.'

The completion of the work is to be the token that
the 'angel who spake with me' was God's messenger.
We can know that before the fulfilment, but we cannot
but know it after. Better to be sure that the message
is from God while yet the certainty is the result of
faith, than to be sure of it afterwards, when the issue
has shattered and shamed our doubts.

If we realise that God's Spirit is the guarantee for
the success of work done for God, we shall escape the
vulgar error of measuring the importance of things by
their size, as, no doubt, many of these builders were
doing. No one will help on the day of great things
who despises that of small ones. They say that the

seeds of the 'big trees' in California are the smallest
of all the conifers. I do not vouch for the truth of the
statement, but God's work always begins with little
seeds, as the history of the Church and of every good
cause shows. 'What do these feeble Jews?' sneered
the spectators of their poor little walls, painfully piled
up, over which a fox could jump. They did very little,
but they were building the city of God, which has
outlasted all the mockers.

Men might look with contempt on the humble beginning, but other eyes than theirs looked at it with
other emotions. The eyes which in the last vision
were spoken of as directed on the foundation stone,
gaze on the work with joy. These are the seven eyes
of 'the Lord,' which are 'the seven Spirits of God,
sent forth into all the earth' (Rev. v. 6). The
Spirit is here contemplated in the manifoldness of His
operations rather than in the unity of His person.
Thus the closing assurance, which involves the success
of the work, since God's eyes rest on it with delight,
comes round to the first declaration, 'Not by might, not
by power, but by My Spirit.' Note the strong contrast
between 'despise' and 'rejoice.' What matter the
scoffs of mockers, if God approves? What are they
but fools who look at that which moves His joy, and
find in it only food for scorn? What will become of
their laughter at last? If we try to get so near God
as to see things with His eyes, we shall be saved from
many a false estimate of what is great and what is
small, and may have our own poor little doings invested
with strange dignity, because He deigns to behold and
bless them.

THE FOUNDER AND FINISHER OF THE TEMPLE

'The hands of Zerubbabel have laid the foundation of this house; his hands shall also finish it.'—ZECHARIAH iv. 9.

I AM afraid that Zerubbabel is very little more than a grotesque name to most Bible-readers, so I may be allowed a word of explanation as to him and as to the original force of my text. He was a prince of the blood royal of Israel, and the civil leader of the first detachment of returning exiles. With Joshua, the high priest, he came, at the head of a little company, to Palestine, and there pathetically attempted, with small resources, to build up some humble house that might represent the vanished glories of Solomon's Temple. Political enmity on the part of the surrounding tribes stopped the work for nearly twenty years. During all that time, the hole in the ground, where the foundations had been dug and a few courses of stones been laid, gaped desolate, a sad reminder to the feeble band of the failure of their hopes. But with the accession of a new Persian king, new energy sprang up, and new, favourable circumstances developed themselves. The Prophet Zechariah came to the front, although quite a young man, and became the mainspring of the renewed activity in building the Temple. The words of my text are, of course, in their plain, original meaning, the prophetic assurance that the man, grown an old man by this time, who had been honoured to take the first spadeful of soil out of the earth should be the man 'to bring forth the headstone with shoutings of Grace, grace unto it!'

But whilst that is the original application, and whilst

the words open to us a little door into long years of
constrained suspension of work and discouraged hope,
I think we shall not be wrong if we recognise in them
something deeper than a reference to the Prince of
David's line, concerning whom they were originally
spoken. I take them to be, in the true sense of the
term, a Messianic prophecy; and I take it that, just
because Zerubbabel, a member of that royal house
from which the Messiah was to come, was the builder
of the Temple, he was a prophetic person. What was
true about him primarily is thereby shown to have a
bearing upon the greater Son of David who was to
come thereafter, and who was to build the Temple of
the Lord. In that aspect I desire to look at the words
now: 'His hands have laid the foundation of the
house, and His hands shall also finish it.'

I. There is, then, here a large truth as to Christ, the
true Temple-builder.

It is the same blessed message which was given from
His own lips long centuries after, when He spoke from
heaven to John in Patmos, and said, 'I am Alpha
and Omega, the First and the Last.' The first letter
of the Greek alphabet, and the last letter of the Greek
alphabet, and all the letters that lie between, and all
the words that you can make out of the letters—they
are all from Him, and He underlies everything.

Now that is true about creation, in the broadest and
in the most absolute sense. For what does the New
Testament say, with the consenting voice of all its
writers? 'In the beginning was the Word, and the
Word was with God, and the Word was God. Without
Him was not anything made that was made.' His
hands laid the foundations of this great house of the
universe, with its 'many mansions.' And what says

Paul? 'He is the Beginning, in Him all things consist' . . . 'that in all things He might have the pre-eminence.' And what says He Himself from heaven? 'I am the First and the Last.' So, in regard to everything in the universe, Christ is its origin, and Christ is its goal and its end. He 'has laid the foundation, and His hands shall also finish it.'

But, further, we turn to the application which is the more usual one, and say that He is the Beginner and Finisher of the work of redemption, which is His only from its inception to its accomplishment, from the first breaking of the ground for the foundations of the Temple to the triumphant bringing forth of the last stone that crowns the corner and gleams on the top-most pinnacle of the completed structure. There is nothing about Jesus Christ, as it seems to me, more manifest, unless our eyes are blinded by prejudice, than that the Carpenter of Nazareth, who grew up amidst the ordinary conditions of infant manhood, was trained as other Jewish children, increased in wisdom, spoke a language that had been moulded by man, and inherited His nation's mental and spiritual equipment, yet stands forth on the pages of these four Gospels as a perfectly original man, to put it on the lowest ground, and as owing nothing to any prede-cessor, and not as merely one in a series, or naturally accounted for by reference to His epoch or conditions. He makes a new beginning; He presents a perfectly fresh thing in the history of human nature. Just as His coming was the introduction into the heart of humanity of a new type, the second Adam, the Lord from heaven, so the work that He does is all His own. He does it all Himself, for all that His servants do in carrying out the purposes dear to His heart is done by

His working in and through them, and though we are
fellow-labourers with Him, His hands alone lay every
stone of the Temple.

Not only does my text, in its highest application,
point to Jesus Christ as the Author of redemption from
its very beginning, but it also declares that all through
the ages His hand is at work. 'Shall also finish it'—
then He is labouring at it now; and we have not to
think of a Christ who once worked, and has left to us
the task of developing the consequences of His completed activity, but of a Christ who is working on and
on, steadily and persistently. The builders of some
great edifice, whilst they are laying its lower courses,
are down upon our level, and as the building rises the
scaffolding rises, and sometimes the platform where
they stand is screened off by some frail canvas
stretched round it, so that we cannot see them as
they ply their work with trowel and mortar. So
Christ came down to earth to lay the courses of His
Temple that had to rest upon earth, but now the
scaffolding is raised and He is working at the top
stories. Though out of our sight, He is at work as
truly and energetically as He was when He was
down here. You remember how strikingly one of
the Evangelists puts that thought in the last words
of his Gospel—if, indeed, they are his words. 'He was
received up into heaven, and sat at the right hand of
God, and they went everywhere, preaching the word.'
Well, that looks as if there were a sad separation
between the Commander and the soldiers that He
had ordered to the front, as if He were sitting at ease
on a hill overlooking the battle-field from a safe
distance and sending His men to death. But the next
words bring Him and them together—'The Lord also

working with them, and confirming the word with signs following.' And so, brethren, a work begun, continued, and ended by the same immortal Hand, is the work on which the redemption of the world depends.

II. Notice, secondly, that we have here the assurance of the triumph of the Gospel.

No doubt, in the long-forgotten days in which my text was spoken, there were plenty of over-prudent calculators in the little band of exiles who said, 'What is the use of our trying to build in face of all this opposition and with these poor resources of ours?' They would throw cold water enough on the works of Zerubbabel, and on Zechariah who inspired them. But there came the great word of promise to them, 'He shall bring forth the headstone with shoutings.' The text is the cure for all such calculations by us Christian people, and by others than Christian people. When we begin to count up resources, and to measure these against the work to be done, there is little wonder if good men and bad men sometimes concur in thinking that the Gospel of Jesus Christ has very little chance of conquering the world. And that is perfectly true, unless you take Him into the calculation, and then the probabilities look altogether different. We are but like a long row of ciphers, but put one significant figure in front of the row of ciphers and it comes to be of value. And so, if you are calculating the probabilities of the success of Christianity in the world and forget to start with Christ, you have left out the principal factor in the problem. Churches lose their fervour, their members die and pass away. He renews and purifies the corrupted Church, and He liveth for ever. Therefore, because we may say, with calm confidence, 'His hands have laid the foundation of the house, and His hands are at work on all the courses of it as it rises,' we may be perfectly sure that the Temple which He founded, at which He still toils, shall be completed, and not stand a gaunt ruin, looking on which passers-by will mockingly say, 'This man began to build and was not able to finish.' When Brennus conquered Rome, and the gold for the city's ransom was being weighed, he clashed his sword into the scale to outweigh the gold. Christ's sword is in the scale, and it weighs more than the antagonism of the world and the active hostility of hell. 'His hands have laid the foundation ; His hands shall also finish it.'

III. Still further, here is encouragement for despondent and timid Christians.

Jesus Christ is not going to leave you half way across the bog. That is not His manner of guiding us. He began; He will finish. Remember the words of Paul which catch up this same thought: 'Being confident of this very thing, that He which hath begun a good work in you will perfect the same until the day of Jesus Christ.' Brethren ! if the seed of the kingdom is in our hearts, though it be but as a grain of mustard seed, be sure of this, that He will watch over it and bless the springing thereof. So, although when we think of ourselves, our own slowness of progress, our own feeble resolutions, our own wayward hearts, our own vacillating wills, our many temptations, our many corruptions, our many follies, we may well say to ourselves, 'Will there ever be any greater completeness in this terribly imperfect Christian character of mine than there is to-day?' let us be of good cheer, and not think only of ourselves, but much rather of Him who works on and in and for us. If we lift up our hearts to Him, and keep ourselves near Him, and let Him work, He will work. If we do not—like the demons in the old monastic stories, who every night pulled down the bit of walling that the monks had in the daytime built for their new monastery—by our own hands pull down what He, by His hand, has built up, the structure will rise, and we shall be 'builded together for a habitation of God through the Spirit.' Be of good cheer, only keep near the Master, and let Him do what He desires to do for us all. God is 'faithful who hath called us to the fellowship of His Son,' and He also will do it.

IV. Lastly, here is a striking contrast to the fate which attends all human workers.

There are very few of us who even partially seem to be happy enough to begin and finish any task, beyond the small ones of our daily life. Authors die, with books half finished, with sentences half finished sometimes, where the pen has been laid down. No man starts an entirely fresh line of action; he inherits much from his past. No man completes a great work that he undertakes; he leaves it half-finished, and coming generations, if it is one of the great historical works of the world, work out its consequences for good or for evil. The originator has to be contented with setting the thing going and handing on unfinished tasks to his successors. That is the condition under which we live. We have to be contented to do our little bit of work, that will fit in along with that of a great many others, like a chain of men who stand between a river and a burning house, and pass the buckets from end to end. How many hands does it take to make a pin? How many did it take to make the cloth of our dress? The shepherd out in Australia, the packer in Melbourne, the

sailors on the ship that brought the wool home, the
railwaymen that took it to Bradford, the spinner, the
weaver, the dyer, the finisher, the tailor—they all had
a hand in it, and the share of none of them was fit to
stand upright by itself, as it were, without something
on either side of it to hold it up.

So it is in all our work in the world, and eminently
in our Christian work. We have to be contented with
being parts of a mighty whole, to do our small piece of
service, and not to mind though it cannot be singled
out in the completed whole. What does that matter,
as long as it is there? The waters of the brook are lost
in the river, and it, in turn, in the sea. But each drop
is there, though indistinguishable.

Multiplication of joy comes from division of labour.
'One soweth and another reapeth,' and the result is
that there are two to be glad over the harvest instead
of one—'that he that soweth and he that reapeth may
rejoice together.' So it is a good thing that the hands
that laid the foundations so seldom are the hands that
finish the work; for thereby there are more admitted
into the social gladness of the completed results. The
navvy that lifted the first spadeful of earth in excavat-
ing for the railway line, and the driver of the loco-
motive over the completed track, are partners in the
success and in the joy. The forgotten bishop who, I
know not how many centuries ago, laid the foundations
of Cologne Cathedral, and the workmen who, a few
years since, took down the old crane that had stood for
long years on the spire, and completed it to the slender
apex, were partners in one work that reached through
the ages.

So let us do our little bit of work, and remember that
whilst we do it, He for whom we are doing it is doing

it in us, and let us rejoice to know that at the last we shall share in the 'joy of our Lord,' when He sees of the travail of His soul and is satisfied. Though He builds all Himself, yet He will let us have the joy of feeling that we are labourers together with Him. 'Ye are God's building'; but the Builder permits us to share in His task and in His triumph.

THE PRIEST OF THE WORLD AND KING OF MEN

'He shall build the Temple of the Lord . . . and He shall be a Priest upon His throne.'—ZECHARIAH vi. 13.

A HANDFUL of feeble exiles had come back from their Captivity. 'The holy and beautiful house' where their fathers praised Him was burned with fire. There was no king among them, but they still possessed a representative of the priesthood, the other great office of divine appointment. Their first care was to rear some poor copy of the Temple; and the usual difficulties that attend reconstruction of any sort, and dog every movement that rests upon religious enthusiasm, beset them —strong enemies, and half-hearted friends, and personal jealousies weakening still more their weak forces. In this time of anarchy, of toil at a great task with inadequate resources, of despondency that was rapidly fulfilling its own forebodings, the Prophet, who was the spring of the whole movement, receives a word in season from the Lord. He is bidden to take from some of the returned exiles the tribute-money which they had brought, and having made of it golden and silver crowns—the sign of kingship—to set them on the high priest's head, thus uniting the sacerdotal and regal offices, which had always been jealously separated in Israel. This singular action is explained, by the words which he is commanded to speak, as being a symbolic prophecy of Him who is 'the Branch'—the well-known name which older prophets had used for the Messiah— indicating that in Him were the reality which the priest- hood shadowed, and the rule which was partly dele- gated to Israel's king as well as the power which should rear the true temple of God among men.

It is in accordance with the law of prophetic develop- ment from the beginning, that the external circum- stances of the nation at the moment should supply the mould into which the promise is run. The earliest of all Messianic predictions embraced only the existence of evil, as represented by the serpent, and the conquest of it by one who was known but as a son of Eve. When the history reaches the patriarchal stage, wherein the family. is the predominant conception, the prophecy proportionately advances to the assurance, 'In thy seed shall all the families of the earth be blessed.' When the mission of Moses had made the people familiar with the idea of a man who was the medium of revela- tion, then a further stage was reached—'a Prophet shall the Lord your God raise up unto you, of your brethren, like unto me.' The kingdom of David pre- pared the way for the prediction of the royal dignity of the Messiah, as the peaceful reign of Solomon for the expectation of one who should bring peace by righteousness. The approach of national disaster and sorrow was reflected in Isaiah's vision of the suffering Messiah, and that prophet's announcements of exile had for their counterpoise the proclamation of Him who should bring liberty to the captive. So, here, the kingless band of exiles, painfully striving to rear again

the tabernacle which had fallen down, are heartened
for their task by the thought of the priest-king of the
nation, the builder of an imperishable dwelling-place
for God.

To-day we need these truths not less than Zechariah's
contemporaries did. And, thank God! we can believe
that, for every modern perplexity, the blessed old
words carry the same strength and consolation. If
kings seem to have perished from among men, if authorities are dying out, and there are no names of power
that can rally the world—yet there is a Sovereign. If
old institutions are crumbling, and must still further
decay ere the site for a noble structure be cleared, yet
He shall build the Temple. If priest be on some lips a
name of superstitious folly, and on others a synonym
for all that is despised as effete in religion, yet this
Priest abideth for ever, the guide and the hope for the
history of humanity and for the individual spirit. Let
us, then, put ourselves under the Prophet's guidance,
and consider the eternal truths which he preaches to
us too.

I. The true hope of the world is a priest.

The idea of priesthood is universal. It has been distorted and abused ; it has been made the foundation of
spiritual tyranny. The priest has not been the teacher
nor the elevator of the people. All over the world he
has been the ally of oppression and darkness, he has
hindered and cramped social and intellectual progress.
And yet, in spite of all this, there the office stands, and
wherever men go, by some strange perversity they
take with them this idea, and choose from among themselves those who, being endowed with some sort of
ceremonial and symbolic purity, shall discharge for
their brethren the double office of representing them

before God, of representing God to them. That is what
the world means, with absolute and entire unanimity,
by a priest—one who shall be sacrificer, intercessor,
representative; bearer of man's worship, channel of
God's blessing. How comes it, that, in spite of all the
cruelties and lies that have gathered round the office,
it lives, indestructible, among the families of men?
Why, because it springs from, and corresponds to, real
and universal wants in their nature. It is the result of
the universal consciousness of sin. Men feel that there
is a gulf betwixt them and God. They know themselves
to be all foul. True, as their knowledge of God dims
and darkens, their conscience hardens and their sense
of sin lessens; but, as long as there is any notion of
God at all, there will be a parallel and corresponding
conviction of moral evil. And so, feeling that, and feeling it, as I believe, not because they are rude and barbarous, but because, though rude and barbarous, they
still preserve some trace of their true relation to God,
they lay hold upon some of their fellows, and say,
'Here! be thou for us this thing which we cannot be
for ourselves—stand thou there in front of us, and be
at once the expression of our knowledge that we dare
not come before our gods, and likewise, if it may be,
the medium by which their gifts may come on us,
unworthy.'

That is a wide-spread and all but universally expressed instinct of human nature. Argue about it as
you like, explain it away how you choose, charge the
notions of priesthood and sacrifice with exaggeration,
immorality, barbarism, if you will—still the thing
remains. And I believe for my part that, so far from
that want being one which will be left behind, with
other rude and savage desires, as men advance in

civilisation—it is as real and as permanent as the craving of the understanding for truth, and of the heart
for love. When men lose it, it is because they are
barbarised, not civilised, into forgetting it. On that
rock all systems of religion and eminently all theories
of Christianity, that leave out priest and sacrifice, will
strike and split. The Gospel for the world must be one
which will meet all the facts of man's condition. Chief
among these facts is this necessity of the conscience, as
expressed by the forms in which for thousands of years
the worship of mankind has been embodied all but
everywhere—an altar, and a priest standing by its
side.

I need not pause to remind you how this Jewish
people, who have at all events taught the world the
purest Theism, and led men up to the most spiritual
religion, had this same institution of a priesthood for
the very centre of its worship. Nor need I dwell at
length on the fact that the New Testament gives-in its
full adhesion to the same idea. We are told that all
these sacerdotal allusions in it are only putting pure
spiritual truth in the guise of the existing stage of
religious development—the husk, not the kernel. It
seems to me much rather that the Old Testament ceremonial—Temple, priesthood, sacrifice—was established
for this along with other purposes, to be a shadow
of things to come. Christ's office is not metaphorically
illustrated by reference to the Jewish ritual; but the
Jewish ritual is the metaphor, and Christ's office the
reality. He is the Priest.

And what is the priest whom men crave?

The first requisite is oneness with those whom he
represents. Men have ever felt that one of themselves
must fill this office, and have taken from among their

brethren their medium of communication with God.
And we have a Priest who, 'in all things, is made like
unto His brethren,' having taken part of their flesh and
blood, and being 'in all points tempted like as we are.'
The next requisite is that these men, who minister at
earth's altars, should, by some lustration, or abstinence,
or white robe, or other external sign, be separated from
the profane crowd, and possess, at all events, a symbolic
purity—expression of the conviction that a priest must
be cleaner and closer to God than his fellows. And we
have a Priest who is holy, harmless, undefiled, radiant
in perfect purity, lustrous with the light of constant
union with God.

And again, as in nature and character, so in function,
Christ corresponds to the widely expressed wants of
men, as shown in their priesthoods. They sought for
one who should offer gifts and sacrifices on their behalf,
and we have One who is 'a merciful and faithful High
Priest to make reconciliation for the sins of the people.'
They sought for a man who should pass into the awful
presence, and plead for them while they stood without,
and we lift hopeful eyes of love to the heavens, 'whither
the Forerunner is for us entered, even Jesus, made an
High Priest for ever.' They sought for a man who
should be the medium of divine blessings bestowed
upon the worshippers, and we know who hath gone
within the veil, having ascended up on high, that He
might give gifts unto men.

The world needs a priest. Its many attempts to find
such show how deep is the sense of need, and what he
must be who shall satisfy them. We have the Priest
that the world and ourselves require. I believe that
modern Englishmen, with the latest results of civilisa-

tion colouring their minds and moulding their characters, stand upon the very same level, so far as this matter is concerned, as the veriest savage in African wilds, who has darkened even the fragment of truth which he possesses, till it has become a lie and the parent of lies. You and I, and all our brethren, alike need a brother who shall be holy and close to God, who shall offer sacrifices for us, and bring God to us. For you and me, and all our brethren alike, the good news is true, 'we have a great High Priest that is passed into the heavens, Jesus, the Son of God.' That message quenches the fire on every other altar, and strips the mitre from every other head. It, and it alone, meets fully and for ever that strange craving, which, though it has been productive of so many miseries and so many errors, though it has led to grinding tyranny and dark superstitions, though it has never anywhere found what it longs for, remains deep in the soul, indestructible and hungry, till it is vindicated and enlightened and satisfied by the coming of the true Priest, 'made not after the law of a carnal commandment, but after the power of an endless life.'

II. Our text tells us, secondly, that 'the priest of the world is the king of men.' 'He shall be a Priest upon His throne.'

In Israel these two offices were jealously kept apart, and when one monarch, in a fit of overweening self-importance, tried to unite in his own person the kingly and the priestly functions, 'the leprosy rose up in his forehead,' even as he stood with the censer in his hand, and 'Uzziah the king was a leper unto the day of his death.' And the history of the world is full of instances, in which the struggles of the temporal and spiritual power have caused calamities only less intolerable than those which flowed from that alliance of priests and kings which has so often made monarchy a grinding tyranny, and religion a mere instrument of statecraft. History being witness, it would seem to be a very doubtful blessing for the world that one man should wield both forms of control without check or limitation, and be at once king and priest. If the words before us refer to any one but to Christ, the prophet had an altogether mistaken notion about what would be good for men, politically and ecclesiastically, and we may be thankful that his dream has never come true. But if they point to the Son of David who has died for us, and declare that because He is Priest, He is therefore King—oh! then they are full of blessed truth concerning the basis and the nature and the purpose of His dominion, which may well make us lift up our heads and rejoice that in the midst of tyranny and anarchy, of sovereignties whose ultimate resort is force, there is another kingdom—the most absolute of despotisms and yet the most perfect democracy, whose law is love, whose subjects are every one the children of a King, the kingdom of that Priest-ruler on whose head is Aaron's mitre, and more than David's crown.

He does rule. 'The kingdom of Christ' is no unreal fanciful phrase. Take the lowest ground. Who is it that, by the words He spoke, by the deeds He did, by the life He lived, has shaped the whole form of moral and religious thought and life in the civilised world? Is there One among the great of old, the dead yet sceptred sovereigns, who still rule our spirits from their urns, whose living power over thought and heart and deed among the dominant races of the earth is to be compared with His? And beyond that, we believe that, as the result of His mighty work on earth, the dominion of the whole creation is His, and He is King of kings, and Lord of lords, that His will is sovereign and His voice is absolute law, to which all the powers of nature, all the confusions of earth's politics, all the unruly wills of men, all the pale kingdoms of the dead, and all the glorious companies of the heavens, do bow in real though it be sometimes unconscious and sometimes reluctant obedience.

The foundation of His rule is His sacrifice; or in other words—no truer though a little more modern in their sound—men will do anything for Him who does *that* for them. Men will yield their whole souls to the warmth and light that stream from the Cross, as the sunflower turns itself to the sun. He that can give an anodyne which is not an opiate, to my conscience— He that can appeal to my heart and will, and say, 'I have given Myself for thee,' will never speak in vain to those who accept His gift, when He says, 'Now give thyself to Me.'

Brethren! it is not the thinker who is the true king of men, as we sometimes hear it proudly said. We need One who will not only show but be the Truth; who will not only point, but open and be, the Way; who will not only communicate thought, but give, because He is, the Life. Not the rabbi's pulpit, nor the teacher's desk, still less the gilded chairs of earthly monarchs, least of all the tents of conquerors, are the throne of the true King. He rules from the Cross. The one dominion worth naming, that over men's inmost spirits, springs from the one sacrifice which alone calms and quickens men's inmost spirits. 'Thou art the King of Glory, O Christ,' for Thou art 'the Lamb of God, which taketh away the sin of the world.'

His rule is wielded in gentleness. Priestly dominion has ever been fierce, suspicious, tyrannous. 'His words were softer than oil, yet were they drawn swords.' But the sway of this merciful and faithful High Priest is full of tenderness. His sceptre is not the warrior's mace, nor the jewelled rod of gold, but the reed— emblem of the lowliness of His heart, and of authority guided by love. And all His rule is for the blessing of His subjects, and the end of it is that they may be made free by obedience, emancipated in and for service, crowned as kings by submission to the King of kings, consecrated as priests by their reliance on the only Priest over the house of God, whose loving will rests not until it has made all His people like Himself.

Then, dear brethren! amid all the anarchic chaos of this day, when old institutions are crumbling or crash- ing into decay, when the whole civilised world seems slowly and painfully parting from its old moorings, and like some unwieldy raft, is creaking and straining at its chains as it feels the impulse of the swift current that is bearing it to an unknown sea, when venerable names cease to have power, when old truths are flouted as antiquated, and the new ones seem so long in making their appearance, when a perfect Babel of voices stuns us, and on every side are pretenders to the throne which they fancy vacant, let us joyfully welcome all change, and hopefully anticipate the future. Lifting our eyes from the world, let us fix them on the likeness of a throne above the firmament that is above the cherubs, and rejoice since there we behold 'the likeness as the appearance of a man upon it.' 'Shout, O daughter of Jerusalem; behold, thy King cometh unto thee.'

III. Our text still further reminds us that the

Priest-King of men builds among men the Temple of God.

The Prophet and his companions had become familiar in their captivity with the gigantic palaces and temples which Assyrian and Babylonian monarchs had a passion for rearing. They had learned to regard the king as equally magnified by his conquests and by his buildings. Zechariah foretells that the true King shall rear a temple more lasting than Solomon's, more magnificent than those which towered on their marble-faced platforms over the Chaldean plain.

Christ is Himself the true Temple of God. Whatsoever that shadowed Christ is or gives. In Him dwelt all the fulness of the Godhead. 'The glory' which once dwelt between the cherubim, 'tabernacled among us' in His flesh. As the place of sacrifice, as the place where men meet God, as the seat of revelation of the divine will, the true tabernacle which the Lord hath pitched is the Manhood of our Lord.

Christ builds the temple. By faith, the individual soul becomes the abode of God, and into our desecrated spirits there comes the King of Glory. 'Know ye not that ye are the temples of God?' By faith, the whole body of believing men 'are builded together for an habitation of God through the Spirit.'

Christ builds this temple because He is the Temple. By His incarnation and work, He makes our communion with God and God's dwelling in us possible. By His death and sacrifice He draws men to Himself, and blends them in a living unity. By the gift of His Spirit and His life, He hallows their wills, and makes them partakers of His own likeness; so that 'coming to Him, we also are built up a spiritual house.'

Christ builds the temple, and uses us as His servants

in the work. Our prophecy was given to encourage faint-hearted toilers, not to supply an excuse for indolence. Underlying all our poor labours, and blessing them all, is the power of Christ. We may well work diligently who work in the line of His purposes, after the pattern of His labours, in the strength of His power, under the watchfulness of His eye. The little band may be few and feeble; let them not be fearful, for He, the throned Priest, even *He*, and not they with their inadequate resources, shall build the temple.

Christ builds on through all the ages, and the prophecy of our text is yet unfulfilled. Its fulfilment is the meaning and end of all history. For the present, there has to be much destructive as well as constructive work done. Many a wretched hovel, the abode of sorrow and want, many a den of infamy, many a palace of pride, many a temple of idols, will have to be pulled down yet, and men's eyes will be blinded by the dust, and their hearts will ache as they look at the ruins. Be it so. The finished structure will obliterate the remembrance of poor buildings that cumbered its site. This Emperor of ours may indeed say, that He found the city of brick and made it marble. Have patience if His work is slow; mourn not if it is destructive; doubt not, though the unfinished walls, and corridors that seem to lead nowhere, and all the confusion of unfinished toils puzzle you, when you try to make out the plan. See to it, my brother, that you lend a hand and help to rear the true temple, which is rising slowly through the ages, at which successive generations toil, and from whose unfinished glories they dying depart, but which shall be completed, because the true Builder 'ever liveth,' and is 'a priest for ever after the order of Melchizedek.' Above all, brethren!

take heed that you are yourselves builded in that temple. Travellers sometimes find in lonely quarries long abandoned or once worked by a vanished race, great blocks squared and dressed, that seem to have been meant for palace or shrine. But there they lie, neglected and forgotten, and the building for which they were hewn has been reared without them. Beware lest God's grand temple should be built up without you, and you be left to desolation and decay. Trust your souls to Christ, and He will set you in the spiritual house which the King greater than Solomon is building still.

In one of the mosques of Damascus, which has been a Christian church, and before that was a heathen temple, the portal bears, deep cut in Greek characters, the inscription, 'Thy kingdom, O Christ, is an everlasting kingdom, and Thy dominion endureth throughout all generations.' The confident words seem contradicted by the twelve centuries of Mohammedanism on which they have looked down. But though their silent prophecy is unheeded and unheard by the worshippers below, it shall be proved true one day, and the crescent shall wane before the steady light of the Sun of Righteousness. The words are carven deep over the portals of the temple which Christ rears; and though men may not be able to read them, and may not believe them if they do, though for centuries traffickers have defiled its courts, and base-born usurpers have set up their petty thrones, yet the writing stands sure, a dumb witness against the transient lies, a patient prophet of the eternal truth. And when all false faiths, and their priests who have oppressed men and traduced God, have vanished; and when kings that have prostituted their great and godlike office to personal advancement

x

and dynastic ambition are forgotten; and when every shrine reared for obscene and bloody rites, or for superficial and formal worship, has been cast to the ground, then from out of the confusion and desolation shall gleam the temple of God, which is the refuge of men, and on the one throne of the universe shall sit the Eternal Priest—our Brother, Jesus the Christ.

MALACHI

A DIALOGUE WITH GOD

'A son honoureth his father, and a servant his master: if then I be a Father, where is Mine honour? and if I be a master, where is My fear? saith the Lord of Hosts unto you, O priests, that despise My Name. And ye say, Wherein have we despised Thy Name? 7. Ye offer polluted bread upon Mine altar. And ye say, Wherein have we polluted Thee?'—MALACHI i. 6, 7.

A CHARACTERISTIC of this latest of the prophets is the vivacious dialogue of which our text affords one example. God speaks and the people question His word, which in reply He reiterates still more strongly. The other instances of its occurrence may here be briefly noted, and we shall find that they cover all the aspects of the divine speech to men, whether He charges sin home upon them or pronounces threatenings of judgment, or invites by gracious promises the penitent to return. His charges of sin are repelled in our text and in the following verse by the indignant question, 'Wherein have we polluted Thee?' And similarly in the next chapter the divine accusation, 'Ye have wearied the Lord with your words,' is thrown back with the contemptuous retort, 'Wherein have we wearied Him?' And in like manner in the third chapter, 'Ye have robbed Me,' calls forth no confession but only the defiant answer, 'Wherein have we robbed Thee?' And in a later verse, the accusation, 'Your words have been stout against Me,' is traversed by the question, 'What have we spoken so much against Thee?' Similarly the threatening of judgment that the Lord will 'cut off'

the men that 'profane the holiness of the Lord' calls
forth only the rebutting question, 'Wherefore?' (ii.
14). And even the gracious invitation, 'Return unto
Me, and I will return unto you,' evokes not penitence,
but the stiff-necked reply, 'Wherein shall we return?'
(iii. 7). In this sermon we may deal with the first of
these three cases, and consider, God's Indictment, and
man's plea of 'Not guilty.'

I. God's Indictment.

The precise nature of the charge is to be carefully considered. The Name is the sum of the revealed character,
and that Name has been despised. The charge is not
that it has been blasphemed, but that it has been neglected, or under-estimated, or cared little about. The
pollution of the table of the Lord is the overt act by
which the attitude of mind and heart expressed in
despising His Name is manifested; but the overt act is
secondary and not primary—a symptom of a deeper-
lying disease. And herein our Prophet is true to the
whole tenor of the Old Testament teaching, which draws
its indictment against men primarily in regard to their
attitude, and only as a manifestation of that, to their
acts. The same deed may be, if estimated in relation to
human law, a crime: if estimated in relation to godless
ethics, a wrong; and if estimated in the only right way,
namely, the attitude towards God which it reveals, a
sin. 'The despising of His Name' may be taken as the
very definition of sin. It is usual with men to-day to
say that 'Sin is selfishness'; but that statement does
not go deep enough unless it be recognised that self-
regard only becomes sin when it rears its puny self in
opposition to, or in disregard of, the plain will of God.
The 'New Theology,' of course, minimises, even where
it does not, as it to be consistent should, deny the

possibility of sin : for, if God is all and all is God, there can be no opposition, there can be no divine will to be opposed, and no human will to oppose it. But the fact of sin certified by men's own consciences is the rock on which Pantheism must always strike and sink. A superficial view of human history and of human nature may try to explain away the fact of sin by shallow talk about 'heredity' and 'environment,' or about 'ignorance' and ' mistakes '; but after all such euphemistic attempts to rechristen the ugly thing by beguiling names, the fact remains, and conscience bears sometimes unwilling witness to its existence, that men do set their own inclinations against God's commands, and that there is in them that which is 'not subject to the law of God, neither indeed can be.' The root of all sin is the despising of His Name.

And as sin has but one root, it has many branches, and as working backwards from deed to motive, we find one common element in all the various acts; so working outwards from motive to deed, we have to see one common character stamped upon a tragical variety of acts. The poison-water is exhibited in many variously coloured and tasted draughts, but however unlike each other they may be, it is always the same.

The great effort of God's love is to press home this consciousness of despising His Name upon all hearts. The sorrows, losses, and disappointments which come to us all are not meant only to make us suffer, but through suffering to lead us to recognise how far we have wandered from our Father, and to bring us back to His heart and our home. The beginning of all good in us is the contrite acknowledgment of our evil. Christ's first preaching was the continuation of John's message, 'Repent ye, for the kingdom of

heaven is at hand'; and His tenderest revelation of
the divine love incarnated in Himself was meant to
arouse the penitent confession, 'I am no more worthy
to be called Thy son,' and the quickening resolve, 'I
will arise and go to my Father.' There is no way
to God but through the narrow gate of repentance.
There is no true reception of the gift of Christ which
does not begin with a vivid and heart-broken consciousness of my own sin. We can pass into, and
abide in, the large room of joyous acceptance and
fellowship, but we must reach it by a narrow path
walled in by gloomy rocks and trodden with bleed-
ing feet. The penitent knowledge of our sin is the
first step towards the triumphant knowledge of
Christ's righteousness as ours. Only they who have
called out in the agony of their souls, 'Lord, save us,
we perish,' have truly learned the love of God, and
truly possess the salvation that is in Christ.

II. Man's plea of 'Not Guilty.'

That such an answer should be given to such a
charge is a strange, solemn fact, which tragically confirms the true indictment. The effect of all sin is to
make us less conscious of its presence, as persons in an
unventilated room are not aware of its closeness. It
is with profound truth that the Apostle speaks of being
hardened by the 'deceitfulness' of sin. It comes to us
in a cloud and enfolds us in obscure mist. Like white
ants, it never works in the open, but makes a tunnel
or burrows under ground, and, hidden in some piece
of furniture, eats away all its substance whilst it seems
perfectly solid. The man's perception of the standard
of duty is enfeebled. We lose our sense of the moral
character of any habitual action, just as a man who
has lived all his life in a slum sees little of its hideous-

ness, and knows nothing of green fields and fresh air.
Conscience is silenced by being neglected. It can be
wrongly educated and perverted, so that it may regard
sin as doing God's service; and the only judgment in
which it can be absolutely trusted is the declaration
that it is right to do right, while all its other decisions
as to what is right may be biassed by self-interest; but
the force with which it pronounces its only unalterable
decision depends on the whole tenor of the life of the
man. The sins which are most in accordance with our
characters, and are therefore most deeply rooted in us,
are those which we are least likely to recognise as sins.
So, the more sinful we are, the less we know it; therefore there is need for a fixed standard outside of us.
The light on the deck cannot guide us; there must be
the lighthouse on the rock. This sad answer of the
heart untouched by God's appeal prevents all further
access of God's love to that heart. That love can only
enter when the reply to its indictment is, 'I have
despised Thy name.'

Let us not forget the New Testament modification of
the divine accusation. 'In Christ' is the Name of God
fully and finally revealed to men. For us who live in
the blaze of the ineffable brightness of the revelation,
our attitude towards Him who brings it is the test of
our 'hallowing of the Name' which He brings. He
Himself has varied Malachi's indictment when He said,
'He that despiseth Me despiseth Him that sent Me.'
Our sin is now to be measured by our under-estimate and
neglect of Him, and chiefly of His Cross. That Cross prevents our consciousness of sin from becoming despair
of pardon. Judas went out, and with bitter weeping,
himself ended his traitorous life. If God's last word to
us were, 'Ye have despised My Name,' and it sank into

our souls, there would be no hope for any of us. But the message which begins with the universal indictment of sin passes into the message which holds forth forgiveness and freedom as universal as the sin, and 'God hath concluded all in unbelief that He may have mercy upon all.'

BLEMISHED OFFERINGS

'Offer it now unto thy governor; will he be pleased with thee, or accept thy person? saith the Lord of Hosts.'—MALACHI i. 8.

A WORD of explanation may indicate my purpose in selecting this, I am afraid, unfamiliar text. The Prophet has been vehemently rebuking a characteristic mean practice of the priests, who were offering maimed and diseased animals in sacrifice. They were probably dishonest as well as mean, because the worshippers would bring sound beasts, and the priests, for their own profit, slipped in a worthless animal, and kept the valuable one for themselves. They had become so habituated to this piece of economical religion, that they saw no harm in it, and when they offered the lame and the sick and the blind for sacrifice they said to themselves, 'It is not evil.' And so Malachi, with the sudden sharp thrust of my text, tries to rouse their torpid consciences. He says to them: 'Take that diseased creature that you are not ashamed to lay on God's altar, and try what the governor'—the official appointed by the Persian Kings to rule over the returned exiles—'will think about it. Will an offering of that sort be considered a compliment or an insult? Do you think it will smooth your way or help your suit with him? Surely God deserves as much reverence

as the deputy of Artaxerxes. Surely what is not good
enough for a Persian satrap is not good enough for the
Lord of Hosts. Offer it to the governor, will he be
pleased with it? Will he accept thy person?'

Now, it seems to me that this cheap religion of the
priests, and this scathing irony of the Prophet's counsel
need little modification to fit us very closely. You will
bear me witness, I think, that I do not often speak to
you about money. But I am going to try to bring out
something about the great subject of Christian administration of earthly possessions from this text, because I
believe that the Christian consciousness of this generation does need a great deal of rousing and instructing
about this matter.

I. We note the startling and strange contrast which
the text suggests.

The diseased lamb was laid without scruple or hesitation on God's altar, and not one of these tricky priests
durst have taken it to Court in order to secure favour
there. Generalise that, and it comes to this—the gifts
that we lavish on men are the condemnation of the
gifts that we bring to God; and further, we should be
ashamed to offer to men what we are not in the least
ashamed to bring to God. Let me illustrate in one or
two points.

Let us contrast in our own consciences, for instance,
the sort of love that we give to one another with the
sort of love that we bring to Him. How strong, how
perennially active, how delighting in sacrifice and
service, what a felt source of blessedness is the love
that knits many husbands and wives, many parents
and children, many lovers and friends together! And
in dreadful contrast, how languid, how sporadic and
interrupted, how reluctant when called upon for service

and sacrifice, how little operative in our lives is the love
we bring to God! We durst not lay upon the altar of
family affection, of wedded love, of true friendship, a
love of such a sort as we take to God and expect Him
to be satisfied with. It would be an insult if offered to
'the governor,' but we think it good enough for the
King of kings. Here a gushing flood, there a straitened
trickle coming drop by drop; here a glowing flame
that fills life with warmth and light, there a few dying
embers. Measure and contrast the love that is lavished
by men upon one another, and the love that is coldly
brought to Him. And I think we must all bow our
heads penitently.

Contrast the trust that we put in one another, and the
trust that we direct to Him. In the one case it is absolute. 'I am as sure as I am of my own existence that
so-and-so will always be as true as steel to me, and will
never fail me, and whatever he, or she, does, or fails to
do, no shadow of suspicion, or mist of doubt, will creep
across the sunshine of our sky.' And in contrast to the
firm grasp with which we clasp an infirm human hand,
there is a tremulous touch, scarcely a grasp at all,
which we lay upon the one Hand that is strong enough
always to be outstretched for our defence and our
blessing. Contrast your confidence in men, and your
confidence in God. Are we not all committing the
absurdity of absolutely trusting that which has no
stability or stay, and refusing so to trust that which is
the Rock of Ages? God's faithfulness is absolute, our
faith in it is tremulous. Men's faithfulness is uncertain,
our faith in it is entire.

We might contrast the submission and obedience
with which we follow those who have secured our confidence and evoked our love, as contrasted with the

rebellion, the reluctance, the self-will, which come in to break and mar our submission to God. Men that will not take Jesus Christ for their Master, and refuse to follow Him when He speaks, will bind themselves to some human teacher, and enrol themselves as disciples in some school of thought or science or philosophy, with a submission so entire, that it puts to shame the submission which Christians render to the Incarnate Truth Himself.

And so I might go on, all round the horizon of our human nature, and signalise the difference that exists between the blemished sacrifices which each part of our being dares to bring to God and expects Him to accept, and the sacrifices, unblemished and spotless, which we carry to one another.

But let me say a word more directly about the subject of which Malachi is speaking. It seems to me that we may well take a very condemnatory contrast between what we offer to God in regard to our administration of earthly good, and what we offer on other altars. Contrast what you give, for directly beneficent and Christian purposes, with what you spend, without two thoughts, on your own comfort, indulgence, recreation, tastes—sometimes doubtful tastes—and the like. Contrast England's drink bill and England's missionary contribution. We spend £10,000,000 on some wretched war, and some of you think it is cheap at the price, and the whole contributions of English Christians to missionary purposes in a twelvemonth do not amount to a tenth of that sum. You offer that to the spread of Christ's kingdom. 'Offer it to your Government,' and try to compound for your share of the ten millions that you are going to spend in shells and gunpowder by the amount you give to Christian

missions, and you will very soon have the tax-gatherer
down on you. 'Will he be pleased with it?'

This one Missionary Society with which we are nomi-
nally connected has an income of £70,000 a year. I
suppose that is about a shilling per head from the
members of our congregations. Of this congregation
there are many that never give us a farthing, except,
perhaps, the smallest coin in their pockets when the
collecting-box comes round. I do not suppose that
there is one of us that applies the underlying principle
in our text, of giving God our best, to this work. I
am not going to urge you. It is my business now
simply to state, as boldly and strongly as I can, the fact;
and I say with all sadness, with self-condemnation, as
well as bringing an indictment against my brethren,
but with the clearest conviction that I am not exaggerating in the smallest degree, that the contrast between
what we lavish on other things and what we give for
God's work in the world, is a shameful contrast, like
that other which the Prophet gibbeted with his indignant eloquence.

II. And now let me come to another point—viz., that
we have here suggested and implied the true law and
principle on which all Christian giving of all sorts is to
be regulated.

And that is—give the best. The diseased animal
was no more fit for the altar of God than it was for the
shambles of the viceroy. It was the entire and unblemished one that would be accepted in either case.
But for us Christian people that general principle has
to be expanded. Let me do it in two or three sentences.

The foundation of all is 'the unspeakable Gift.' Jesus
Christ has given Himself, God has given His Son. And
Jesus Christ and God, in giving, gave up that we might

receive. Do you believe that? Do you believe it about
yourself? If you do, then the next step becomes
certain. That gift, truly received by any man, will
infallibly lead to a kindred (though infinitely inferior)
self-surrender. If once we come within the circle of
the attraction of that great Sun, if I might so say, it
will sweep us clean out of our orbit, and turn us into
satellites reflecting His light. To have self for our
centre is death and misery, to have Christ for our centre
is life and blessedness. And the one power that decen-
tralises a man, and sweeps him into an orbit around
Jesus, is the faithful acceptance of His great gift. Just
as some little State will give up its independence in
order to be blessedly absorbed into a great Empire, on
the frontiers of which it maintains a precarious existence, so a man is never so strong, never so blessed,
never so truly himself, as when the might of Christ's
sacrifice has melted down all his selfishness, and has
made it flow out in rivers of self-surrender, self-absorp-
tion, self-annihilation, and so self-preservation. 'He
that loseth his life shall find it.'

Then the next step is that this self-surrender, consequent upon my faithful acceptance of the Lord's
surrender for me, changes my whole conception as to
what I call my possessions. If I, in the depths of my
soul, have yielded myself to Jesus Christ, which I shall
have done if I have truly accepted Him as yielding
Himself for me, then the yielding of self draws after it,
necessarily, and without a question, a new relation
between me and all that I have and all that I can do.
Capacities, faculties, means, opportunities, powers of
brain and heart and mind, and everything else—they
all belong to Him. As in old times a nobleman came
and put his hands between the King's hands, and

kneeling before him surrendered his lands, and all his property, to the over-lord, and got them back again for his own, so we shall do, in the measure in which we have accepted Christ as our Saviour and our Guide. And so, because I am His, I shall feel that I am His steward to administer what He gives me, not for myself, but for men and for God.

Then there follows another thing, and that is, that Christian giving, not of money only, but of money in a very eminent degree, is only right and truly Christian when you give yourself with your gift. A great many of us put our sixpence, or our half-crown, or our sovereign, into the plate, and no part of ourselves goes with it, except a little twinge of unwillingness to part with it. That is how they fling bones to dogs. That is not how you have to give your money and your efforts to God and God's cause. Farmers nowadays sow their seed-corn out of a machine with a number of little conical receptacles at the back of it and a small hole in the bottom of each, and as the thing goes bumping along over the furrows, out they fall. That drill does as well as, and better than, the hand of the sower scattering the seed, but it does not do near as well in the Christian agriculture in sowing the seed of the Kingdom. Machine-work will not do there; we have to have the sower's hand, and the sower's heart with his hand, as he scatters the seed. Brethren! apply the lesson to yourselves, and let your sympathies and your prayers and your wishes to help go along with your gifts, if you intend them to be of any good.

And there is another thing, and that is that, somehow or other, if not in the individual gifts, at all events in their aggregate, there must be present the fact of sacrifice. 'I will not offer unto the Lord burnt offer-

ings of that which doth cost me nothing,' said the old
king. And we do not give as we ought, unless our
gifts involve some measure of sacrifice. From many a
subscription list some of the biggest donations would
disappear, like the top-writing in one of those old
manuscripts where the Gospel has been half-erased
and written over with some foolish legend, which
vanishes when the detergent liquid is applied to the
parchment, if that thought were brought to bear upon
it. God asks how much is kept, not how much is given.

Now, dear friends, these are all threadbare, elementary, 'A.B.C.' truths. Are they the alphabet of our
stewardship and administration of our possessions?

III. One last suggestion I would make on this text is
that it brings before us the possible blessing and possible
grave results of right or wrong Christian giving.

'Will he be pleased with it? Or will he accept thy
person?' Will the governor think the hobbling creature,
blind of an eye, and infected with some sickness, to be
a beautiful addition to his flock? Will it help your
suit with him? No!

It is New Testament teaching that our faithfulness in
the administration of earthly possessions of all sorts
has a bearing on our spiritual life. Remember our
Lord's triple illustration of this principle, when He
speaks about faithfulness 'in that which is least,' leading on to the possession of that which is the greatest;
when He speaks of faithfulness in regard to 'the unrighteous Mammon' leading on to being intrusted with
the true riches; when He speaks of faithfulness in our
administration of that which is another's—alien to ourselves, and which may pass into the possession of a
thousand more—leading on to our firmer hold, and our
deeper and fuller possession of the riches which, in the

deepest sense of the word, are our own. One very
important element in the development and advance of
the religious life is our right use of these earthly things.
I have seen many a case in which a man was far better
when he was a poor man than he was when a rich one,
in which slowly, stealthily, certainly, the love of wealth
has closed round a man like an iron band round a
sapling, and has hindered the growth of his Christian
character, and robbed him of the best things. And,
God be thanked! one has seen cases, too, in which, by
their Christian use of outward possessions, men have
weakened the dominion of self upon themselves, have
learned the subordinate value of the wealth that can be
counted and detached from its possessor, and have
grown in the grace and knowledge of the Lord and
Saviour Jesus Christ. Dear friends, God has given all
of us something in charge, the faithful use of which is a
potent factor in the growth of our Christian characters.

It is New Testament teaching that our faithful
administration of earthly possessions has a bearing on
the future. Remember what Jesus Christ said, 'That
when ye fail they may receive you into everlasting
habitations.' Remember what His Apostle says, 'Laying
up in store for themselves a good foundation against
the time to come, that they may lay hold on eternal
life.' Let no fear of imperilling the great truth of
salvation by faith lead us to forget that the faith
which saves manifests its vitality and genuineness, by
its effects upon our lives, and that no small part of our
lives is concerned with the right acquisition and right
use of these perishable outward gifts. And let us take
care that we do not, in our dread of damaging the free
grace of God, forget that although we do not earn
blessedness, here or hereafter, by gifts whilst we are

living or legacies when we are dead, the administration of money has an important part to play in shaping Christian character, and the Christian character which we acquire here settles our hereafter.

Brethren! we all need to revise our scale of giving, especially in regard to missionary operations. And if we will do that at the foot of the Cross, then we shall join the chorus, 'Worthy is the Lamb that was slain to receive *riches*,' and we shall come to Him 'bringing our silver and our gold with us,' rejoicing that He gives us the possibility of sharing His blessedness, 'according to the word of the Lord Jesus which He spake, It is more blessed to give than to receive.'

A DIALOGUE WITH GOD

'The Lord will cut off the man that doeth this . . . out of the tents of Jacob, . . . 14. Yet ye say, Wherefore? Because the Lord hath been witness between thee and the wife of thy youth.'—MALACHI ii. 12, 14 (R.V.).

IT is obvious from the whole context that divorce and foreign inter-marriage were becoming increasingly prevalent in Malachi's time. The conditions in these respects were nearly similar to that prevailing in the times of Ezra and Nehemiah. It is these sins which the Prophet is here vehemently condemning, and for which he threatens to cut off the transgressors out of the tents of Jacob, and to regard no more their offerings and simulated worship. They might cover 'the altar of the Lord with tears,' but the sacrifice which they laid upon it was polluted by the sins of their daily domestic life, and therefore was not 'regarded by Him any more.' Malachi is true to the prophetic spirit when he denounces a religion which has the form of godliness without its power over the practical

Y

life. But his sharp accusations have their edge turned
by the question, 'Wherefore?' which again calls out
from the Prophet's lips a more sharply-pointed accusation, and a solemner warning that none should 'deal
treacherously against the wife of his youth,' 'for I hate
putting away, saith the Lord.' We may dismiss any
further reference to the circumstances of the text, and
regard it as but one instance of man's way of treating
the voice of God when it warns of the consequences
of the sin of man. Looked at from such a point of
view the words of our text bring before us God's merciful threatenings and man's incredulous rejection of
them.

I. God's merciful threatenings.

The fact of sin affects God's relation to and dealings
with the sinner. It does not prevent the flowing forth
of His love, which is not drawn out by anything in us,
but wells up from the depths of His being, like the
Jordan from its source at Dan, a broad stream gushing
forth from the rock. But that love which is the out-
going of perfect moral purity must necessarily become
perfect opposition to its own opposite in the sinfulness
of man. The divine character is many-sided, and whilst
'to the pure' it 'shows itself pure,' it cannot but be that
'to the froward' it 'will show itself froward.' Man's sin
has for its most certain and dreadful consequence that,
if we may so say, it forces God to present the stern
side of His nature which hates evil. But not merely
does sin thus modify the fact of the divine relation to
men, but it throws men into opposition in which they
can see only the darkness which dwells in the light of
God. To the eye looking through a red tinted medium
all things are red, and even the crystal sea before the
throne is 'a sea of glass mingled with fire.'

No sin can stay our reception of a multitude of good gifts appealing to our hearts and revealing the patient love of our Father in heaven, but every sin draws after it as certainly as the shadow follows the substance, evil consequences which work themselves out on the large scale in nations and communities, and in the smaller spheres of individual life. And surely it is the voice of love and not of anger that comes to warn us of the death which is the wages of sin. It is not God who has ordained that 'the soul that sinneth it shall die,' but it is God who tells us so. The train is rushing full steam ahead to the broken bridge, and will crash down the gulph and be huddled, a hideous ruin, on the rocks; surely it is care for life that holds out the red flag of danger, and surely God is not to be blamed if in spite of the flag full speed is kept up and the crash comes.

The miseries and sufferings which follow our sins are self-inflicted, and for the most part automatic. 'Whatsoever a man soweth, that'—and not some other crop—'will he also reap.' The wages of sin are paid in ready money; and it is as just to lay them at God's door as it would be to charge Him with inflicting the disease which the dissolute man brings upon himself. It is no arbitrary appointment of God's that 'he that soweth to the flesh shall of the flesh reap corruption'; nor is it His will acting as that of a jealous despot which makes it inevitably true that here and hereafter, 'Every transgression and disobedience shall receive its just recompense of reward,' and that to be parted from Him is death.

If then we rightly understand the connection between sin and suffering, and the fact that the sorrows which are but the echoes of preceding sins have all a

distinctly moral and restorative purpose, we are prepared rightly to estimate how tenderly the God who
warns us against our sins by what men call threatenings loves us while He speaks.

II. Man's rejection of God's merciful threatenings.

It is the great mystery and tragedy of life that men
oppose themselves to God's merciful warnings that
all sin is a bitter, because it is an evil, thing. He has
to lament, ' I have smitten your children, and they have
received no correction.' The question ' Wherefore?' is
asked in very various tones, but none of them has in it
the accent of true conviction; and there is a whole
world of difference between the lowly petition, 'Show
me wherefore Thou contendest with me,' and the
curt, self-complacent brushing aside of God's merciful
threatenings in the text. The last thing which most
of us think of as the cause of our misfortunes is ourselves; and we resent as almost an insult the word,
which if we were wise, we should welcome as the
crowning proof of the seeking love of our Father in
heaven. We are more obstinate and foolish than
Balaam, who persisted in his purpose when the angel
with the drawn sword in his hand would have barred
his way, not to the tree of life, but to death. The
awful mystery that a human will can, and the yet sadder
mystery that it does, set itself against the divine, is
never more unintelligible, never so stupid, and never so
tragic as when God says, 'Turn ye, turn ye, why will
ye die?' and we say, 'Why need I die ? I will not turn.'

The ' Wherefore?' of our text is widely asked in the
present day as an expression of utter bewilderment
at the miseries of humanity, both in the wide area of
this disordered world and in the narrower field of individual lives. There are whole schools of so-called

political and social thinkers who have yet to learn that the one thing which the world and the individual need is not a change of conditions or environment, but redemption from sin. Man's sorrows are but a symptom of his disease, and he is no more to be healed by tinkering with these than a fever-stricken patient can be restored to health by treating the blotches on his skin which tell of the disease that courses through his veins.

But sometimes the question is more than an expression of bewilderment; it conceals an arraignment of God's justice, or even a denial that there is a God at all. There are men among us who hesitate not to avow that the miseries of the world have rooted out of their minds a belief in Him; and who point to all the ills under which humanity staggers as conclusive against the ancient faith of a God of love. They, too, forget that that love is righteousness, and that if there be sin in the world and God above it, He must necessarily war against it and hate it.

Our right response to God's merciful threatenings is to ask this question in the right spirit. We are not wise if we turn a deaf ear to His warnings, or go on in a headlong course which He by His providences declared to be dangerous and fatal. We use them as wise men should, only if our 'Wherefore?' is asked in order to learn our evil, and having learned it, to purge our bosoms of the perilous stuff by confession and to seek pardon and victory in Christ. Then we shall 'know the secret of the Lord' which is 'with them that fear Him'; and the mysteries that still hang over our own histories and the world's destiny will have shining down upon them the steadfast light of that love which seeks to make men blessed by making them good.

THE LAST WORD OF PROPHECY

' Behold, I will send My messenger, and he shall prepare the way before Me : and the Lord, whom ye seek, shall suddenly come to His temple, even the Messenger of the covenant, whom ye delight in : behold, He shall come, saith the Lord of Hosts. 2. But who may abide the day of His coming? and who shall stand when He appeareth? for He is like a refiner's fire, and like fullers' soap : 3. And He shall sit as a refiner and purifier of silver : and He shall purify the sons of Levi, and purge them as gold and silver, that they may offer unto the Lord an offering in righteousness. 4. Then shall the offering of Judah and Jerusalem be pleasant unto the Lord, as in the days of old, and as in former years. 5. And I will come near to you to judgment ; and I will be a swift Witness against the sorcerers, and against the adulterers, and against false swearers, and against those that oppress the hireling in his wages, the widow, and the fatherless, and that turn aside the stranger from his right, and fear not Me, saith the Lord of Hosts. 6. For I am the Lord, I change not ; therefore ye sons of Jacob are not consumed. 7. Even from the days of your fathers ye are gone away from mine ordinances, and have not kept them. Return unto Me, and I will return unto you, saith the Lord of Hosts. But ye said, Wherein shall we return? 8. Will a man rob God? Yet ye have robbed Me. But ye say, Wherein have we robbed Thee? In tithes and offerings. 9. Ye are cursed with a curse : for ye have robbed Me, even this whole nation. 10. Bring ye all the tithes into the storehouse, that there may be meat in Mine house, and prove Me now herewith, saith the Lord of Hosts, if I will not open you the windows of heaven, and pour you out a blessing, that there shall not be room enough to receive it. 11. And I will rebuke the devourer for your sakes, and he shall not destroy the fruits of your ground ; neither shall your vine cast her fruit before the time in the field, saith the Lord of Hosts. 12. And all nations shall call you blessed : for ye shall be a delightsome land, saith the Lord of Hosts.'
—MALACHI iii. 1-12.

DEEP obscurity surrounds the person of this last of the prophets. It is questioned whether Malachi is a proper name at all. It is the Hebrew word rendered in verse 1 of our passage ' My messenger,' and this has led many authorities to contend that the prophecy is in fact anonymous, the name being only a designation of office. Whether this is so or not, the name, if it is a name, is all that we know about him. The tenor of his prophecy shows that he lived after the restoration of the Temple and its worship, and the sins which he castigates are substantially those with which Ezra and Nehemiah had to fight. One ancient Jewish authority asserts that he was Ezra ; but the statement has no confirmation, and if it had been correct, we should not have expected that such an author would have been anonymous. This dim figure, then, is the last of the mighty line of prophets, and gives strong utterance to the 'hope of Israel'! One clear voice, coming from we scarcely know whose lips, proclaims for the last time, ' He comes! He comes!' and then all is silence for four hundred years. Modern critics, indeed, hold that the bulk of the Psalter is of later date; but that contention has much to do before it can be regarded as established.

The first point worthy of notice in this passage, then, is the concentration, in this last prophetic utterance, of that element of forward-looking expectancy which marked all the earlier revelation. From the beginning, the selectest spirits in Israel had set their faces and pointed their fingers to a great future, which gathered distinctness as the ages rolled, and culminated in the King from David's line, of whom many psalms sung, and in the suffering Servant of the Lord, who shines out from the pages of the second part of Isaiah's prophecy. This Messianic hope runs through all the Old Testament, like a broadening river. 'They that went before cried, Hosanna! Blessed is He that cometh.'

That hope gives unity to the Old Testament, whatever criticism may have to teach about the process of its production. The most important thing about the book is that one purpose informs it all; and the student who misses the truth that 'the testimony of Jesus is the spirit of prophecy' has a less accurate conception of the meaning and inter-relations of the Old Testament than the unlearned who has accepted that great truth. We should be willing to learn all that modern scholarship has to teach about the course of revelation. But we should take care that the new knowledge does not darken the old certainty that the prophets 'testified beforehand of the sufferings of Christ and of the glory that should follow.' Here, at the very end, stands Malachi, reiterating the assurance which had come down through the centuries. The prophets, as it were, had lit a beacon which flamed through the darkness. Hand after hand had flung new fuel on it when it burned low. It had lighted up many a stormy night of exile and distress. Now we can dimly see one more, the last of his order, casting his brand on the fire, which leaps up again; and then he too passes into the darkness, but the beacon burns on.

The next point to note is the clear prophecy of a forerunner. 'My messenger' is to come, and to 'prepare the way before Me.' Isaiah had heard a voice calling, 'Prepare the way of the Lord,' and Malachi quotes his words, and ascribes the same office to the 'messenger.' In the last verses of his prophecy he calls this messenger 'Elijah the prophet.' Here, then, we have a remarkable instance of a historical detail set forth in prophecy. The coming of the Lord is to be immediately preceded by the appearance of a prophet, whose function is to effect a moral and religious reformation, which shall prepare a path for Him. This is no vague ideal, but definite announcement of a definite fact, to be realised in a historical personality. How came this half-anonymous Jew, four hundred years beforehand, to hit upon the fact that the next prophet in Israel would herald the immediate coming of the Lord? There ought to be but one answer possible.

Another point to note is the peculiar relation between Jehovah and Him who comes. Emphatically and broadly it is declared that Jehovah Himself 'shall suddenly come to His temple'; and then the prophecy immediately passes on to speak of the coming of 'the Messenger of the covenant,' and dwells for a time exclusively on his work of purifying; and then again it glides, without conscious breach of continuity or mark of transition, into, 'And *I* will come near to you in judgment.' A mysterious relationship of oneness and yet distinctness is here shadowed, of which the solution is only found in the Christian truth that the Word, which was God, and was in the beginning with God, became flesh, and that in Him Jehovah in very deed tabernacled among men. The expression 'the Messenger (or Angel) of the covenant' is connected with the remarkable representations in other parts of the Old Testament, of 'the Angel of Jehovah,' in whom many commentators recognise a pre-incarnate manifestation of the eternal Word. That 'Angel' had redeemed Israel from Egypt, had led them through the desert, had been the 'Captain of the Lord's host.' The name of Jehovah was 'in Him.' He it is whose coming is here prophesied, and in His coming Jehovah comes to His temple.

We next note the aspect of the coming which is prominent here. Not the kingly, nor the redemptive, but the judicial, is uppermost. With keen irony the Prophet contrasts the professed eagerness of the people for the appearance of Jehovah and their shrinking terror when He does come. He is 'the Lord whom ye seek'; the Messenger of the covenant is He 'whom ye delight in.' But all that superficial and partially insincere longing will turn into dread and unwillingness to abide His scrutiny. The images of the refiner's fire and the fullers' soap imply painful processes, of which

the intention is to burn out the dross and beat out the
filth. It sounds like a prolongation of Malachi's voice
when John the Baptist peals out his herald cry of one
whose 'fan was in His hand,' and who should plunge
men into a fiery baptism, and consume with fire that
destroyed what would not submit to be cast into the
fire that cleansed. Nor should we forget that our
Lord has said, 'For judgment am I come into the
world.' He came to 'purify'; but if men would not
let Him do what He came for, He could not but be
their bane instead of their blessing.

The stone is laid. If we build on it, it is a sure
foundation; if we stumble over it, we are broken.
The double aspect and effect of the gospel, which was
meant only to have the single operation of blessing,
are clearly set forth in this prophecy, which first
promises purging from sin, so that not only the 'sons
of Levi' shall offer in righteousness, but that the
'offerings of Judah and Jerusalem shall be pleasant,'
and then passes immediately to foretell that God will
come in judgment and witness against evil-doers.
Judgment is the shadow of salvation, and constantly
attends on it. Neither Malachi nor the Baptist gives
a complete view of Messiah's work, but still less do
they give an erroneous one; for the central portion of
both prophecies is His purifying energy which both
liken to cleansing fire.

That real and inward cleansing is the great work of
Christ. It was wrought on as many of His contemporaries as believed on Him, and for such as did not
He was a swift Witness against them. Nor are we to
forget that the prophecy is not exhausted yet; for
there remains another 'day of His coming' for judgment. The prophets did not see the perspective of the

future, and often bring together events widely separated in time, just as, to a spectator on a mountain, distances between points far away towards the horizon are not measurable. We have to allow for foreshortening.

This blending of events historically widely apart is to be kept in view in interpreting Malachi's prediction that the coming would result in Judah's and Israel's offerings being 'pleasant unto the Lord as in former years.' That prediction is not yet fulfilled, whether we regard the name of Israel and the relation expressed in it as having passed over to the Christian Church, or whether we look forward to that bringing in of all Israel which Paul says will be as 'life from the dead.' But by slow degrees it is being fulfilled, and by Christ men are being led to offer up spiritual sacrifices, acceptable to God.

The more directly Messianic part of this prophecy is closed in verse 6 by a great saying, which at once gives the reason for the coming and for its severe aspect of witness against sin. The unchangeableness of God, which is declared in His very name, guarantees the continued existence of Israel. As Paul says in regard to the same subject, 'The calling of God is without change of purpose' (on His part). But it is as impossible that God should leave them to their sins, which would destroy them, as that He should Himself consume them. Therefore He will surely come; and coming, will deliver from evil. But they who refuse to be so delivered will forfeit that title and the pledge of preservation which it implies.

A new paragraph begins with verse 7, which is not closely connected with the promises preceding. It recurs to the prevailing tone of Malachi, the rebuke

of negligence in attending to the legal obligations of
worship. That negligence is declared to be a reason
for God's withdrawal from them. But the 'return,'
which is promised on condition of their renewed
obedience, can scarcely be identified with the coming
just foretold. That coming was to bring about offerings of righteousness which should be pleasant to the
Lord. This section (vs. 7-12) promises blessings as
results of such offerings, and a 'return' of Jehovah
to His people contingent upon their return to Him.
If the two sections of this passage are taken as closely
connected, this one must describe the consequences of
the coming. But, more probably, this accusation of
negligence and promise of blessing on a change of
conduct are independent of the previous verses. We,
however, may fairly take them as exhibiting the
obligations of those who have received that great
gift of purifying from Jesus Christ, and are thereby
consecrated as His priests.

The key-word of the Christian life is 'sacrifice'—
surrender, and that to God. That is to be stamped
on the inmost selves, and by the act of the will, on
the body as well. 'Yield yourselves to God, and your
members as instruments of righteousness to Him.' It
is to be written on possessions. Malachi necessarily
keeps within the limits of the sacrificial system, but
his impetuous eloquence hits us no less. It is still
possible to 'rob God.' We do so when we keep anything as our own, and use it at our own will, for our
own purposes. Only when we recognise His ownership of ourselves, and consequently of all that we call
'ours,' do we give Him His due. All the slave's chattels
belong to the owner to whom he belongs. Such
thorough-going surrender is the secret of thorough

possession. The true way to enjoy worldly goods is to give them to God.

The lattices of heaven are opened, not to pour down, as of old, fiery destruction, but to make way for the gentle descent of God's blessing, which will more than fill every vessel set to receive it. This is the universal law, not always fulfilled in increase of outward goods, but in the better riches of communion and of larger possession in God Himself. He suffers no man to be His creditor, but more than returns our gifts, as legends tell of some peasant who brought his king a poor tribute of fruits of his fields, and went away from the presence-chamber with a jewel in his hand.

THE UNCHANGING LORD

'I am the Lord, I change not; therefore ye sons of Jacob are not consumed.'
MALACHI iii. 6.

THE scriptural revelations of the divine Name are always the basis of intensely practical admonition. The Bible does not think it worth while to proclaim the Name of God without building on the proclamation promises or commandments. There is no 'mere theology' in Scripture; and it does not speak of 'attributes,' nor give dry abstractions of infinitude, eternity, omniscience, unchangeableness, but lays stress on the personality of God, which is so apt to escape us in these abstract conceptions, and thus teaches us to think of this personal God our Father, as infinite, eternal, knowing all things, and never changing. There is all the difference in our attitude towards the very same truth if we think of the unchange-

ableness of God, or if we think that our Father God
is unchangeable. In our text the thought of Him
as unchanging comes into view as the foundation of
the continuance of the unfaithful sons of Jacob in
their privileges and in their very lives. 'I am the
Lord,' Jehovah, the Self-existent, the Eternal whose
being is not under the limitations of succession and
time. 'Because I am Jehovah, I change not'; and
because Jehovah changes not, therefore our finite and
mortal selves abide, and our infinite and sinful selves
are still the objects of His steadfast love.

Let us consider, first, the unchangeable God, and
second, the unchanging God as the foundation of our
changeful lives.

I. The unchangeable God.

In the great covenant-name Jehovah there is revealed
an existence which reverses all that we know of finite
and progressive being, or finite and mortal being, or
finite and variable nature. With us there are muta-
tions arising from physical nature. The material must
needs be subject to laws of growth and decadence.
Our spiritual nature is subject to changes arising from
the advancement in knowledge. Our moral nature is
subject to fluctuations; circumstances play upon us,
and 'nothing continueth in one stay.' Change is the
condition of life. It means growth and happiness;
it belongs to the perfection of creatures. But the
unchangeableness of God is the negation of all imper-
fection, it is the negation of all dependence on circumstances, it is the negation of all possibility of decay or
exhaustion, it is the negation of all caprice. It is the
assurance that His is an underived, self-dependent
being, and that with Him is the fountain of light: it
is the assurance that, raised above the limits of time

and the succession of events, He is in the eternal present, where all things that were and are, and are to come, stand naked and open. It is the assurance that the calm might of His eternal will acts, not in spasms of successive volitions preceded by a period of indecision and equilibrium between contending motives, but is one continuous uniform energy, never beginning, never bending, never ending; that the purpose of His will is 'the eternal purpose which He hath purposed in Himself.' It is the assurance that the clear vision of His infinite knowledge, from the heat of which nothing is hid, has no stages of advancement, and no events lying nebulous in a dim horizon by reason of distance, or growing in clearness as they draw nearer, but which pierces the mists of futurity and the veils of the past and the infinities of the present, and 'from the beginning to the end knoweth all things.' It is the assurance that the mighty stream of love from the heart of God is not contingent on the variations of our character and the fluctuations of our poor hearts, but rises from His deep well, and flows on for ever, 'the river of God' which 'is full of water.' It is the assurance that round all the majesty and the mercy which He has revealed for our adoration and our trust there is the consecration of permanence, that we might have a rock on which to build and never be confounded. Is there anywhere in the past an act of His power, a word of His lip, a revelation of His heart which has been a strength or a joy or a light to any man? It is valid for me, and is intended for my use. 'He fainteth not, nor is weary.' The bush burns and is not consumed. 'I will not alter the thing that has gone out of my lips.' 'By two immutable things in which it is impossible for God to lie, we have strong consolation.'

II. The unchanging God as the foundation of our changeful lives.

In the most literal sense our text is true. Because He lives we live also. He is the same for ever, therefore we are not consumed. The foundation of our being lies beyond and beneath all the mutable things from which we are tempted to believe that we draw our lives, and is in God. The true lesson to be drawn from the mutable phenomena of earth is—heaven. The many links in the chain must have a staple. Reason requires that behind all the fleeting shall be the permanent. There must be a basis which does not partake of change. The lesson from all the mutable creation is the immutable God.

Since God changes not, the life of our spirits is not at the mercy of changing events. We look back on a lifetime of changing scenes through which we have passed, and forward to a similar succession, and this mutability is sad to many of us, and in some aspects sad to all, so powerless we are to fix and arrest any of our blessings. Which we shall keep we know not; we only know that, as certainly as buds and blossoms of spring drop, and the fervid summer darkens to November fogs and December frosts, so certainly we shall have to part with much in our passage through life. But if we let God speak to us, the necessary changes that come to us will not be harmful but blessed, for the lesson that the mutability of the mutual is meant to impress upon us is, the permanency of the divine, and our dependence, not on them, but on Him. We may look upon all the world of time and chance and think that He who Himself is unchanging changeth all. The eye of the tempest is a point of rest. The point in the heavens towards which, according to some astronomers, the whole of the solar system is drifting, is a fixed point. If we depend on Him, then change is not all sad ; it cannot take God away, but it may bring us nearer to Him. We cannot be desolate as long as we have Him. We know not what shall be on the morrow. Be it so ; it will be God's to-morrow. When the leaves drop we can see the rock on which the trees grow; and when changes strip the world for us of some of its waving beauty and leafy shade, we may discern more clearly the firm foundation on which our hopes rest. All else changes. Be it so ; that will not kill us, nor leave us utterly forlorn as long as we hear the voice which says, 'I am the Lord ; I change not ; therefore ye are not consumed.'

God's purposes and promises change not, therefore our faith may rest on Him, notwithstanding our own sins and fluctuations. It is this aspect of the divine immutability which is the thought of our text. God does not turn from His love, nor cancel His promises, nor alter His purposes of mercy because of our sins. If God could have changed, the godless forgetfulness of, and departure from, Him of 'the Sons of Jacob' would have driven Him to abandon His purposes ; but they still live—living evidences of His longsuffering. And in that preservation of them God would have them see the basis of hope for the future. So this is the confidence with which we should cheer ourselves when we look upon the past, and when we anticipate the future. The sins that have been in our past have deserved that we should have been swept away, but we are here still. Why are we ? Why do we yet live ? Because we have to do with an unchanging love, with a faithfulness that never departs from its word, with a purpose of blessing that will not be turned aside. So let us look back

z

with this thought and be thankful; let us look forward
with it and be of good cheer. Trust yourself, weak and
sinful as you are, to that unchanging love. The future
will have in it faults and failures, sins and shortcomings,
but rise from yourself to God. Look beyond the light
and shade of your own characters, or of earthly events
to the central light, where there is no glimmering
twilight, no night, 'no variableness nor shadow of
turning.' Let us live in God, and be strong in hope.
Forward, not backward, let us look and strive; so our
souls, fixed and steadied by faith in Him, will become
in a manner partakers of His unchangeableness; and
we too in our degree will be able to say, 'The Lord is
at my side; I shall not be moved.'

A DIALOGUE WITH GOD

'Return unto Me, and I will return unto you, saith the Lord of Hosts. But ye
say, Wherein shall we return?'—MALACHI iii. 7 (R.V.).

IN previous sermons we have considered God's indictment of man's sin met by man's plea of 'not guilty,' and
God's threatenings brushed aside by man's question.
Here we have the climax of self-revealing and patient
love in God's wooing voice to draw the wanderer back,
met by man's refusing answer. These three divine
utterances taken together cover the whole ground of
His speech to us; and, alas! these three human utterances but too truly represent for the most part our
answers to Him.

I. God's invitation to His wandering child.

The gracious invitation of our text presupposes a
state of departure. The child who is tenderly recalled
has first gone away. There has been a breach of love.

Dependence has been unwelcome, and cast off with the vain hope of a larger freedom in the far-off land; and this is the true charge against us. It is not so much individual acts of sin but the going away in heart and spirit from our Father God which describes the inmost essence of our true condition, and is itself the source of all our acts of sin. Conscience confirms the description. We know that we have departed from Him in mind, having wasted our thoughts on many things and not having had Him in the multitude of them in us. We have departed from Him in heart, having squandered our love and dissipated our desires on many objects, and sought in the multiplicity of many pearls—some of them only paste—a substitute for the all-sufficient simplicity of the One of great price. We have departed from Him in will, having reared up puny inclinations and fleeting passions against His calm and eternal purpose, and so bringing about the shock of a collision as destructive to us as when a torpedo-boat crashes in the dark against a battle-ship, and, cut in two, sinks.

The gracious invitation of our text follows, 'I am the Lord, I change not; therefore ye sons of Jacob are not consumed.' Threatenings, and the execution of these in acts of judgment, are no indication of a change in the loving heart of God; and because it is the same, however we have sinned against it and departed from it, there is ever an invitation and a welcome. We may depart from Him, but He never departs from us. Nor does He wait for us to originate the movement of return, but He invites us back. By all His words in His threatenings and in His commandments, as in the acts of His providence, we can hear His call to return. The fathers of our flesh never cease to long for their prodigal child's return; and their patient persistence of hope is but brief and broken when contrasted with the infinite longsuffering of the Father of spirits.   We have heard of a mother who for long empty years has nightly set a candle in her cottage window to guide her wandering boy back to her heart; and God has bade us think more loftily of the unchangeableness of His love than that of a woman who may forget, that she should not have compassion upon the son of her womb.

II. Man's answer to God's invitation.

It is a refusal which is half-veiled and none the less real.   There is no unwillingness to obey professed, but it is concealed under a mask of desiring a little more light as to how a return is to be accomplished.   There are not many of us who are rooted enough in evil as to be able to blurt out a curt 'I will not' in answer to His call.   Conscience often bars the way to such a plain and unmannerly reply; but there are many who try to cheat God, and who do to some extent cheat themselves, by professing ignorance of the way which would lead them to His heart.   Some of us have learned only too well to raise questions about the method of salvation instead of accepting it, and to dabble in theology instead of making sure work of return.   Some of us would fain substitute a host of isolated actions, or apparent moral or religious observance, for the return of will and heart to God; and all who in their consciences answer God's call by saying, 'Wherein shall we return?' with such a meaning are playing tricks with themselves, and trying to hoodwink God.

But the question of our text has often a nobler origin, and comes from the depths of a troubled heart. Not seldom does God's loving invitation rouse the dormant conscience to the sense of sin.   The man, lying broken at the foot of the cliff down which he has

fallen, and seeing the brightness of God far above, has
his heart racked with the question: How am I, with
lame limbs, to struggle back to the heights above?
'How shall man be just with God?' All the religions
of the world, with their offerings and penances and
weary toils, are vain attempts to make a way back
to the God from whom men have wandered, and that
question, 'Wherein shall we return?' is really the
meaning of the world's vain seeking and profitless
effort.

God has answered man's question; for Christ is at
once the way back to God, and the motive which
draws us to walk in it. He draws us back by the mag-
netism of His love and sacrifice. We return to God
when we cling to Jesus. He is the highest, the tenderest
utterance of the divine voice; and when we yield to His
invitation to Himself we return to God. He calls to
each of us, 'Come unto Me, and I will give you rest.'
What can we reply but, 'I come; let me never wander
from Thee'?

'STOUT WORDS,' AND THEIR CONFUTATION

'Your words have been stout against Me, saith the Lord: yet ye say, What have
we spoken so much against Thee? 14. Ye have said, It is vain to serve God; and
what profit is it that we have kept His ordinance, and that we have walked
mournfully before the Lord of Hosts? 15. And now we call the proud happy; yea,
they that work wickedness are set up; yea, they that tempt God are even delivered.
16. Then they that feared the Lord spake often one to another: and the Lord
hearkened, and heard it; and a book of remembrance was written before Him for
them that feared the Lord, and that thought upon His name. 17. And they shall be
Mine, saith the Lord of Hosts, in that day when I make up My jewels; and I will
spare them, as a man spareth his own son that serveth him. 18. Then shall ye return, and discern between the righteous and the wicked; between him that serveth
God and him that serveth Him not. iv. 1. For, behold, the day cometh that shall burn
as an oven; and all the proud, yea, and all that do wickedly, shall be stubble: and
the day that cometh shall burn them up, saith the Lord of Hosts, that it shall leave
them neither root nor branch. 2. But unto you that fear My Name shall the sun of
righteousness arise with healing in his wings; and ye shall go forth, and grow up

as calves of the stall. 3. And ye shall tread down the wicked; for they shall be ashes under the soles of your feet, in the day that I shall do this, saith the Lord of Hosts. 4. Remember ye the law of Moses My servant, which I commanded unto him in Horeb for all Israel, with the statutes and judgments. 5. Behold, I will send you Elijah the prophet before the coming of the great and dreadful day of the Lord: 6. And he shall turn the heart of the fathers to the children, and the heart of the children to their fathers, lest I come and smite the earth with a curse.'—MALACHI iii. 13-18; iv. 1-6.

THIS passage falls into three parts,—the 'stout words' against God which the Prophet sets himself to confute (verses 13-15); the prophecy of the day which will show their falsehood (verse 16 to iv. 3); and the closing exhortation and prediction (iv. 4-6).

I. The returning exiles had not had the prosperity which they had hoped. So many of them, even of those who had served God, began to let doubts darken their trust, and to listen to the whispers of their own hearts, reinforced by the mutterings of others, and to ask: 'What is the use of religion? Does it make any difference to a man's condition?' Here had they been keeping God's charge, and going in black garments 'before the Lord,' in token of penitence, and no good had come to them, while arrogant neglect of His commandments did not seem to hinder happiness, and 'they that work wickedness are built up.' Sinful lives appeared to have a firm foundation, and to rise high and palace-like, while righteous ones were like huts. Goodness seemed to spell ruin.

What was wrong in these 'stout words'? It was wrong to attach such worth to external acts of devotion, as if these were deserving of reward. It was wrong to suspend the duty of worship on the prosperity resulting from it, and to seek 'profit' from 'keeping his charge.' Such religion was shallow and selfish, and had the evils of the later Pharisaism in germ in it. It was wrong to yield to the doubts which the apparently unequal distribution of worldly pros-

perity stirred in their hearts. But the doubts themselves were almost certain to press on Old Testament
believers, as well as on Old Testament scoffers,
especially under the circumstances of Malachi's time.
The fuller light of Christianity has eased their pressure, but not removed it, and we have all had to face
them, both when our own hearts have ached with sorrow
and when pondering on the perplexities of this con-
fused world. We look around, and, like the psalmist,
see 'the prosperity of the wicked,' and, like him, have
to confess that our 'steps had wellnigh slipped' at the
sight. The old, old question is ever starting up. 'Doth
God know?' The mystery of suffering and the mystery
of its distribution, the apparent utter want of connection between righteousness and wellbeing, are still
formidable difficulties in the way of believing in a
loving, all-knowing, and all-powerful God, and are
stock arguments of the unbeliever and perplexities of
humble faith. Never to have felt the force of the
difficulty is not so much the sign of steadfast faith
as of scant reflection. To yield to it, and still more,
to let it drive us to cast religion aside, is not merely
folly, but sin. So thinks Malachi.

II. To the stout words of the doubters is opposed
the conversation of the godly. ' *Then* they that feared
the Lord spake one with another,' nourishing their faith
by believing speech with like-minded. The more the
truths by which we believe are contradicted, the more
should we commune with fellow-believers. Attempts
to rob us should make us hold our treasure the faster.
Bold avowal of the faith is especially called for when
many potent voices deny it. And, whoever does not
hear, God hears. Faithful words may seem lost, but
they and every faithful act are written in His remem-

brance, and will be recompensed one day. If our
names and acts are written there, we may well be content to accept scanty measures of earthly good, and not
be 'envious of the foolish' in their prosperity.

Malachi's answer to the doubters leaves all other
considerations which might remove the difficulty un-
mentioned, and fixes on the one, the prophecy of a
future which will show that it is not all the same
whether a man is good or bad. It was said of an
English statesman that he called a new world into
existence to redress the balance of the old, and that is
what the Prophet does. Christianity has taught us
many other ways of meeting the doubters' difficulty,
but the sheet anchor of faith in that storm is the un-
conquerable assurance that a day comes when the
righteousness of providence will be vindicated, and the
eternal difference between good and evil manifested in
the fates of men. The Prophet is declaring what will be
a fact one day, but he does not know when. Probably
he never asked himself whether 'the day of the Lord'
was near or far off, to dawn on earth or to lie beyond
mortal life. But this he knew—that God *was* righteous,
and that sometime and somewhere character would
settle destiny, and even outwardly it would be good
to be good. He first declares this conviction in general
terms, and then passes on to a magnificent and terrible
picture of that great day.

The promise, which lay at the foundation of Israel's
national existence, included the recognition of it as 'a
peculiar treasure unto Me above all people,' and Malachi
looks forward to that day as the epoch when God will
show by His acts how precious the righteous are in His
sight. Not the whole Israel, but the righteous among
them, are the heirs of the old promise. It is an antici-

pation of the teaching that 'they are not all Israel, which are of Israel.' And it bids us look for the fulfilment of every promise of God's to that great day of the Lord which lies still before us all, when the gulf between the righteous and the wicked shall be solemnly visible, wide, and profound. There have been many 'days which I make' in the world's history, and in a measure each of them has re-established the apparently tottering truth that there is a God who judgeth in the earth, but the day of days is yet to come.

No grander vision of judgment exists than Malachi's picture of 'the day,' lurid, on the one hand, with the fierce flame, before which the wicked are as stubble that crackles for a moment and then is grey ashes, or as a tree in a forest fire, which stands for a little while, a pillar of flame, and then falls with a crash, shaking the woods; and on the otherhand, radiant with the early beams of healing sunshine, in whose sweet morning light the cattle, let out from their pent-up stalls, gambol in glee. But let us not forget while we admire the noble poetry of its form that this is God's oracle, nor that we have each to settle for ourselves whether that day shall be for us a furnace to destroy or a sun to cheer and enlighten.

We can only note in a sentence the recurrence in verse 1 of the phrases 'the proud' and they 'that work wickedness,' from verse 15 of chapter iii. The end of those whom the world called happy, and who seemed stable and elevated, is to be as stubble before the fire. We must also point out that 'the sun of righteousness' means the sun which is righteousness, and is not a designation of the Messiah. Nor can we dwell on the picture of the righteous treading down the wicked, which seems to prolong the previous metaphor of the leaping young cattle. Then shall 'the upright have dominion over them in the morning.'

III. The final exhortation and promise point back-wards and forwards, summing up duty in obedience to the law, and fixing hope on a future reappearance of the leader of the prophets. Moses and Elijah are the two giant figures which dominate the history of Israel. Law and prophecy are the two forms in which God spoke to the fathers. The former is of perpetual obligation, the latter will flash up again in power on the threshold of the day. Jesus has interpreted this closing word for us. John came 'in the spirit and power of Elijah,' and the purpose of his coming was to 'turn the hearts of the fathers to the children' (Luke i. 16, 17); that is, to bring back the devout dispositions of the patriarchs to the existing generations, and so to bring the 'hearts of the children to their fathers,' as united with them in devout obedience. If John's mission had succeeded, the 'curse' which smote Israel would have been stayed. God has done all that He can do to keep us from being consumed by the fire of that day. The Incarnation, Life, and Death of Jesus Christ made a day of the Lord which has the twofold character of that in Malachi's vision, for He is a ' savour of life unto life' or 'of death unto death,' and must be one or other to us. But another day of the Lord is still to come, and for each of us it will come burning as a furnace or bright as sunrise. Then the universe shall 'discern between the righteous and the wicked, between him that serveth God and him that serveth Him not.'

THE LAST WORDS OF THE OLD AND NEW TESTAMENTS

'Lest I come and smite the earth with a curse.'—MALACHI iv. 6.
'The grace of our Lord Jesus Christ be with you all. Amen '—REVELATION xxii. 21.

IT is of course only an accident that these words close the Old and the New Testaments. In the Hebrew Bible Malachi's prophecies do not stand at the end; but he was the last of the Old Testament prophets, and after him there were 'four centuries of silence.' We seem to hear in his words the dying echoes of the rolling thunders of Sinai. They gather up the whole burden of the Law and of the prophets; of the former in their declaration of a coming retribution, of the latter in the hope that that retribution may be averted.

Then, in regard to John's words, of course as they stand they are simply the parting benediction with which he takes leave of his readers; but it is fitting that the Book of which they are the close should seal up the canon, because it stands as the one prophetic book of the New Testament, and so reaches forward into the coming ages, even to the consummation of all things. And just as Christ in His Ascension was taken from them whilst His hands were lifted up in the act of blessing, so it is fitting that the revelation of which He is the centre and the theme should part from us as He did, shedding with its final words the dew of benediction on our upturned heads.

I venture, then, to look at these significant closing words of the two Testaments as conveying the spirit of each, and suggesting some thoughts about the con-

trast and the harmony and the order that subsist
between them.

I. I ask you, first, to notice the apparent contrast
and the real harmony and unity of these two texts.

'Lest I come and smite the land with a curse.' That
last awful word does not convey, in the original, quite
the idea of our English word 'curse.' It refers to a
somewhat singular institution in the Mosaic Law
according to which things devoted, in a certain sense,
to God were deprived of life. And the reference
historically is to the judgments that were inflicted
upon the nations that occupied the land before the
Israelitish invasion, those Canaanites and others who
were put under 'the ban' and devoted to utter destruction. So, says my text, Israel, which has stepped into
their places, may bring down upon its head the same
devastation; and as they were swept off the face of
the land that they had polluted with their iniquities,
so an apostate and God-forgetting Judah may again
experience the same utter destruction falling upon
them. If instead of the word 'curse' we were to
substitute the word 'destruction,' we should get the
true idea of the passage.

And the thought that I want to insist upon is this,
that here we have distinctly gathered up the whole
spirit of millenniums of divine revelation, all of which
declare this one thing, that as certainly as there is a
God, every transgression and disobedience receives,
and must receive, its just recompense of reward.

That is the spirit of law, for law has nothing to say,
except, 'Do this, and thou shalt live; do not this, and
thou shalt die.'

And then turn to the other. 'The grace of our Lord
Jesus Christ be with you all.' What has become of

the thunder? All melted into dewy rain of love and pity and compassion. Grace is love that stoops; grace is love that foregoes its claims, and forgives sins against itself. Grace is love that imparts, and this grace, thus stooping, thus pardoning, thus bestowing, is a universal gift. The Apostolic benediction is the declaration of the divine purpose, and the inmost heart and loftiest meaning of all the words which from the beginning God hath spoken is that His condescending, pardoning, self-bestowing mercy may fall upon all hearts, and gladden every soul.

So there seems to emerge, and there is, a very real and a very significant contrast. 'I come and smite the earth with a curse' sounds strangely unlike 'The grace of our Lord Jesus Christ be with you all.' And, of course, in this generation there is a strong tendency to dwell upon that contrast and to exaggerate it, and to assert that the more recent has antiquated the more ancient, and that now the day when we have to think of and to dread the curse that smites the earth is past, 'because the true Light now shineth.'

So I ask you to notice that beneath this apparent contrast there is a real harmony, and that these two utterances, though they seem to be so diverse, are quite consistent at bottom, and must both be taken into account if we would grasp the whole truth. For, as a matter of fact, nowhere are there more tender utterances and sweeter revelations of a divine mercy than in that ancient law with its attendant prophets. And as a matter of fact, nowhere, through all the thunderings and lightnings of Sinai, are there such solemn words of retribution as dropped from the lips of the Incarnate Love. There is nothing anywhere so dreadful as Christ's own words about what comes, and

must come, to sinful men. Is there any depth of darkness in the Old Testament teaching of retribution half
as deep, half as black, and as terrible, as the gulf that
Christ opens at your feet and mine? Is there anything so awful as the threatenings of Infinite Love?

And the same blending of the widest proclamation
of, and the most perfect rejoicing confidence in, the
universal and all-forgiving love of God, with the teaching of the sharpest retribution, lies in the writings of
this very Apostle about whose words I am speaking.
There are nowhere in Scripture more solemn pictures
than those in that book of the Apocalypse, of the inevitable consequences of departure from the love and
the faith of God, and John, the Apostle of love, is
the preacher of judgment as none of the other writers
of the New Testament are.

Such is the fact, and there is a necessity for it.
There must be this blending; for if you take away
from your conception of God the absolute holiness
which hates sin, and the rigid righteousness which
apportions to all evil its bitter fruits, you have left
a maimed God that has not power to love but is nothing but weak, good-natured indulgence. Impunity
is not mercy, and punishment is never the negation of
perfect love, but rather, if you destroy the one you
hopelessly maim the other. The two halves are
needed in order to give full emphasis to either. Each
note alone is untrue; blended, they make the perfect
chord.

II. And now, let me ask you to look with me at
another point, and that is, the relation of the grace to
the punishment.

Is it not love which proclaims judgment? Are not
the words of my first text, if you take them all,

merciful, however they wear a surface of threatening? 'Lest I come.' Then He speaks that He may
not come, and declares the issue of sin in order that
that issue may never need to be experienced by us
that listen to Him. Brethren! both in regard to the
Bible and in regard to human ministrations of the
Gospel, it is all-important, as it seems to me at present,
to insist that it is the cruellest kindness to keep back
the threatenings for fear of darkening the grace; and
that, on the other hand, it is the truest tenderness to
warn and to proclaim them. It is love that threatens;
it is mercy to tell us that the wrath will come.

And just as one relation between the grace and the
retribution is that the proclamation of the retribution
is the work of the grace, so there is another relation—
the grace is manifested in bearing the punishment,
and in bearing it away by bearing it. Oh! there is no
adequate measure of what the grace of the Lord Jesus
Christ is except the measure of the smiting destruction from which He frees us. It is because every
transgression receives its just recompense of reward,
because the wages of sin is death, because God cannot
but hate and punish the evil, that we get our truest
standard of what Christ's love is to every soul of us.
For on Him have met all the converging rays of the
divine retribution, and burnt the penal fire into His
very heart. He has come between every one of us, if
we will, and that certain incidence of retribution for
our evil, taking upon Himself the whole burden of our
sin and of our guilt, and bearing that awful death
which consists not in the mere dissolution of the tie
between soul and body, but in the separation of the
conscious spirit from God, in order that we may stand
peaceful, serene, untouched, when the hail and the fire

of the divine judgment are falling from the heavens and running along the earth. The grace depends for all our conceptions of its glory, its tenderness, and its depth, on our estimate of the wrath from which it delivers.

So, dear brethren, remember, if you tamper with the one you destroy the other; if there be no fearful judgment from which men need to be delivered, Christ has borne nothing for us that entitles Him to demand our hearts; and all the ascriptions of praise and adoration to Him, and all the surrender of loving hearts, in utter self-abandonment, to Him that has borne the curse for us, fade and are silent. If you strike out the truth of Christ's bearing the results of sin from your theology, you do not thereby exalt, but you fatally lower the love; and in the interests of the loftiest conceptions of a divine lovingkindness and mercy that ever have blessed the world, I beseech you, be on your guard against all teachings that diminish the sinfulness of sin, and that ask again the question which first of all came from lips that do not commend it to us—'*Hath God said?*' or advance to the assertion—'Ye shall *not* surely die.' If 'I come to smite the earth with a curse' ceases to be a truth to you, 'the grace of our Lord Jesus Christ' will fade away for you likewise.

III. Now, still further, let me ask you to consider, lastly, the alternative which these texts open for us.

I believe that the order in which they stand in Scripture is the order in which men generally come to believe them, and to feel them. I am old-fashioned enough and narrow enough to believe in conversion; and to believe further that, as a rule, the course through which the soul passes from darkness into light is the course which divine revelation took: first, the unveiling of sin and its issues, and then the glad leaping up of the trustful heart to the conception of redeeming grace.

But what I seek briefly to suggest now is, not only the order of manifestation as brought out in these words, but also the alternative which they present to us, one branch or other of which every soul of you will have to experience. You must have either the destruction or the grace. And, more wonderful still, the same coming of the same Lord will be to one man the destruction, and to another the manifestation and reception of His perfect grace. As it was in the Lord's first coming, 'He is set for the rise and the fall of many in Israel.' The same heat softens some substances and bakes others into hardness. A bit of wax and a bit of clay put into the same fire—one becomes liquefied and the other solidified. The same light is joy to one eye and torture to another. The same pillar of cloud was light to the hosts of Israel, and darkness and dismay to the armies of Egypt. The same Gospel is 'a savour of life unto life, or of death unto death,' by the giving forth of the same influences killing the one and reviving the other; the same Christ is a Stone to build upon or a Stone of stumbling; and when He cometh at the last, Prince, King, Judge, to you and me, His coming shall be prepared as the morning; and ye 'shall have a song as when one cometh with a pipe to the mountain of the Lord'; or else it shall be a day of darkness and not of light. He comes to me, to you; He comes to smite or He comes to glorify.

Oh, brethren! do not believe that God's threatenings are wind and words; do not let teachings that sap the very foundations of morality and eat all the power out of the Gospel persuade you that the solemn words, 'The soul that sinneth it shall die,' are not simple verity.

And then, my brethren, oh! then, do you turn yourselves to that dear Lord whose grace is magnified in this most chiefly, that 'He hath borne our sins and carried our sorrows'; and taking Him for your Saviour, your King, your Shield, your All, when He cometh it will be life to you; and the grace that He imparts will be heaven for ever more.

CPSIA information can be obtained
at www.ICGtesting.com
Printed in the USA
LVOW08*2237260217

525507LV00003B/56/P